W9-ADP-625

Dr. GEORGIA HARKNESS is one of the most widely known women in the Christian Church. Since 1950 she has been a professor at the Pacific School of Religion in Berkeley, California. Previously, she taught at Garrett Biblical Institute, Mount Holyoke and Elmira College. She has been active in the World Council of Churches and has held a number of distinguished lectureships. In 1947 she was awarded the $7,500 prize as co-winner of the Abingdon-Cokesbury Award.

Dr. Harkness's TOWARD UNDERSTANDING THE BIBLE was published recently by Scribners.

KANSAS BIBLE CHAIR
MYERS HALL,   Lawrence, Kansas
PRIVATE LIBRARY

The Sources

of Western Morality

KANSAS BIBLE CHAIR
MYERS HALL,   Lawrence, Kansas
PRIVATE LIBRARY

BJ 101
.H35
1954

GEORGIA HARKNESS

The Sources
of Western Morality

FROM PRIMITIVE SOCIETY

THROUGH THE BEGINNINGS

OF CHRISTIANITY

KANSAS SCHOOL OF RELIGION
UNIVERSITY OF KANSAS
1300 OREAD AVENUE
LAWRENCE, KANSAS 66044

Charles Scribner's Sons, New York, 1954

KANSAS BIBLE CHAIR
MYERS HALL,   Lawrence, Kansas
PRIVATE LIBRARY

Copyright, 1954, by
GEORGIA HARKNESS

Printed in the United States of America

*All rights reserved. No part of this book
may be reproduced in any form without
the permission of Charles Scribner's Sons*

A

LIBRARY OF CONGRESS CATALOGUE NO. 54–10370

TO

two good men, my brothers

CHARLES MERRILL HARKNESS

and

EDWARD EVERETT HARKNESS

ACKNOWLEDGMENTS

THE material in this book is drawn from many sources—so many, in fact, that it would be impossible to identify all of them. Since its object is not to present the fruits of "research" in the usual specialized meaning of that term but rather to give a simple, organic presentation of the major historical currents that have shaped our moral ideals and culture, it has not seemed wise or necessary to include extensive footnotes. Direct quotations and the citing of interpretations from a specific source have, of course, been identified.

Most of what is here included has been gathered during the process of teaching it—first as a course in the history of ethical theory given for ten years at Elmira College, more recently as a study of the origins of Christian ethics at the Pacific School of Religion. Lectures by Reinhold Niebuhr on the evolution of moral ideals to which I listened at Union Seminary during the autumn of 1936 gave me many valuable insights. Three of my colleagues at the Pacific School of Religion have graciously read sections of the book: Jack Finegan, the chapters on Egypt and the Mesopotamian Valley; John Herbert Otwell, those on the Old Testament; and Robert E. Fitch, those on Greek and Roman philosophy and Christian ethics. I have found their scrutiny most helpful and, needless to say, any remaining errors are not to be charged against them.

In Biblical citations I have used the Revised Standard Version of the Bible, copyrighted 1946 and 1952, unless there was some reason for preferring a more familiar rendering. For permission to quote from it I am indebted to the owners of the copyright, the Division of Christian Education of the National Council of the Churches of Christ in the United States of America.

GEORGIA HARKNESS.

CONTENTS

I. A PREVIEW BY RETROSPECT   1

II. MORALS IN PRIMITIVE SOCIETY   9
    1. The Family
    2. Economic Organization
    3. Civic Relations
    4. Religion
    5. Achievements

III. EGYPT AND THE BEGINNINGS OF
      CIVILIZATION   35
    1. The Emergence of Civilization
    2. The Cycle of Egyptian History
    3. Egyptian Religion
    4. Egyptian Morals

IV. THE MESOPOTAMIAN VALLEY   59
    1. The Physical Setting
    2. The Cycle of History
    3. Babylonian Religion
    4. Morality by Law
    5. Conclusion

V. EARLY HEBREW MORALITY   86
    1. God and Hebrew Morals
    2. Periods of Hebrew History
    3. Pre-prophetic Morality

VI. ISRAEL'S PROPHETS AND SAGES   116

    1. Before the Exile

    2. The Great Reformation

    3. The Exile

    4. The Rise of Judaism

    5. Post-exilic Literature

    6. Contributions to Morality

VII. THE GREEK IDEAL   151

    1. Hebrew versus Greek

    2. The Birth of Democracy

    3. The Greek Moral Consciousness

    4. Early Greek Morality

    5. The Sophists

    6. Socrates

    7. Cyrenaics and Cynics

VIII. SYSTEM BUILDERS OF GREECE AND ROME   179

    1. Plato

    2. Aristotle

    3. The Epicureans

    4. Stoicism

    5. The Roman Temper

    6. Contributions of Roman Stoicism

IX. THE BEGINNINGS OF CHRISTIAN ETHICS   212

    1. The Meaning of Christian Ethics

    2. Jesus and the Ideals of Greece and Rome

    3. Jesus and His Hebrew Background

    4. Distinctive Elements in the Ethics of Jesus

5. *Jesus' Economic Ethics*

6. *Jesus and the State*

7. *Jesus and the Family*

8. *Are Jesus' Teachings Practical?*

9. *The Ethics of Paul*

SELECTED BIBLIOGRAPHY   245

INDEX   249

The Sources

of Western Morality

CHAPTER ONE

A PREVIEW
BY RETROSPECT

THE purpose of this book is to present a survey of the origins of Western morality. In one sense, this is a most ambitious task, before which an author who is not a specialist in the history of civilization must have either courage or fool-hardiness to plunge in. Yet if our concern is not with an intricate mass of detail but with main currents and movements—for these are what matter most—it is not an impossible task. Beginning with the undifferentiated but powerful moral sanctions of primitive society and taking concrete form in the early civilizations of Egypt and the Mesopotamian Valley, coming to clearer and higher focus in Hebrew morality and among the great system-makers of Greece and Rome, giving to the world that was later to be called Christendom the matchless moral imperative of Jesus and the New Testament, the moral undergirding of Western society took shape. At these streams of development we are now to look.

Whether the task is difficult or easy is irrelevant in the face of the fact that it is a needed one. It is a platitude to say that the accepted moral standards of Christendom are now being put to a greater strain than at any time since Constantine made Christianity the official religion of the Roman Empire. This does not mean that we are living in the worst era of our history. In many respects there is more kindness, more humaneness, more social wisdom, more intelligent and broad-visioned concern for all the peoples of the earth than there has ever been before. But there is also an attack both by communism from without and by secularism from within which imperils much of what has been wrought out in centuries of moral progress.

If this be the case, then why not look at the present instead of the past? The present needs to be looked at. With many others who have written on various aspects of the present situation, I have tried to do this with regard to the secularism all around us in *The Modern Rival of Christian Faith*. Others, seeking to temper with intelligent understanding the current tendency to brand everything liberal as communistic, have written effectively and persuasively on communism's threat to Christianity.[1] Nevertheless, the field is wide open for an attempt to dig down to the roots from which came the moral standards now so much under fire.

That our present morals are in transition few would deny. I shall not attempt very extensively in this book to analyze current trends, and where there are morals to be pointed, we shall for the most part let the past speak to the present such lessons as it has for us. But since we shall be turning in a moment to the long past, let us look briefly at the recent past. What has happened within the memories of persons now in middle life may give some index both as to what undergirds our moral standards and why these foundations at so many points seem now to be melting away.

[1]Notably John C. Bennett in *Christianity and Communism;* Alexander Miller in *The Christian Significance of Karl Marx;* and Charles Lowry in *Communism and Christ.*

In the spring of 1929, before most people glimpsed the fact that a stock-market crash in October of that year would usher in a world depression, Walter Lippmann gave the reading public a brilliant analysis of the way in which the "acids of modernity" had eaten into the old patterns of moral and religious thinking. This is worth getting down off the shelf to look into again, for no one has done it better since. Nor has the picture he presented been materially altered since 1929. After a world depression, a Second World War, the emergence of the atomic age, the rise and fall of Naziism, the coming to power over vast areas of the earth of Soviet communism, the Korean stalemate, the ups and downs of the New Deal and the Fair Deal and now the resurgence of the Republican party, the acids of modernity still keep eating away. Political and economic changes have affected them, yes, but not vitally and centrally. The primary catalytic agent in these acids does not lie in the field of politics and economics, but in religion and in personal moral ideals. It is still true that "Whirl is king, having driven out Zeus," and there is no great evidence that the gods Lippmann wished to substitute, Maturity and Disinterestedness, have been enthroned.

Many factors, which can here be only briefly suggested, have tended toward this transition from the old order.[2] It is an oversimplification to attribute to the two World Wars everything that has happened in the past four decades; yet one would be blind who failed to see that the demons of nationalism and militarism let loose in 1914 have not been chained. It is impossible to glorify mass murder and international hatred year after year without leaving moral scars. Nor can the normal processes of world trade be upset without leaving economic confusion which runs into moral turbulence. In the two postwar periods the immoralities of a machine-made, profit-dominated society became more virulent, as in the depression years

[2]They are treated in greater fullness in *The Recovery of Ideals*, Chapter II and *The Modern Rival of Christian Faith*, Part II.

they became more evident. Men are not more acquisitive or more blind to human values than they have been all through the history of human relations; but as society becomes more complex, and the means of production and distribution and the range of goods for consumption become more and more extended, so do the temptations to illicit money-making and the occasions for a rationalization of selfishness.

In times of confusion—political, economic, or as in our times both together—there is a natural tendency to turn to anything which seems to put ground under one's feet. Most people, if confronted with a choice between security and freedom, will choose security. This fact, given concreteness by a union of deceptive promises with dynamic faith, largely accounts for the phenomenal spread of communism. But it accounts also for the fact that in countries professedly democratic, the ideals of liberty, equality and brotherhood so deeply imbedded in a democratic heritage become subordinated to economic and military security—or at least, to what in the mind of the public and its leaders is thought to offer security. When this urge for security is joined with a psychological erection of the State into the place of primary loyalty, what we have is "nationalism, man's other religion."[3]

Man's perennial source of inner security has been his religion. Has this stood by him—or has he stood by it—in the midst of turmoil and the tragic events of our time? There are frequent announcements of an upturn in religious interest, and religious interest whether in or out of the churches is by no means dead or dying. Nevertheless, it must be said that there are millions of people in the so-called Christian West who find no foothold in it.

The weakening hold of theistic religion, due to causes both intellectual and practical, has been accompanied by a relaxation of the moral ideals which were supported by it in the past.

[3]From a book by this title by Edward Shillito.

This loss of religious dynamic has been in part compensated for by increasing social intelligence, but only in part, for a humanistic social idealism unmotivated by the vigor of the old faith has often shed more light than heat, and has failed to generate power for living.

At the same time that religion has been declining in vitality, the propagation of a deterministic theory of morals along with a naturalistic or Freudian psychology has placed many in a curious moral paradox. On the one hand, they have felt emancipated from moral responsibility on the ground that the individual, being merely the creature of heredity and environment, has no freedom; on the other, they have felt impelled to give free expression to their impulses in order to avoid the dire effects of inhibition.

This becomes the more serious because the type of education under which the younger generation has grown up has had in it less of challenge to discipline than the older types. In theory it has attempted to substitute self-discipline for external discipline—this needs to be recognized by those who see in the Dewey system of progressive education nothing but undisciplined liberty. Yet in practice, it may be doubted whether it has achieved this end as effectively as did some of the older forms of control. The young persons of today, growing up as they have had to in the midst of an adult generation in turmoil and with a war and military service ever in the offing, can hardly be blamed for lack of consistent moral ideals and a settled purpose. During the same period, the increase in the range of knowledge taught in the schools, in the movies and over the radio and television has not always carried with it a corresponding depth. The tendency in both secondary and higher education to subordinate liberal culture to technical skills has left many with more of such skills than with moral incentives for using them. All of these forces and numerous others have converged at one time upon an already upset generation.

The result is a new tyranny in personal living which masquerades under the guise of freedom. The liberated individual finds his moral freedom nerve-racking. Society's nerves are shattered also, and the characteristic attitude of our day is one of confusion and bewilderment. Many voices are calling for a reassessment of moral values.

But we seem to be beginning at the end of the story. The object of this book is to survey the genesis of moral ideals, describing how the old morality, now in a state of flux, came into being. It is because a great deal is to be learned from historic morality, both as to what to let slip and what to preserve, that this study is undertaken. It is safe to predict that our moral heritage will not wholly pass, for it is too deeply grounded.

There are many ways to study ethics, and if one chooses the historical route there are still two main approaches. One way is to study and weigh the systems of the philosophers who have speculated upon the good life, trying to recapture their insights and appropriate what is true in their theories. The other way is to see what has motivated the masses of the people when they were not trying to be ethical theorists at all, but simply human beings living at least partially according to their consciences and the customs of their day. Sometimes the two routes converge but not always, and if one's concern is to know how morals came to be, the second is the more trustworthy, for people must live before they can speculate. It is often possible to learn more about the morals of a people from their religion, literature and art than from the theorizing of their philosophers.

This book is a study of moral ideals. An ideal is an idea which so grips an individual or a social group as to determine by an inner authority the direction taken in action. This means that we shall have to make a synthesis of these approaches through theory and life. Some ideas which become ideals are born in speculation; most of the materials of speculation came into being through religious experience, the turn of historical circumstance or the pressure of economic need. Normally all these elements are intertwined. They can be separated for purposes of analysis, but never in actuality. We shall not in general attempt to separate them, for it is better to see them—as life is lived—in a composite whole.

To write the history of moral ideals is to write the history of civilization, for what men have dreamed they have lived by, and what they have lived by they have transmitted. However, the function of this book is more modest. It will attempt to outline, with some interpretation relevant to the present, the foundations on which the morality of the Western world was built. That it deals only with the morals of the ancient world is due to no discrediting of the movements which have taken place since the beginning of the Christian era. To write the history of these developments is a different task, already done a number of times in classic form.[4] What is attempted here is to bring together the most significant facts about the birth of the great ideals on which all Western morality rests —ideals and systems which have many times been elaborated and adapted to changing circumstance, but never superseded.

This explanation will, I trust, make clear also why I have not attempted to deal with the secular or semi-secular systems of morality which have emerged within Christendom. To do so adequately even in outline would require the writing of another book as long as this, or longer. In particular, the rise of modern science laid the foundations of the type of moral thought espoused by John Dewey and other contemporary exponents of naturalistic social theory. This is certainly a

---

[4]Cf. especially W. E. H. Lecky, *History of European Morals,* Vols. I and II; Ernst Troeltsch, *Die Soziallehren der Christlichen Kirchen und Gruppen;* T. C. Hall, *History of Ethics Within Organized Christianity.* Virtually every history of philosophy deals with the various forms taken by ethical theory in the development of Western thought.

source of present-day Western morality, and an important one. But the book must stop somewhere, and since its object is to set forth as faithfully as possible the deep rootage and the long past of our Western heritage, it has seemed best to carry the survey only through the New Testament and there let the story rest.

To this story—so ancient, yet in many respects so contemporary—we now turn. Ours is not the first period of moral transition. Out of every change amongst the many in history has come a mixture of good and evil with the preservation of something vital from the past. No one can hope intelligently to understand the present or prepare for the future—much less have an effective part in its making—unless he knows this past. The signposts of history exist to be read.

CHAPTER TWO

MORALS

IN PRIMITIVE SOCIETY

W‌HEN one discusses what *was* or *is* in primitive society, it is hard to know which tense to use, for it is evidence of the oneness of the human world that the same conditions revealed to the anthropologist in early cave drawings, tools, pottery, ruins of places of worship and other archaeological treasures are also found today among primitive tribes living still in the less developed regions of the earth. Since it is our purpose to survey beginnings we shall speak mainly of the past.

It is not the purpose of this chapter to give a detailed anthropological account of the morals of early society. Those who wish such an account will find it in the monumental works of Westermarck and Hobhouse.[1] Ours is the more limited enterprise of tracing the outlines of early moral development in order to examine, first, the foundations on which civilization had to build, and second, the elements which are not only

[1] E. A. Westermarck, *The Origin and Development of the Moral Ideas,* Vols. I and II (London and New York: Macmillan, 1906–08); L. T. Hobhouse, *Morals in Evolution* (New York: Holt, 1921).

primitive but permanent. We shall note some phenomena which by a combination of historical events, economic forces, rational reflection and ethical idealism have been abolished or radically transformed; others which are as potent today, though in modified forms, as in their genesis. In establishing norms for our own day it is equally important to know what society has eradicated and what—at least to the present—seems ineradicable.

There are certain fundamental institutions which have apparently existed in some form, however primitive, throughout the entire range of human society from its earliest beginnings. These are the family and the agencies for economic, political and religious pursuits. Perhaps education should be added to this list, for the passing on of the lore and the moral attitudes of the older to the younger generations has never been absent. However, as an institution, education remained in a very undifferentiated form long after there was a fairly well developed organization in these other fields. Significantly, these are still the dominant institutions in which center most of our social problems.

1. *The Family*

In primitive society the family is the key to all social organization. Men have lived in groups since human life began, and the first group was the one established biologically for the preservation of the species. The British philosopher Thomas Hobbes worked out an interesting and fantastic *social contract* theory of the State, in which he represented primitive men as living in a state of individualism, each actuated by a desire for his own gain, glory and safety and thus impelled to destroy one another, until men came together and voluntarily formed a social contract to restrain their egoistic impulses for mutual self-protection. A century later Jean Jacques Rousseau developed his social contract theory in terms of the "noble savage" corrupted and drawn away from an ideal state of nature by the entanglements of civilization. It can hardly be thought that either of these philosophers intended to give a historically accurate picture of human society, though in both are very suggestive analyses of perennial human traits. In any case, society did not begin in this way. It began in families, in which the lines between blood kinship and social kinship were not very closely drawn, and while there must have been plenty of egoism of impulse, there was from the earliest times a great deal of social regimentation of action. Individualization was a late and painfully wrought out development.

It is not to be assumed that the family in primitive society existed exactly along the lines of the father-mother-and-children unit with which we are familiar. The family was usually much larger, consisting of many in-laws, grandparents, aunts, uncles and cousins, besides others added to the clan through capture or adoption whose actual relationship was very vague but who were assumed nevertheless to be descended from a common ancestor. This ancestor might be a god, a legendary hero, or an animal rather than a real person, but the significant thing was that the members of the clan *felt* themselves to be kindred, and therefore bound to one another by ties which could not be broken with impunity.

Kinship organization seems to have passed through three over-lapping but fairly distinguishable stages: the primitive horde,[2] the maternal family, and the patriarchal, or paternal, family. In the first of these there is very little organization of any kind, the group being restricted to the biological family or a few families living in close proximity. Caves, trees or rude windbreaks furnish shelter; berries, roots, and other food supplied by Nature furnish sustenance. Disputes are usually set-

---

[2]This term is adopted from anthropological usage but is misleading, since the units at this stage though unorganized are usually small. The term "savage" is also misleading, for an undeveloped moral sense lacks the savagery of more advanced stages.

tled by fighting or by the influence of dominant personalities. Cannibalism is not uncommon, the motive being humanitarian (to spare aged parents pain), economic (to get food in the dearth of other supplies), sanitary (to dispose of the corpses of relatives), protective (to lay the ghost of a murdered man), magical (to acquire the qualities of the victim), religious (to offer the gods a human sacrifice)—or perhaps simply to take revenge. There is no developed sense of duty, yet there is a strong conviction that some things are permitted and others taboo.

The life of the "noble savage" has often been disproportionately lauded, yet it does reveal some admirable traits. Family life is usually monogamous, and is characterized by filial affection, obedience to elders and mutual protection. There are strong loyalties toward friends, with treachery toward strangers and enemies. Courage, cooperativeness and a rudimentary sense of justice are often much in evidence. This type of organization is found today among the Pygmies of the Congo, the Rock Veddahs of Ceylon, the Negritoes of the Philippines, and elsewhere, and, with picturesque exaggerations, is a familiar theme in the movies.

In the second stage, the maternal family (often incorrectly called the matriarchate), the mother does not rule, but she remains among her own kin, she and her children being supported by her brothers rather than her husband, and descent is traced through the mother's side of the house. The husband is a comparatively unimportant member and may not even live with his family, for he must care for his own sisters and their sons, to whom pass his possessions and titles upon his death.

The phenomenon of totemism, clearly exemplified among the American Indians, often accompanies the maternal system. Members of a totem group believe themselves to be descended from a common ancestor, often a material object, plant, or animal, and the totem gives its name to the group. The life of the totem animal in certain Australian tribes is very sacredly guarded, as one would protect that of a beloved relative, and its flesh is eaten only in a solemn ceremonial feast, the *intichiuma*. In this, the partakers believe they acquire in their own persons the qualities of the totem, and it is said to have an effect not unlike that of the Christian Eucharist in developing corporate unity and religious feeling.

With totemism is found usually *exogamy*,[3] the requirement that one must marry outside of his totem. To do otherwise would be like marrying a brother or sister. Exogamy was based partly on an almost universal aversion to incest[4] and probably partly also on the practical discovery that inbreeding is biologically harmful. There are survivals in our present prohibition upon marriage between near relatives. But there was *endogamy* with reference to the tribe—one might marry only within his own tribal group. Of this there are conspicuous survivals in our aversion to miscegenation. One finds it in Jewish endogamy which has had the effect of preserving Judaism, in Hitler's ban upon the marriage of Jews and Aryans, in the caste system of India, in the fear of intermarriage between Negroes and whites in this country which thwarts many efforts toward race equality. Among the royal houses of Europe there is a class endogamous system which transcends racial, national and religious lines of cleavage.

These totemic-tribal relations were sources of unity, and made cooperation possible over a wide area. The most famous historical example is the League of the Iroquois, uniting five tribes (at one time six), in each of which there were eight totems. This organization brought under one government at least fifteen thousand persons.[5] Yet the totem arrangement had

[3]See J. G. Frazer's *Totemism and Exogamy* for a classic account of this relationship. *Laughing Boy* by Oliver LaFarge gives a clear picture in story form.

[4]Westermarck, who holds in general to a theory of the relativity of morals, regards aversion to incest as having been practically universal.

[5]William K. Wright, *General Introduction to Ethics*, p. 29.

in it the seeds of dissolution, for situations were bound to arise in which it was not possible at the same time to be loyal to totem and tribe. The conflict between small-group and large-group loyalties which an individual now feels in war when torn between service to family and state was a disruptive force, and war was an almost constant enterprise.

Furthermore, the maternal family did not rest on a sound economic basis. Family affection is possessive in an economic as well as a spiritual sense, and it is against nature in any age to expect a man to work as hard for his sister's sons as for his own. The maternal system gave way, leaving few vestiges persisting to the present, and the patriarchal family took its place.

Up to the recent past, Chinese peasant life gave a striking picture of the patriarchal family. In it one found the characteristic dominance of the father over his sons and their families, polygamy, concubinage, treatment of girls as chattels to be virtually bought and sold in marriages arranged for them, the faithful but often unrequited service of the wife to her husband, exaltation of filial obedience and reverence for ancestors.[6] Under a different setting but with very similar traits this type of social organization is portrayed in the patriarchal stories of the Old Testament and in somewhat more advanced form in the Greek Homeric tales.[7]

The patriarchal family is the most common form of kinship organization, and it laid foundations which survived to permeate the civilized world. Under it the bride, bought by gifts of cattle, jewelry or other goods, sometimes by services if the groom were poor, went to live in her husband's home and be-

----

[6] A propaganda play of the new regime entitled "Between Husband and Wife" pictures a wife as belonging to the Housewives' Homework Team, bringing home a banner for being a Public Health Work Model, and leaving her husband to tend the baby while she goes off to meetings! Supplement to *China Reconstructs*, No. 6, 1953.

[7] In the latter monogamy with concubinage, rather than polygamy, is the rule, but there is the same paternal dominance, forerunner of the *patria potestas*.

came his property. Such purchase not only transferred possession of the bride from her own family to her husband's, but gave reassuring evidence of the groom's ability to support her. Of Isaac's wooing of Rebekah we read:

> And the servant took ten camels of the camels of his master, and departed; for all the goods of his master were in his hand.[8]

When Jacob sought a bride, he must give his father-in-law seven years of service for each of his wives, though the concubines were secured more easily. These incidents are characteristic of the custom, still widely prevalent in the Orient, of having marriages arranged by relatives. Concubines often, and wives sometimes, were acquired by capture rather than purchase, as in the Biblical story of the seizure of the daughters of Shiloh to provide wives for the Benjamites.[9]

Inheritance, under the patriarchal setting, acquires great importance. Here lie the roots of the union of acquisitiveness with family loyalty which so extensively corrupts our present economic system. The living must lay up goods for their sons, who in turn must hold sacred the memory of their dead ancestors. The sons inherited their father's name (not a surname, but the right to be called "the son of" Abraham, Isaac or Jacob, as today we have John*son*, Peter*sen*, Mendels*sohn*, *Fitz*patrick); also their father's titles, lands, ambitions and ancestors. The daughters, marrying into other families, submerged their lot in that of the husbands' people.

Under the paternal system, there was an economic advance. Society passed from the nomadic to the agricultural stage, the possession of lands became more stable, developing sometimes into great ancestral estates, and the degree of authority exercised by the patriarch made for internal stability. Most

[8]Gen. 24:10.
[9]*Cf. Judges* 21:16–24.

of the features of economic, political and religious life to be discussed later in the chapter are characteristic of this stage of development.

But in one important respect, there was retrogression. While it is easy to idealize the position of woman under the maternal system, she undoubtedly had more freedom than in the subsequent period. A few women of the Old Testament stories, such as Rebekah and Rachel, Deborah and Hannah, appear to have been given esteem and honor for their own sakes; but woman became, in general, the property of her husband. It was her duty to satisfy his sex desires, bear him many sons to perpetuate his name, rear his children, labor in his house or fields. Her industry and chastity were prized that she might bring reward and honor to her husband. The husband who could afford to do so took plural wives to give him sexual novelty, to bear him more sons, to serve him as unpaid laborers, to give him prestige among the people. Sex equality was unheard of. Long after polygamy gave way to monogamy and purchase to romance in the Western world, this patriarchal idea of male dominance continued. It is not yet ended.

As a corrective to an over-idealistic theory of morals, it is necessary to note that monogamy did not supplant polygamy because of any developed sense of the wrongness of the latter. Monogamy begins in the inability of the poor man to support more than one wife, and is reinforced by a combination of practical exigency and crude reflection which gradually eliminates polygamy because of the jealousy it breeds. But never wholly. Its vestigial remnant is prostitution and there is no civilized country which does not have it still, just as there is no country in which women have full sex equality. Both polygamy and male dominance have very deep roots—psychologically in superior physical power which generates social power, culturally in mores which stretch back to the dawn of civilization. To recognize these facts is not to accept the situation as unchangeable, but any attack which disregards them is foredoomed to frustration.

All of these family customs were surrounded with religious sanctity. They changed slowly because to affront them was to affront the gods, and only economic factors were powerful enough to modify them. There is an anticipation here of the power over family life which religion has maintained to the present but which under the impact of secularism is now in dissolution—power, on the one hand, to stabilize and enrich the marriage relation and on the other, to reinforce social conservatism in such matters as birth control and the equal partnership of the sexes. In regard to positions of leadership the Church is one of the last strongholds of male dominance, due to a deep-seated ecclesiastical tradition which is imbedded in a much older religious sanctification of male superiority.

2. Economic Organization

In primitive society are found three of the four main stages of economic development; the hunting, pastoral (or nomadic) and agricultural, while the fourth, the industrial, was a development emerging much closer to our own times. In all three of these stages the dominant note is group solidarity. Primitive society reveals a degree of cooperation and collectivism in economic activities which is virtually communistic. There is an *Urwir*, a "primeval we," which has great coercive power.

It is not to be supposed that this state was arrived at reflectively. Society began on the basis of joint ownership and group activity. Nature and its bounty belonged to everybody long before it belonged to anybody in particular. Of ownership in the modern legal sense, there was none in the early days, though it was generally recognized that a man had a right to his movable goods, as to his wives and children. Primitive communism seems never to have been absolute, probably because in possession of tools and weapons (instruments of power), clothes and ornaments (symbols of prestige), and wives and concubines (agencies of sex expression) there is a spontaneous outcropping of an individualism more deep-rooted than any collectivist tendency. Warfare was a powerful uniting force, and the loot taken in battle was the joint property of the tribe. The story of the stoning of Achan for appropriating "a goodly Babylonish mantle" makes clear what happened to one who appropriated to himself the spoils.[10]

This collectivism, emerging from natural conditions and the demands of war, was reinforced by the need of joint action for economic success. It was imperative in the hunting stage that all the men of the tribe participate in the hunt for big game, for one could do little by himself, and an elemental sense of justice forbade that any be permitted to sit at home in idleness to participate in the fruit of others' effort. That this was the product of practical exigency rather than moral compunction is shown by the fact that small game need not thus be shared except under compulsion of the demands of hospitality.

In the pastoral period, there was generally individual or family ownership of flocks, but the land was not a fixed possession and corporate effort was necessary both for defense and plunder. The custom of holding grazing lands in common lasted on for many centuries into a more advanced civilization. It persisted in Europe until the time of the enclosures[11] in the Renaissance period, and there are still occasional vestiges of it among peasants who pasture their herds on common lands belonging to their village.

In the agricultural stage, individual activity and therefore ownership began to supplant collectivistic. First the harvest, then the land, became the property of him who (in John

[10]Joshua 7.

[11]One of the marks of an advancing capitalism which helped to cause Wat Tyler's Rebellion and the Peasants' War.

Locke's phrase) "mixes his labor with nature." Yet communal occupancy, if not ownership, remained a common form of agricultural life until the break-up of the feudal system, and family ownership prevailed for a long time before individual ownership supplanted it. This was due in part to the difficulty of dividing inheritances, in part to a spontaneous assumption that the land belonged to all members of the group who lived upon and tilled it. We find Caesar in his Gallic Wars thus describing the situation among the Germanic tribes:

> No one possesses privately a definite extent of land; no one has limited fields of his own; but every year the magistrates and chiefs distribute the land to the clans and kindred groups and to those who live together.[12]

In the maintenance of this primitive communism there was a degree of social coercion unsurpassed today in Soviet Russia. Not only the individual who tried to overstep its requirements, but his whole family, fell under condemnation. Achan and *his sons and daughters and cattle* were stoned, and his possessions burned. Though there was rigid insistence upon the preservation of collective property rights within the group, there was slight compunction about stealing from other groups. A great deal of plundering of neighboring tribes was expected and, except as the other tribe resisted, was permitted, thus becoming the occasion for many a border squabble. This difference between the property rights of the "in-group" and the "out-group" is, of course, no outworn phenomenon. Petty thievery from tourists, either overtly or by over-charging for services, is common in many if not most parts of the world; and one needs to look no further than the last war to note with what moral indifference an army of occupation, either in individual looting or in official requisition, appropriates whatever it desires from the inhabitants of a conquered country.

[12]*De Bello Gallico*, VI, 22.

In the midst of primitive communism, with its sharp lines of distinction between "our people" and all others, there is a very attractive feature which marks the first step toward a broadening of moral outlook beyond the kinship relation. This is the obligation of hospitality.

At just what point in moral evolution it became a social obligation to receive kindly the defenseless stranger, set food before him, give him lodging for a time, and send him on his way refreshed, it is not easy to determine. Logically it should have been a late development, but it appears as a pervasive element among the customs of many primitive peoples. It could not have emerged until there was enough individuation for the lone traveler to be journeying abroad; when it appeared it was an implicit recognition that an individual, or a small group of persons, had rights in a peaceful enterprise that would have been immediately cancelled in a mass movement or in war. It is not only one of the most attractive, but one of the most socially useful, expressions of the "primeval we."

In this primitive economic communism, as in modern sophisticated forms, there was much suppression of individual freedom, much cruelty, much disregard of the rights of outsiders. However, on the whole it was an effective system which enabled society cooperatively to get an economic footing and make a start in the direction of the mastery of Nature.

Class equality and class differentiations roughly parallel economic status, but are more primary. Possessions give prestige but prestige gives the right to possess. The priest or chief—particularly the military chieftain—by virtue of his function might hold property forbidden to others. The fact that in early society religious and military prestige creates greater opportunity for dominance than does wealth disproves the Marxist contention that all power is at bottom economic.

Slavery, combining economic with social servitude, is the earliest institutional departure from an equalitarian society.

Slaves had rights, but never equal rights with freemen—a fact which illustrates the union of moral considerations with the callousness begotten by power which runs throughout social history. Within slavery, social distinctions were drawn, debt slaves holding a higher station than those acquired by capture. To challenge social discrimination in the present is to challenge something very deeply inbedded in the past.

With the emergence of private property in the agricultural stage came a parallel development of stratification based on economic power. The small landowner was pushed under and the landed aristocrat increased both in opulence and arrogance. Agrarian societies are usually also military societies, military prowess being rewarded by large gifts or seizures of land. Power begets power, and the small landholder must struggle for his existence against the soldier tax-collector.

All these developments were a gradual process, for in history there are few if any absolute beginnings. In general, primitive society is characterized by economic communism rather than by the private ownership which persistently bursts through it, and by a relatively unstratified society within which social distinctions continually emerge to increase in virulence. A "state of nature" is by no means an idyllic, equalitarian Golden Age of Innocence. Yet early society was less corrupted by distinctions in possessions and prestige, and at the same time less modified by intelligent moral concern, than that which was to follow it.

The question naturally arises as to the relation of this early communistic society to the communism of the present. Is what is taking place behind the Iron and the Bamboo Curtains simply a reversion to primitivism? If it were, it would be far less baneful. At least four aspects mark it off as radically different. First, it is not "natural," but consciously manipulated by shrewd and powerful leaders. Second, it is linked with a political attempt at world dominance, as primitive communism with its border squabbles never was. Third, it is a powerful atheistic faith, a religion which without a god enlists sacrificial devotion but is unredeemed by the inchoate yet real religious adoration of primitive polytheism. And fourth, it has at its command all the instrumentalities of modern technology, mass communication, propaganda and censorship to make its totalitarian control far more complete and dangerous than was ever possible in any primitive society.

3. Civic Relations

In primitive society there was no real State, in the modern sense of the term, yet the clan and tribe formed political units in that they exercised authority over their members, administered justice, and waged war. Membership in the group gave protection and imposed duties. Between the clan, composed of people bearing the same name, and the tribe—the wider social unit consisting of people living in the same general locality and regarding themselves descended from a common ancestor, there was no very sharp distinction. Sometimes, but not always, the clan was a totem group: sometimes, as among the Israelites, clan and tribe were merged. Political organization in many parts of the world seems to have started on this kinship basis, giving rise to the Hebrew tribe, the Greek genos and phyle, the Roman gens and curia, the Scottish clan, the Irish sept, the German Sippe.

Control within the groups was exercised by a powerful sentiment of public opinion, by religious taboos and ceremonials, by the stern use, when deemed necessary, of chastisement, exile or death. Authority came very early to be vested in dominating personalities—chiefs, sachems, war-lords, priests, "judges" (not among the Hebrews judicial officers, but local chieftains, usually military heroes). Often in the paternal system the *paterfamilias*, exercising complete authority over his own family, extended his power to those whose kinship was a matter of inference rather than evidence. Sometimes, as among the early Greeks and Romans and the Iroquois Indians, a council of elders decided the destinies of the group, and thus laid the foundations of democratic government. In various ways authority passed into the hands of certain strong individuals who sometimes became hereditary rulers, but who more often surrendered their power, at death or defeat, to some other strong leader. Dynasties were usually short-lived.

Crime in early society falls into three general categories: offenses against the family and the mores of sex, against property, and against life. The Hebrew commandments, "Thou shalt not commit adultery," "Thou shalt not steal," "Thou shalt not kill" epitomize these prohibitions. Offenses against the gods, as we shall note presently, have a mixture of social and religious reference, and have a seriousness commensurate with the importance of deity.

We have remarked upon the almost universal aversion to incest. There is no evidence that this was commonly practiced. But adultery was, as in every society to the present, and it had to be dealt with. Both honor and property rights were at stake. To commit adultery with the wife of another was to appropriate his goods, as with a virgin it was to decrease her marriage value. Within the tribe or clan it was a punishable —and often a severely punishable—offense. No such restrictions held regarding alien women—a situation which one needs to look no farther than the last World War or the Korean conflict to find reproduced, and which accounts for a great deal of mixture of white with Negro blood in this country. The early codes usually indicate greater severity toward the adulteress than the adulterer, and death by stoning was not uncommon.[13] Then as now, the community was protecting itself

[13]In Lev. 20:10 the death penalty is imposed on both adulterer and adulteress. The penalty is less severe (Lev. 19:20) if the woman is a slave.

against illegitimacy by its rigor toward the one more obviously the parent of unwanted offspring. Through a combination of biological function and age-long tradition, the double standard at this point is likely to be one of the last injustices to surrender before an advancing moral sensitivity.

Punishment for crimes against property show the widest variation—from no punishment and even encouragement for stealing from an outsider to the death penalty for sheep-stealing. Man is by nature acquisitive, and in a relatively property-less state of society there is little sense of wrong in appropriating whatever one finds at hand and can make use of. Travelers today among primitive peoples must expect anything left unguarded to be stolen, not from malice but from simple-mindedness. When a property sense develops, rigid penalties begin to be imposed for theft from one's peers, sometimes multiple restitution,[14] sometimes death. The frontier code which made a horse-thief one of the most despicable of offenders runs true to form. Yet in every country today, some forms of theft are condoned. The most universal element in the early attitude has undergone slight change; namely, that in war the property of the enemy alien is free plunder to be joyously appropriated. From the ravaging army to the individual soldier's glee in taking home some loot to his family or his sweetheart, the practice persists.

In every society there appears to be an elemental reverence for life which makes the deliberate killing of another person a punishable offense. In all societies there are exceptions, such as infanticide in earlier stages (lasting even into the Roman mores) and the acceptance of war and of capital punishment to the present. Yet aversion to murder is probably the most universal of all moral attitudes.

Primitive justice roots in the vengeance to be meted out to the murderer. If this seems like a low origin for high ethics, it is sobering to reflect that no murder trial to the present,

[14]*Cf.* Exod. 22:1.

whether of individual offenders or of war criminals, has been free from vindictiveness in popular attitudes. Vengeance, then as now, was in part the outcropping of a wholesome moral aversion, in part the result of natural and uncurbed impulses to hate and to like to see others suffer for their real or alleged misdeeds.

Like all early activities, punishment for offenses against life or person was a group matter. With the emergence of civilized society among the Egyptians and Babylonians we shall note the appearance of courts and an organized attempt to affix blame and mete out penalties. Antedating this, the leader of the tribe gave the word and the group executed it.

The history of social progress is sometimes grouped in three stages: kinship, authority and citizenship. This division is useful in suggesting trends of development, but it is evident that no sharp line of cleavage can be drawn between them. The kinship period manifests much authority and at least the beginnings of a sense of civic responsibility.

The most striking evidence of a feeling of civic unity is found in the phenomenon of *collective responsibility,* with the related, but not identical, concept of *blood revenge.* Whenever any member of one group injured a member of another, it was the duty of every individual in the injured person's group to exact punishment, if not from the offender, then from any of his kinsmen. If the injury were the taking of a life, then a life must be taken in return, and the debt was often paid many times over. As an humanitarian restriction against overexaction of the penalty, both the Code of Hammurabi formulated in Babylon in the twentieth century B.C. and the Hebrew Covenant Code of about twelve hundred years later state the *lex talionis,* "Thou shalt give life for life, eye for eye, tooth for tooth, hand for hand, foot for foot, burning for burning, wound for wound, stripe for stripe."[15] This doubtless exercised restraint among members of the same group, but little toward

15Exodus 21:23, 24.

outsiders. Chief Justice Taney's dictum that "a Negro has no rights that a white man is bound to respect"[16] expresses aptly the primitive conception of one kinship group's relation to another, and a movement of revenge, once started, had no terminus.

There is a story in Judges 19–21 which gives a vivid picture of the operation of collective responsibility. A Levite and his concubine, coming at nightfall to Gibeah, among the people of Benjamin, were received hospitably by an old man who gave them food and shelter. Some rowdies besieged the house and demanded the guest, but the host, placing the obligation of hospitality above feminine chastity, offered his virgin daughter instead. When the men refused to listen, the guest in self-protection gave them his concubine. The text states dramatically the result:

> [They] abused her all the night until the morning: and when the day began to spring, they let her go. Then came the woman in the dawning of the day, and fell down at the door of the man's house where her lord was, till it was light.
>
> And her lord rose up in the morning, and opened the doors of the house, and went out to go his way; and behold, the woman his concubine was fallen down at the door of the house, and her hands were upon the threshold. And he said unto her, Up, and let us be going. But none answered. . . .
>
> And when he was come into his house, he took a knife, and laid hold on his concubine, and divided her, together with her bones, into twelve pieces, and sent her into all the coasts of Israel.[17] And it was so, that all that saw it said, There was no such deed done nor seen from the day

[16]In connection with the famous Dred Scott case, prior to the outbreak of the Civil War.

[17]Cf. the sending of the fiery cross through the Scottish clans as described in Scott's Lady of the Lake.

that the children of Israel came up out of the land of Egypt unto this day: consider it, take advice, and speak your minds.[18]

Incensed at the outrage committed by the men of Benjamin at Gibeah (the unchivalrous conduct of the Levite and his host apparently caused no disturbance!), "all the children of Israel went out, and the congregation was gathered together as one man, from Dan even to Beersheba, with the land of Gilead, unto the Lord in Mizpeh."[19] The husband of the concubine addressed a great company that included the chiefs of all the tribes and four hundred thousand fighting men; and the people, "knit together as one man," vowed not to return to their tents till the injury was avenged upon the men of Benjamin. The Benjamites, in turn, rallied their forces, refused to give up the "base fellows" of Gibeah, and won two victories. Thereupon the rest of the Israelites, empowered by fasting and the counsel of Jehovah, deceived and smote the Benjamites, killed twenty-five thousand men, drove the rest into hiding, burned the city of Gibeah, and exterminated its inhabitants.

An interesting sequel tells how the Israelites, unwilling to have one of the tribes disappear, yet prevented by a vow from marrying their own daughters to the Benjamites, destroyed Jabesh-Gilead to seize four hundred virgins for them; and told the remnant not thus provided to "catch you every man his wife of the daughters of Shiloh" when these maidens came out to dance in the annual feast of Jehovah. The concluding statement in the account is suggestive:

In those days there was no king in Israel: every man did that which was right in his own eyes.[20]

[18]Judges 19:25–30.
[19]Judges 20:1.
[20]Judges 21:25.

This story illustrates not only the power of collective responsibility but the low position of woman, the binding force of the vow, the obligation of hospitality, and the tendency to invest human bellicose impulses with divine sanction—all current concepts among primitive peoples. And as a matter of fact, while "there was no king in Israel," at that time, the tale reveals a condition of unified effort far removed from anarchy.

The practice of blood revenge was not wholly a social loss. It probably produced enough fear of consequences to serve as somewhat of a deterrent, and it certainly generated a high degree of solidarity of feeling within the clan. But like its modern parallel in the feuds of the Scottish highlands and Kentucky mountains, it was much more of a divisive than uniting force. Under it ghastly perversions of justice could take place. No proof of guilt was asked or offered; punishments fell more often on the innocent than the guilty; no distinction was drawn between offenses committed by accident and design; no freedom of choice was permitted as to whether an individual would participate in the revenge; life and property in another clan were held in slight esteem; there was no way to end the process of retaliation except by the defeat or extermination of the weaker party. As a result, early society was weakened by incessant wars and the foundations were laid for attitudes and practices which have not yet been eradicated.

4. Religion

Religion was a very important thing in the life of primitive man. To be sure, the forms it took were often so different from those to which we are accustomed that it is scarcely distinguishable as religion. Yet beneath a wide disparity of practices, wherever men have been religious, they have sought to relate themselves to a power, or powers, higher than themselves. To this superhuman, supernatural Other they must give reverence, adoration and praise. To It (or Him or Them) they must yield moral obedience, these moral sanctions being unconsciously colored by the prevailing mores but in force and urgency pointing beyond them. From this Power they believed they could receive help, both material and spiritual. This attitude of worshipful dependence on and moral obedience to the Unseen permeates primitive society.

It is sometimes charged that fear creates the gods. Fear is an element in leading man to seek support outside himself, and primitive man had plenty of things to be afraid of—enemy tribes, hostile animal life, cold, hunger, pestilence, disaster of all sorts from an unconquered physical and social environment. Yet fear is not the only source of religion. If we may draw inferences from the myths that arose among every people, curiosity in a world of mystery, and reverence and wonder in a world of awe-inspiring scenes, were quite as much responsible as fear for the tendency of man to people his world with deities. These gods and spirits did whatever man in his ordinary powers could not. Not only did they create the world: they sent the rain to water it, gave it fertility, stirred the sea with mighty storms, caused the volcano to belch forth lava and rivers to flow in torrents over waterfalls. The tendency among primitive peoples to deify the powers of nature, particularly the sun and moon and "bright and shining" elements, is rooted not only in the feeling that from these powers come sustenance, but in the conviction, at least dimly conceived, that nature's mysteries require a more-than-human explanation.

And religion is born, not only in fear and curiosity and awe, but in an ethical urge. Primitive man, like every other man, must regulate his life in a social group. Born in a world of social compulsion, his main course was marked out for him, but these very compulsions—"thou shalts" and "thou shalt nots" —required for their fullest efficacy a sanction coming from be-

yond the society on which they were imposed. Nothing was
more natural than that the untutored mind should fail to
distinguish between the commands laid down by the social
group and by the unseen powers, and that human ordinances
should be uttered with the authority of "Thus saith the Lord."
However to maintain, as some do, that the imputation of
divine authority to human edicts was a deliberate form of
deception by rulers to enhance their own power is to misread
the evidence. Both in early cultures and in undeveloped communities today, religion is a potent force in putting into effect
the current moral standards—some of them unethical enough,
from our viewpoint—and it is a potent force because the people are impregnated with the idea that the unseen powers
make ethical demands. Otherwise, "thus saith the Lord" would
fall on unresponsive ears.

So the world of primitive man was peopled with unseen
spirits, some good, some evil, to be coerced by magical incantations or appeased with offerings. In the beginning religion was thoroughly animistic, with all sorts of inanimate
objects conceived as having spirits akin to that which man
believed he himself possessed. Some objects of special potency
became fetiches—charms to ward off evil, like the rabbit's foot,
or household gods, like the Roman Lares and Penates. Some
objects of special aversion, like a dead body, or of special
sanctity, like the interior of the place of worship, became
taboo—forbidden to the common touch.[21]

An elaborate system of sacrifices by which to appease, to
persuade, and in higher forms to reverence the gods grew up,
and with them arose an elaborate priesthood to be the cus-
todians of these rites and the intermediaries between the gods
and the people. The priesthood very early became a class set

[21]Schweitzer in *The Forest Hospital at Lambarene* tells of his difficulty
in finding natives who would bury the dead from his hospital. An example of the second type of taboo is the Hebrew "holy of holies," the
inner court of the temple which could be entered only by the high priest.

apart, given their living and special privileges in return for
their religious, educational, and often political leadership—a
corrupt and lazy lot sometimes, but a group who served a
useful purpose in dramatizing the religious impulses of the
people.

Elaborate ceremonials for the dead were developed, for
it was believed that the soul of man, so apparently separable
from his body in sleep and presumably in death, must be
ushered with fitting honor into the life beyond. Great tombs
were built for the mighty, like that of Tukankhamen—affording the archaeologist today priceless treasures—and in them
were placed food, jewels, chariots, even slaves, that might be
needed in the after life. It was for this purpose that the Pyramids were built, by the labor of many thousand slaves. In
some places, as in China, the tombs were less pretentious but
ancestral tablets were erected to afford the spirit an abiding-
place, and these must be treated with great reverence and
worship offered before them.

The gods did not consist wholly of animistic spirits or deified
ancestors. A very pervasive concept was that of *mana* (also
manitou, or *wakonda*) which was a vague impersonal power,
the source of the hunter's skill, the fields' fertility, and of everything important. This idea was destined to ripen into monotheism, but not until after a long period of anthropomorphism
—of making deities in man's own image. One finds this clearly
illustrated in the jealous, warlike god of the early Old Testament, and in more artistic but less ethical forms in the Greek
and Roman myths. The gods intermarried with humans, quarreled with them, deceived them and each other, and in general
acted much like the people who worshipped them. But not
wholly. Had they not been conceived on a plane above the
human, they could never have inspired men to worship them.

So primitive man through his priests performed ceremonial
rites to these deities, and in his heart rendered homage to

them. Whatever the effect upon the outward conditions which he thought thus to modify, he found in this act security and peace within, and society found reinforcement for its emerging moral sense. Only the cynic can say that his worship was futile.

5. *Achievements*

What, then, did early man achieve in his moral life before the beginning of the great ethnic cultures? We have seen many of the virtues and vices and social mind-sets of the present emerging. There was little in the early days of *conscious* morality, any more than in the early childhood of the individual; yet comparably, the basic habits and attitudes were taking shape which were to condition future growth and lay the foundations for reflective development in maturer years.

Within the family group were fostered the virtues of maternal tenderness (perhaps the basic root of the altruistic impulse), protectiveness, filial reverence, obedience, and a sense of fair play. The members both of the biological family and the larger kinship group learned to work together with hardihood and jointly to wrest a living from Nature. They fought together to avenge wrongs and subdue enemies; they celebrated festal occasions and performed religious rites together. Offenses were punished, exploits were honored, by the group. The lore of the tribe was passed on by the old men to the younger, the memory of deeds of ancestors was kept alive by legend and song, and a feeling of tribal unity strongly akin to patriotism was generated and perpetuated. The interest of one member of the group was the interest of all.

It is not to be supposed that this unity was based upon altruism, in any developed sense. Plenty of petty quarreling and self-seeking there must have been, and the sharp line of cleavage drawn between the in-group and outsiders gives evidence of persisting narrowness of outlook. But the significant thing is that *a cooperative group is biologically the natural group*. By trial and error, unaided by much reflection, primitive men proved through experience that a cooperative society is a more effective social unit than one in which every man is for himself, with the devil—or death—ready to take the hindmost.

We have noted also that within this cooperative society was a growing movement toward individualism. This is most conspicuous in the emergence of property rights and in the increasing stratification of society which came with differentiation of power. On the whole, the results of this movement, though inevitable, were in the direction of injustice, for it was not to any great degree enriched by a sense of the individual's contributions or tempered by a moral concern for his welfare. These—the Greek and Christian concepts of individualism—are very different from the individualism of self-interest which in every age bursts through social restraints.

We saw that in primitive society were laid foundations of a system of restraint of evil-doers—far enough in many cases from justice, but nevertheless the groundwork for all coercive systems since. It was characterized by the mixture of moral vitality and vindictiveness, group loyalty and economic interest, public opinion and physical force which has characterized the agencies of civil order to the present. This does not mean that there has been no progress; but, as in most matters, what is primitive is also in some sense permanent.

Finally, we noted that man's early gropings toward the moral life found reinforcement in his sense of dependence upon and obligation toward the unseen powers. This was of world-transforming importance. Religion was—and is—a powerful cohesive and conserving agency, also a source of social challenge. In every age it has hallowed the *status quo*—a fact which skeptics never tire of pointing out. By doing so, it has thwarted progress and it has stabilized society. Yet also in every age it has laid upon men disturbing and costly demands. Human nature tends to follow the path of least resistance, but religion supervenes. To be stirred out of comfortable self-interest by emotion directed toward higher powers gives evidence that man—even primitive man—does not live by bread alone. This concept is revolutionary. What these beginnings developed into we shall see more clearly as we trace the moral development of the early civilizations.

CHAPTER THREE

EGYPT

AND THE BEGINNINGS

OF CIVILIZATION

THE study of the civilizations which once flourished in lands now semi-barbarous is a sobering pursuit, for it suggests so much of great beginnings and great endings.

> Lo, all our pomp of yesterday
> Is one with Nineveh and Tyre,

we sing. Yet in its dissolution it leaves its residium, as did these and other great centers of the East.

To examine the early cultures of the Far East lies outside the scope of this book, for while their resources stimulated trade and exploration and therefore greatly affected the course of history, they had little influence on Western morals. However, from the Near East the Occident stands in direct succession. The morals of Egypt and the Mesopotamian valley must be surveyed somewhat rapidly to make room for more extended treatment of later and more influential contributions from Palestine and Greece.

1. The Emergence of Civilization

The state of affairs described in the preceding chapter lies for the most part prior to the emergence of civilization. Yet between primitive and civilized society there is no clear line of demarcation. In all societies people live in families, have some means of subsistence, maintain some kind of order, worship some sort of unseen powers. Both the definiteness and the effectiveness with which they do these things is a matter of *less* and *more* rather than of absence and presence. When the development of a people reaches a relatively high degree of systematic organization, historians in retrospect call it civilized. But in every civilized culture, including our own, some elements remain incompletely civilized. We have noted how little advance there has been regarding the ethics of war and how pervasive still is the drawing of sharp distinctions between the in-group and the out-group. Gross perversions of justice in dealing with offenders, lynching and other virulent forms of racial exclusiveness, prostitution and agricultural peonage are hangovers of barbarism persisting into or developing within civilized society.

What causes civilizations to emerge from barbarism? First, economic causes. The theory of economic determinism which regards all historical developments as traceable to material factors is untrue if spread to cover everything, but very important if taken with reservations. Civilization first developed in the Nile and Tigris-Euphrates valleys because these were marvelously fertile areas. Civilizations begin where nature is bountiful; civilizations achieve most where struggle, in moderation, breeds resourcefulness. Egypt, in a relatively sheltered location, developed a different type of civilization from that of Babylon which was more exposed both to enemies and to opportunities for commerce and expansion. Because England is an island, the whole course of her history and culture has been different from that of continental Europe. Because of the frontier, "the American dream" was possible.

Besides the gifts of Nature in favorable location, soil or climate, an economic factor which is both cause and effect of a developing culture is progress in the use of tools. So important is this that anthropologists mark off advancement by reference to the Stone Age, the Bronze Age, the Iron Age. This greater mastery of metals means not only more efficient protection and an improved economic status but—what is more important to morals—better art and craftsmanship by which to express an emerging individuality. The advance from stone to metal implements, as we shall see presently in regard to Egypt, made possible the extensive wall carvings and sculptured figures by which it is possible to learn much about an otherwise buried civilization.

The invention of writing was a forward movement of great consequence. It made possible communication at a distance, therefore bringing larger units under centralization of authority. But its greater effect on morals lay in the opportunity it afforded of codifying customs into laws, thereby binding past to present more securely than was possible through oral tradition only. The tension between the written past and the living present, illustrated in our time by the continual need for reinterpretation of the Constitution by the Supreme Court, is a permanent source both of friction and of growth.

There are many marks of an advancing civilization, among them greater political cohesiveness, the development of a leisure class and with it an interest in learning, the accomplishment of great feats of engineering skill. Political unity affords an organized channel for the securing of justice, but intensifies injustice through dominance of those in power. Leisure and

learning generate, among other kinds of reflection, speculation upon the good life. The building of the "seven wonders
of the world"[1] was at the cost of human blood and toil, possible only because slavery was an accepted and at that time an
ineradicable institution.

But more relevant to morals than any of these was the
emergence from primitive animism of a differentiated form of
religion in each of the great early cultures. Religion has both
stabilizing and revolutionary power. Men may make their gods,
but having made them, they are greatly molded by them. The
dominant god of an area is the god of its dominant group:
but it is always an open question whether without a faith in
its prevailing deity the group itself would have prevailed.
What Yahweh was to the Hebrews, Re and Osiris were to the
Egyptians, though with differences as well as similarities
which stamp the tenor of their developing cultures. To the
present, to renounce one's religious heritage is less apt to be
a mark of emancipation than of self-exile from a great tradition that has shaped the things we should least wish to surrender.

2. The Cycle of Egyptian History

We shall begin our survey of civilizations with Egypt, though
historians differ as to the priority of this or the Mesopotamian
culture. Along the Nile apparently arose, some seven thousand years ago, what the great Egyptologist James H. Breasted
in a fascinating book by this title calls "the dawn of conscience." In one sense the term is somewhat misleading, for
as we saw in the last chapter, conscience had been dawning
for a long time before civilization emerged. But in the sense
of a reflective, broadly sensitive, mature understanding of

---

[1]The pyramids of Egypt; the hanging gardens of Babylon; the temple
of Diana at Ephesus; the Olympian Zeus by Phidias; the mausoleum at
Halicarnassus; the Colossus of Rhodes; the Pharos at Alexandria.

right and wrong, its earliest developments were undoubtedly in Egypt. To travel today in this land which, with all its great monuments, bears so many marks of squalor and a decadent society, is to become vividly aware of the rise and fall of earthly splendor. The sobering question will not down, "It happened to Egypt; could it happen to us?"

The story of Egypt is of particular significance for several reasons. First, it is a civilization of great antiquity, if not the very earliest. Second, it lasted longer than any of the other twenty-one civilizations to the present, and while no man can predict how much time our Western society still has before it, the Egyptian civilization had a duration of three times as long as we have had so far since the rise of Western Christendom from the ruins of the Roman Empire. Third, it marks the emergence of some of the features most vital to our present civilization; notably, writing, centralized government, great engineering exploits. It contains within its scope the dawn of such central religious notes as a major concern for life after death, divine judgment on moral grounds, and salvation through the vicarious act of deity. Fourth, while in many respects it followed the course of developments found repeatedly within civilized societies, in other respects it is unique. "It was without 'parents' and without offspring; no living society can claim it as an ancestor."[2] This does not mean that it left no influences behind it. Rather, the Syriac civilization which superseded it in the fifth century A.D. was mainly formed elsewhere and did not arise out of the Egyptian culture. And fifth, it took a much longer time to die than did most civilizations, having been in a state of disintegration for its last two thousand years, or almost half of its total scope.

The course of Egyptian history, though it can be presented here only in outline, must be surveyed as a basis for under-

[2]Arnold J. Toynbee, *A Study of History*. Abridgement by D. C. Somervell, p. 30.

standing the moral ideas developed within it. We shall in general follow Breasted's chronology and analysis of the sequence of development,[3] but it must be remembered that dates are necessarily only approximate and in some cases in dispute.[4]

The Nile made Egypt. And the Nile country was (and is) in two parts: the Delta, a fan-like, very fertile alluvial plain where the Nile flows into the Mediterranean; and a long strip of land, ten to thirty miles wide, which stretches back along the Nile for many hundreds of miles, bordered by desert on both sides. The Nile is about 4000 miles long, rising just north of the equator and fed by two great tributaries which converge at Khartoum to form this long fertile strip. Its banks periodically overflow but its waters never fail, for one of its sources, the White Nile, is fed by Lake Victoria Nyanza and the other, the Blue Nile, receives the heavy summer rains from the mountains of Abyssinia. A number of cataracts along its course impede navigation and were barriers to the country's southward political and economic expansion.

Our knowledge of Egyptian history, which can be roughly dated as going back to nearly 5000 B.C., reveals an agricultural society already well advanced beyond the primitive kinship stage, with two clearly defined kingdoms. These kingdoms were Lower Egypt, which was the Delta region, and Upper Egypt which extended upstream to the south about 500 miles to the First Cataract. Already an extensive system of irrigation canals had been developed, and the collection and payment of taxes for their use—prototype of the income tax, since

[3]So much of this section is a condensation of Breasted's longer treatment in *The Conquest of Civilization,* Chapters III and IV, that I shall not attempt to acknowledge indebtedness at every point.

[4]For example, Toynbee places the emergence of Egyptian civilization in the fourth millennium B.C., Breasted in the fifth. Another point of difference is as to the existence of a centralized government under Theban control before as well as after the Hyksos invasion in the eighteenth century.

each man must turn in a share of the grain he had gathered
—marks the earliest administration of government. Each kingdom had its own chief ruler and probably royal buildings,
though none were durable enough to have survived. It is believed that in the neighborhood of the forty-third century B.C.,
a powerful king of Lower Egypt conquered Upper Egypt and
inaugurated the period of the First Union.

During the First Union the capital was Heliopolis, the "city
of the sun," which suggests already the prominence of the Sun
God in Egyptian culture. Within this period, which lasted
until approximately 3500 B.C., important developments took
place. The farmer learned to make his wooden hoe into a plow
—the beginnings of agricultural machinery—and so to expand
his production by the use of domestic animals. This plow was
still of wood, but copper was beginning to be mined and used
for axes and chisels. The local canals were united into a national system controlled from the capital by the king's officials
—perhaps the beginnings of bureaucracy, but in any case a
great advance toward centralized government. A twelve-month
calendar was introduced, each month with thirty days and a
five-day feasting and holiday period at the end. This arrangement, which was not such a bad idea in comparison with the
uneven lengths of months later introduced by the Romans,
can be dated by astronomical calculation as introduced in
4236 B.C.—the only precise date in early history.

More important still, a system of phonetic writing was introduced. This was based on a complicated system of signs, or
hieroglyphs, but by the end of the First Union a twenty-four
letter alphabet was known, though not in general use.[5] The
Egyptians learned to make something convenient to write
on out of the vegetable membrane of the river reed called

---

[5]Although this Egyptian alphabet antedates the Phoenician, it was
from the Phoenicians that the Greeks got the alphabet which became the
basis of ours.

papyrus, thus giving both paper and its name to our culture. A mixture of water, gum and soot made ink; a pointed reed made a pen; and mankind was off on an apparently endless adventure!

Though writing was used in the court and temple of the king, this is not to imply that the people in general were as yet reading and writing. They continued to live in their villages, till the neighboring lands and, as many of the pictures on objects excavated from their cemeteries show, to ply a lively trade by boat up and down the Nile. Since in these pictures each boat carries a standard, a symbol of its town, there had apparently developed a sense of local community pride.

After several centuries the First Union fell apart, to be followed after a brief period of division by the Second Union. A king named Menes, the first whose name we know, made himself ruler of Upper Egypt and then about 3400 B.C. annexed Lower Egypt. At this time the dynasties begin by which epochs of Egyptian history are measured.

The period of the Second Union, which lasted approximately for a thousand years, was the most glamorous period in Egyptian history. In it there was a great advance in mining and the use of copper implements; the marvelous engineering feats involving the building of the great Pyramids of Gizeh and many smaller ones; the carving of the Sphinx out of a promontory of rock as King Khafre's head—the largest sculptured portrait ever made; the erection of great temples; the making of seafaring boats. Along with these, which we should call technological advances, went a remarkable development in government, art, and literature.

The grandeur of the Age of the Pyramids would have been impossible without a strong centralized government and a vast backlog of slave labor. The largest of the pyramids, built about 2900 B.C. to be the last resting-place of King Khufu, is a solid mass of masonry which covers thirteen acres and was originally nearly 500 feet high. It is estimated to contain about 600,000,000 tons of stone in 2½ ton blocks. Considering that these great blocks had to be quarried at a distance, transported across the Nile, hoisted into place, and fitted there symmetrically, the feat staggers the imagination. Even with modern cranes and derricks instead of human backs to do the lifting, it would be no small achievement! Herodotus says that it took 100,000 men twenty years to build it, and this does not seem unlikely. Only a combination of great engineering skill with a powerful central authority could have accomplished it.

In view of the amount of human toil expended in such enterprises a popular uprising would not have been strange. It was, however, not the serfs but the nobles that became too strong for the kings. Decentralization set in, until by the middle of the twenty-fifth century Egypt was a set of loosely related feudal states.

The Feudal Age, though less spectacular in its external achievements than the Pyramid Age, contained some important cultural advances. Fragments from the feudal barons' libraries, rolls of papyrus neatly packed in jars, are among the oldest of surviving books. These contain not only stories, songs, hymns, and moral observations, but the drama of Osiris, the god of the Nile. This was a sacred play—a sort of Passion Play—in which the people joined annually to celebrate the life, death, burial and resurrection of Osiris. Some of these rolls indicate at least the beginnings of a knowledge of physiology; others show a considerable development in mathematics and astronomy. During this Feudal Age, also, great earthen dikes and storage basins were made to control the waters of the Nile; census lists were prepared to help in the collection of taxes; and a professional standing army was gathered. A canal was dug from the north end of the Red Sea to the most easterly branch of the Nile at the Delta, thus making it possible— nearly forty centuries before the Suez Canal—to let ships pass from the Mediterranean through the Red Sea. All in all, the achievements of the Feudal Age seem of more significance than the massive monuments of the Age of the Pyramids.

The Feudal Age was at its height about 2000 B.C. Not long after that, in the eighteenth century, its power abruptly came to an end through invasion and conquest by a foreign people, the Hyksos from Asia. The power of the Hyksos kings, with the native Egyptian princes as their vassals, lasted a century or more, during which there is little to record in the way of cultural advancement. However, soon after 1600 B.C. a prince of Thebes rebelled, drove out the foreigners, and again established Egyptian power with the capital at Thebes, where Luxor now is. This ushers in the Age of Empire, which is the period of the Pharaohs.

The Age of the Empire is rich in pictorial and architectural remains. From them we learn of the introduction of horses and chariots from the defeated Hyksos; of a new military spirit and thirst for conquest; of a great standing army by which it was possible to conquer the territory and extend the sway of Egypt from the Fourth Cataract of the Nile to the Euphrates. Much of this expansion took place in the fifteenth century under Thutmose III,[6] the greatest of the Egyptian conquerors. The temple walls at Karnak tell of his crushing of cities and kingdoms in Western Asia, of his fleet of warships that sailed the eastern Mediterranean, of the welding of his conquests into a vast empire. This expansion had in it, to be sure, the seeds of dissolution, for thereafter, as some countries with colonial empires have discovered in our day, Egypt had to fight foreign enemies in the attempt to hold this domain, and the country's internal strength was weakened. But for a time, Egypt was the most far-reaching as well as the most powerful nation of the East.

More permanent than empire was the mammoth Temple of

[6]Also written Thothmes III.

Karnak, which in spite of our Western megalomania contains the largest colonnaded hall ever erected on earth.[7] Behind it is a huge obelisk, a single piece of granite nearly 100 feet high, which was erected by order of Queen Hatshepsut. This queen, the first great woman ruler in history, was the immediate predecessor of Thutmose III and possibly his wife. In any case, Thutmose did not like this display of female prowess, and not only caused many of her monuments to be smashed but had a sheath of stone masonry built around the base of the obelisk to hide her exploits. The masonry has since fallen down and the inscriptions thus revealed proclaim her glory, though much we should like to know about this period was lost to us by Thutmose's iconoclasm. This we know, that so foreign was it to the thinking of the time to have a woman ruling that she is represented in stone with a beard!

To the Age of the Empire belongs the time of the Hebrew bondage, Rameses II being probably the Pharaoh of the oppression and Rameses III of the exodus. Such building enterprises make meaningful the rebellion of the Hebrews at being treated as serfs and forced to make bricks without straw.[8] To it belongs also a brief but shining light—the attempt of King Amenhotep IV, who changed his name to Ikhnaton, in the fourteenth century to establish monotheism throughout his realm.[9] To it belongs the panopy of death-furniture, pottery, jewels and much else of great beauty as well as historic value unearthed a generation ago from the tomb of Ikhnaton's son-in-law, King Tutankhamen. From the tombs of the Empire

[7]Its Great Hall, though it is only one room of the temple, has a floor-space of about the size of the Cathedral of Notre Dame in Paris, with 134 great columns in sixteen rows, and room enough on each of the great capitals that crown the central columns for a hundred men to stand.

[8]Exod. 5:6–21.

[9]Also written Akh-en-Aton. It may be questioned whether what he established was really monotheism, for while the king worshiped only Aton and ordered references to other gods expunged, his subjects continued to worship the king himself as a god. *Cf.* John A. Wilson, *The Burden of Egypt*, p. 223 f.

period have been recovered the papyrus rolls of prayers and magical charms which make up the "Book of the Dead." This with its great Negative Confession, at which we shall look presently, is the most important literary relic of Egyptian history from the standpoint of its disclosure of moral ideals. From this era come also the famous Tell el-Amarna letters, dispatches from the rulers of Western Asia in the outposts of empire to the court of the Pharaoh, the oldest international correspondence of which we have any knowledge and invaluable for the light they throw on the relations between Egypt and the eastern sections of the Empire.

However, Egypt's greatest days were over. Affairs of state fell into the hands of a corrupt bureaucracy of priests, and magic was fast replacing religious vitality. Not far from 1100 B.C., at about the time when the Hebrews were invading Palestine and the Greeks were besieging Troy, the final period of dissolution and decadence set in.

The Empire began to shrink. The Hittites took Syria; the Philistines and Hebrews held Palestine; in the East a great rival empire was growing in power. Egypt remained strong enough to contest with Babylon the right to dominate Palestine through most of the remainder of the Old Testament period; then with the rest of the Eastern world it fell before Alexander's armies and was swept into his vast empire in 332 A.D.

When Alexander's empire after his death split into the rival factions of the Seleucids and the Ptolemies, Egypt remained under the control of the Ptolemies for about three centuries. However, Cleopatra was the last of the Ptolemies. With Antony's defeat by Octavian at the battle of Actium in 31 B.C. and Antony's and Cleopatra's suicides in 30, Egypt became a part of the Roman Empire.

In the centuries adjacent to the beginning of the Christian era northern Egypt, especially the city of Alexandria, became a great center of philosophy and learning. As every student of church history knows, its Christian thinkers played no small part in the development of early Christian thought. The burning of its vast library by order of the Moslem Caliph Omar in 640 A.D. was a major catastrophe to human culture. Nevertheless, Egypt as a nation had forfeited its greatness by the time the civilizations from which we most directly inherit were coming to birth.

Such rise and fall of destiny prove nothing as to the truth of Spengler's theory of "the decline of the West." However, it suggests vividly that no civilization, our own included, should deem itself proof against collapse.

3. Egyptian Religion

The two most dominant aspects of Egyptian civilization are the union of political with religious power, and the importance attached to preparation for the after-life. These meet in the pyramids, great tombs by which kings thought to defeat death and maintain forever both their existence and their prestige. By way of such massive masonry—Egypt's chief surviving monuments—we are led directly to the center of Egyptian faith and culture. This is true both symbolically and historically, for it is from the inscriptions in them (Pyramid Texts) that much of our knowledge of ancient Egypt is derived.

In Egypt it was not the warrior-king of most early civilizations, but the king who claimed religious sanctity, that solidified the state. In any society there are three great sources of unity: a common enterprise with common loyalties, fear, and the rational consent of the governed. It was too early yet for the last to be a dominant force, and to the present it has never been the primary ground of political unity. Fear will hold a state together temporarily, but the unity thus purchased is always in unstable equilibrium. Only a common cause, or the combination of common loyalties to common causes which makes up patriotism, is a secure foundation. Egypt found this common element in a priestly state-religion.

In early Egyptian literature, especially in the hymns, the gods and kings are so mixed together that it is hard to disentangle them. Re[10] is the king and high priest, yet Re is himself the sun-god. The Pharaoh rules by the power of God; the Pharaoh speaks and acts for God; the Pharaoh *is* God. What we have here is somewhat like a doctrine of the divine right of kings plus an orthodox theory of the incarnation. The worshiper-subjects were not troubled by considerations of consistency any more than it has troubled many generations of Christians to think of a certain revered Galilean as "very God of very God."

The Egyptians were polytheists. Each locality had its presiding deity, as is common in a developing religion in the long period between animism and monotheism. As a city rose to prominence, so did its god. Among them nine emerged to constitute a sort of pantheon, and in this Divine Ennead two assumed outstanding importance. These were Re, the Sun-God and presiding deity of Heliopolis, and Osiris, God of the Nile. Osiris came also figuratively to signify verdure and the renewal of vegetative life. These deities were doubtless derived from the two great sources of physical life by which the Egyptians found themselves nourished. In part, though never fully, they were localized in Upper and Lower Egypt respectively and their rivalry symbolizes that of these two areas. There was a long conflict between them, Re being in the ascendancy during the earlier part of Egypt's history and later Osiris, in whom centered a mystery cult which influenced Christianity.

The gods tended to merge into one another. The sky-god Horus, like Re, was god of the sun, and in this capacity was

[10]Also written Rā.

symbolized by the falcon. The Biblical reference to "the sun of righteousness with healing in his wings" reflects this Egyptian background. But Horus was also the son of Osiris, this illustrating the way in which the deities and the mythologies connected with them tended to merge.

According to a widely held and very influential myth, the good Osiris, who, though a god, had assumed mortality for the salvation of mortals, was slain by Set, his evil brother. Horus avenged his death. By the gift to Osiris of his eye, which was wrenched from its socket in the conflict, he enabled Osiris through the help of Isis, the sister and wife of Osiris, to rise from the dead and again to enjoy the immortality befitting a god. Thus the "Horus eye" became a sacred symbol connoting sacrifice,[11] though in the ensuing rites Osiris and Isis have a larger place than Horus. Through the victory of Osiris over death, the power to live immortally was believed to be available to those worshipers also who rightly celebrated the rites commemorating this great event. The re-enactment of this drama, particularly in the springtime when the renewal of vegetative life was a vivid reminder both of the god of vegetation and of a life beyond death, was the central feature both of the Egyptian mysteries and later of the Roman mystery cult of Isis. In Egypt, Osiris held the central place; in Rome, Isis became the primary figure.

How much of this passed over to become the Christian story of death and Resurrection of Jesus Christ for the eternal salvation of mortal men? Opinions, of course, differ. It is easy to make a mistake by going to an extreme position in either direction. The Christian need not hesitate to admit that through the Roman mysteries, this cult had its influence on the ob-

[11]More common symbols are the sun's disk with outstretched wings, thereby constituting a falcon, and the sacred beetle, or scarab. The latter gets its sanctity from being a charm placed over the heart of a dead person to prevent his betraying himself by incautious statement in the Great Judgment. See *infra*, p. 55.

servance of Easter and the retelling of the Resurrection story, and that Isis to some extent has a correlate in the Virgin. Nevertheless, the differences are far greater than the similarities. The Osiris myth lacks the ethical and spiritual richness of the Christian drama of redemption. The fact that there are parallels between mythology and fact in no respect eliminates the essential historicity of the Gospel narrative. To reduce Christianity to its pre-Christian origins, or to discredit its historical foundations because there are mythological parallels in another culture, is a procedure that has no scientific or theological justification.

4. Egyptian Morals

The primary motifs of Egyptian morals center in the worship of Re and Osiris. Though interfused, they must be examined separately. First, let us look at Re worship.

When Heliopolis came to dominate Egypt, Re rose in power, eclipsing other deities. This supremacy was in part due to a transfer of political prestige to religion as the fortunes of the group shifted; it was also due to the fact that as Sun-god Re symbolized a transcendent, universal power. This is characteristic of the way in which historical, physical and spiritual forces often blend. A henotheism—belief in the existence of many gods but supreme worship of one—developed about Re (also called Aton from the sun's disk) as we shall note that it did among the Hebrews about Yahweh. This is morally important because Re was conceived to be not only supreme in power but in righteousness.

This mixture of historical circumstance with religious and moral insight is illustrated in the oldest extant piece of literature in the world, the "Memphite Theology," which dates probably from the first dynasty (about 3400 B.C.). It represents Ptah, the god of Memphis, as the heart and tongue of the gods out of which all the other gods came into being. This reference to heart and tongue, a pictorial way of signifying mind and speech, glimpses behind creation an articulate intelligence, and thus is an early forerunner of a Logos doctrine. Furthermore, the existence of a social criterion of judgment and at least an elementary sense of justice are suggested by the words:

> Indeed, all the divine order came into being through what the heart thought and the tongue commanded . . . (Thus justice was given to) him who does what is desired, (and punishment to) him who does what is not desired. Thus life was given to him who has peace, and death was given to him who has sin.[12]

Though the king in Egyptian thought was intermixed with deity, he was not quite identical. Death stood as a barrier. At death he must make his way eastward to the portals of the sky[13] and there demand admission. The Pyramid Texts abound in descriptions of a glorious hereafter for the king in the Sun-god's presence. There is a neat interplay of subordination and dominance in the king's threat to prevent the rising of the sun if he is halted at the entrance to the Sun-god's realm.

There is much significance in this blending of political, religious and moral functions in the king. It foreshadows the union of Church and State, and with it both the perversions of justice and the attempts to ensure justice by coercive power which have been evoked by such a union through the centuries. Manifestly, it did not prevent the rulers from oppressing the people. Then, as always, the hallowing of earthly power made for gross injustice, as in the building of the pyramids by slave labor that the king might have a glorious life hereafter. Yet Egyptian literature abounds in protests against injustice which are an intimation of growing moral sensitivity.

[12]As quoted by J. A. Wilson in *The Burden of Egypt,* p. 60.
[13]If as children we placed heaven in the sky, this concept has had a long history!

At a number of these we must look briefly, referring the reader to Dr. Breasted's classic *The Dawn of Conscience* for a fuller account.

In the Feudal Age, that is, before 2000 B.C., there was written a meaningful story called "The Eloquent Peasant." Its main point is the unjust treatment of a peasant by a minor official, whereupon the peasant appeals to the Grand Steward of the king. In a series of eight speeches which grow more denunciatory at each round, he reproaches the Steward for failure to give justice to the poor. The importance of this story, aside from its picturesque literary style, is twofold: it makes clear that very early the emergence and vocalization of a sense of social justice had taken place, and it links right doing on earth with immortal destiny. The climax of the story appears in the words:

> For justice (Maat) is for eternity. It descendeth with him that doeth it unto the grave, when he is placed in the coffin and laid in the earth. His name is not effaced on earth, but he is remembered because of right. Such is the uprightness of the word of God.[14]

A second document of about the same period is the "Admonitions of Ipuwer." Its point is very similar, with the difference that it focuses in the need of a just and benevolent king. Ipuwer is represented as a wise man who in the presence of the king delivers a long arraignment of the times and calls for reform. Though the invective centers in portrayal of internal political and economic decay and the consequent danger of foreign invasion, the wise man, with both a nostalgic yearning and a note of messianic hope in his plea, calls for the restoration of peace with justice through an ideal king such as the country once had in a golden age when the Sungod ruled.

In a measure this plea and prophecy were fulfilled centuries

14Breasted, *op. cit.*, p. 191.

later, though without the results hoped for by Ipuwer. We have noted that in the fourteenth century, Amenhotep IV changed his name to Ikhnaton, or Akh-en-Aton, and tried to establish monotheism. This change of name is very significant for Amenhotep means "Amon is satisfied," while Ikhnaton means "He who is serviceable to the Aton."[15] Amon, or Amon-Re, was the old Sun-god about whose worship a powerful priesthood centered, while Aton, the sun's disk, symbolizes a new cultural as well as religious movement. Ikhnaton moved his capital from Thebes, the "City of Amon," to a new rural setting at Tell el-Amarna, ordered references to Amon and the other gods deleted from inscriptions, and tried to exalt Aton as the sole deity. Opinions differ as to how selfless he was in this enterprise. Yet he seems to have been a man of unusual moral probity and religious insight, and a poet of a high order. His "Hymn to Aton," in the mood of the Hebrew psalms, contains passages enough like Psalm 104 so that the latter may have been borrowed from it.

Ikhnaton's reform was unwelcome. Both corruption and conservatism were too strong. He may have tried to exalt himself as well as Aton. In any case, powerful forces opposed him, and he seems to have had no better success in transforming Egypt than did the high-minded Stoic emperor Marcus Aurelius in making over the Roman Empire. At his death, the old cults swept back into power under King Tutankhamen. Ikhnaton's memory lingers as that of a great religious spirit crying in the wilderness for later generations to hear. The demand for righteousness through a union of political and religious power may be either a ghastly substitute for justice, as among the Pyramid builders, or a foregleam of its realization, as with Ikhnaton. Which it is depends on the type of ideals which actuate it, and only a rare sense of the subordination of all earthly power to a righteous, transcendent God is ade-

[15]Or possibly, "It goes well with the Aton." *Cf.* Wilson, *op. cit.,* p. 215.

quate to keep it pure. Yet even when it is pure, it is not always in the historical scene "successful."

One important compilation of moral and spiritual wisdom comes from a period later than Ikhnaton, though it is doubtful that he influenced it. This is the Wisdom of Amenemope, dating from the tenth century B.C. It consists of adages and shrewd moral injunctions, so much like the Hebrew book of Proverbs that the latter was almost certainly influenced by it. It is arranged in thirty chapters, which may account for the "thirty sayings" of Proverbs 22:20 if, as Professor Breasted thinks, the compiler of Proverbs had access to a copy of this book. Though largely in the mood of personal moral advice it also contains injunctions to pray to and honor Aton.

However, the worship of Re or Aton was not the only Egyptian faith which had important moral consequences. Sun worship was challenged by Osiris worship, which centers in individual piety and the hope of personal immortality. As Re was the chief deity of the kings, so Osiris was of the people, and Osiris worship was a popular religion. This is important, for the first major emergence of a sense of the worth of the individual and of the possibility of salvation to personal immortality by divine grace is connected with it.

The Osiris cult developed through several stages. To trace these stages it may be profitable to trace the development of types of belief in immortality. The first of these belongs chiefly to the association of the kings with Re worship; the other three in spite of intermixtures were in the main aspects of the Osiris cult.

The first stage is the *immortality of power*—an immortality possessed by the kings only and not by the masses. Indeed, the ruler from the standpoint of his ultimate destiny was thought of less as an individual than as the incarnation of power and majesty. So great a person could not die! The constant refrain of the Pyramid Texts is the deathlessness of kings. The Pyramids were the instruments of deathlessness, but they were also symbols of the king's enduring life and in a sense they *were* his immortality. It is useless to try to say whether they are more the product of the people's unreasoning reverence for the king's greatness, his own vainglorious desire for earthly prestige, or an authentic though inchoate spiritual impulse. Motives usually come mixed.

The second stage is *immortality through personal goodness.* This is a long step in advance, and did not come suddenly. Social distinctions permeate it; for first the king, then the nobles, and later the common people were thought worthy of immortality through personal purity. But it is a fact of major significance that this moralization and democratization came at all, two thousand years before Christ.

The papyrus rolls found with the mummies in the tombs consistently portray a great judgment scene. In one of its commonest forms the dead person is led by Maat, goddess of truth, justice and righteousness, into the judgment-hall of Osiris, where in the presence of forty-two tutelary deities he must clear himself of the forty-two sins over which these preside. This catalogue of sins, sometimes called the Negative Confession, is preserved in the Egyptian Book of the Dead, a compilation of poems, prayers and affirmations taken from the coffin texts. Though the Book of the Dead contains many magical charms for securing favor in the after-life, it is of great value in reflecting what was thought to be right conduct even if this was not lived up to, and the Negative Confession is its most important chapter.

The Negative Confession is in reality an affirmation of innocence rather than a confession of sin, and the sacred scarab lay on the dead man's breast to keep him from giving himself away. However, it is searching in what it sets forth as the moral ideal—so much so that no Christian could truthfully affirm his freedom from all the sins enumerated! The deceased must declare that he has not done iniquity or violence, stolen from God or man, made light the bushel or acted deceitfully, removed his neighbor's landmark, uttered falsehood, pried into matters or spread evil rumors, given way to wrath, stirred up strife, struck fear into another, caused another to weep, judged hastily, sought for personal distinctions, laid waste the lands or fouled the water, caused a slave to be misused by his master, turned a deaf ear to words of truth and right, committed fornication, committed murder, killed any sacred animal, despoiled the mummies, cursed the king, or blasphemed a god. This searching analysis is followed by an affirmation which contains phrases of an almost Christian tone, "I have given bread to the hungry man, and water to the thirsty man, and offered garments to the naked man, and a boat to the (shipwrecked) mariner. . . . I have made offerings to the gods. I am clean of mouth and clean of hands, therefore let it be said unto me by those who shall behold me, 'Come in peace.' "[16] The final step in the great assize is the weighing of the dead man's heart in the balance against the feather of Truth, the blind goddess of Justice holding the scales. (This still current symbol is at least four thousand years old.) If the heart tips the scales exactly evenly, the deceased receives the name of Osiris and is welcomed by him into the company of the blessed. If not, he passes to oblivion. Egyptian religion had annihilation of the wicked, but no hell.

Since what is thought about death usually mirrors what is thought about life, this judgment-scene with its moral distinctions which reach into the inner aspects of living is highly significant. The belief in immortality both molds, and follows the patterns of, prevailing moral insights. That there was magic mixed with it, and an attempt to circumvent self-revelation,

[16]The Book of the Dead, pp. 258 ff. in The Sacred Books of the East, Vol. II.

should not obscure the existence of a highly developed sense of moral probity.

The third stage is what might in theological terms be called *immortality through grace*—that is, through the gift of Osiris to the undeserving. It is this which was sought in the yearly re-enactment of the sacred drama of Osiris' life, death, burial and resurrection. Just how effective it was in arousing feelings of moral deliverance and the promise of future life is somewhat uncertain, but undoubtedly it kindled religious emotions of personal faith and hope as well as feelings of social solidarity. It would not have been practiced as long as it was, had the people not felt they were gaining from it deliverance from death. But it failed to go deep enough—to be sufficiently moralized or to demand enough of the worshiper—to be self-sustaining, and it never became the dominant note in Egyptian religions.

Since this salvation could be won through the performance of certain esoteric rites, it readily passed over into a fourth and final stage, *immortality through magic*. Magic, to be sure, had never been absent, but it came to overshadow and becloud moral distinctions. It is as a combination of these high elements and low—divine compassion and human manipulation—that Osiris worship became a mystery religion which was later transmitted to the West. Within it, as in Christianity, a system of indulgences was worked out and a corrupt priesthood made a fat living from the human yearning to escape death's terrors.

When a faith reaches this stage, it must either die or be revivified by the radical injection of a new spirit. It was against such sacerdotalism and the use of mechanical magical agencies that Ikhnaton unsuccessfully revolted. A breath of pure poetry and pure religion blows through his hymn to Aton:

I shall breathe the sweet breath
Which comes forth from Thy mouth.
It is my desire that I may hear Thy sweet voice,

Even the North wind, that my limbs may rejuvenate with life
Through love of Thee.
Give me Thy hands, holding Thy spirit,
That I may receive it and may live by it.
Call Thou upon my name throughout eternity
And it shall never fail.[17]

But Egypt's religion had run its course, and it remained for
the Hebrew prophets and psalmists to make permanent what
Ikhnaton glimpsed.

Thus we see why Professor Breasted places the dawn of
conscience in Egypt.[18] The first conscious demand for social
justice in this life, the first clear sense of divine judgment, the
first moralization of the belief that persons have a destiny
beyond the grave, the first idea of vicarious salvation through
the act of a god, the first monotheistic faith, proceed from
Egyptian culture. There is evident here, as in all goodness,
a mixture of high moral impulse with imperialistic pretensions,
self-interest, fear, chicanery and all the more sordid aspects
of human nature. But a start had been made towards something very vital.

[17]From *Lyra Mystica,* ed. C. C. Albertson, p. 1.

[18]Any person with an interest in this field must acknowledge an enormous debt to Breasted for the knowledge of Egyptian culture, religion
and morals which his discoveries have made possible. However, the present writer is obliged to join those who believe that he has greatly over-
estimated the influence of Egypt upon Hebrew literature and religion. Of
this we shall say more in Chapter Five.

CHAPTER FOUR

THE MESOPOTAMIAN

VALLEY

W<small>E</small> have lingered at some length with Egyptian civilization, not because our Western culture stands in direct succession from it, but because it has so many "firsts" that its importance is great for all that came after it. Opinions differ as to how much it influenced the Hebrew faith, and hence all Christendom. It is the author's judgment that except for some such direct borrowings as were noted in the last chapter, its influence was more roundabout than direct. But in any case, no one interested in the development of Western culture, religion or morals can afford to neglect it.

We turn now to a culture that is neither so close-knit, so long lasting, nor so productive of high religious insights. However, through its closer contact with the Hebrew people it is in more direct lineage with the Hebrew-Christian tradition.

1. The Physical Setting

The Tigris-Euphrates valley saw a number of empires rise

and fall, interplaying with each other as conquest succeeded conquest. The foundation that is common to them all is what Professor Breasted nearly forty years ago in a high-school history book called the Fertile Crescent, and the name has stuck.[1]

The Fertile Crescent is the area which lies between the Arabian Desert on the south and the Taurus Mountains on the north, with the Zagros Mountains on the east and the Mediterranean Sea on the west. The Crescent, to be sure, is somewhat skewed, but any topographical map will show that this fertile block of land is undeniably crescent-shaped, with the thickest part lying to the north and the two arms making a semi-circle about the desert, somewhat as if its southern border were the shore of a great inland bay. It contains Palestine and Syria on the west, and of the special topography of Palestine we shall say more in the next chapter. At the southeastern end, the Crescent terminates with the Persian Gulf. However, from the standpoint of what we are now to look at, its most important feature is the watering of this great valley from the Tigris and Euphrates rivers.

These two rivers rise only about 150 miles apart in the mountains of Asia Minor, but follow a very different course. The Tigris to the east flows quite directly toward the Persian Gulf, being fed along the way by many swift streams from the Armenian plateau. The Euphrates, on the contrary, meanders about, flowing first toward the Mediterranean and then bending south-eastward toward the same outlet. They now meet about seventy miles from the Persian Gulf, though in the days of which we are to speak the topography was somewhat different. So much silt has been carried down by the rivers that the gulf has been filled in 150 to 160 miles since early Babylonian days. The ancient "Ur of the Chaldees" on the lower Euphrates may once have been a seaport, though if so, it was before the days of extensive navigation.

[1] *Ancient Times,* 1916.

The Fertile Crescent includes land adjacent to the rivers, extending in the west far beyond the Euphrates. However, it is in the fertile territory between these rivers—whence came the name Mesopotamia which means "between the rivers"— that the Sumerian, Akkadian, Babylonian, Assyrian and Chaldean empires were successively established. This is not to say that they succeeded each other from exactly the same location, for Lower Mesopotamia near the Persian Gulf was the seat of the Sumerian, Akkadian,[2] early Babylonian and later the neo-Babylonian or Chaldean civilizations, while Assur, which we usually call Assyria, was in the north. However, the conquerors as they came along successively took the whole territory and held it until they were supplanted. Thus, there is a mixture of common elements with diversity in the culture that developed.

This entire section, now as decadent as Egypt from the standpoint of its culture, is emerging into importance in world history for a very different reason from that of its ancient grandeur. The reason is—oil. Iraq occupies the greater part of the Mesopotamian valley, and Mosul stands near the site of ancient Nineveh. Whoever controls the oil-wells of Iraq, at the heart of the Middle East, has a strategic advantage in the world contest for power in our time.

Before we move into a survey of the rise and fall of empire in this territory, a look still further back may be of interest. For it is in this valley that the legend of a Garden of Eden, the locus of a golden age of innocence before sin entered to corrupt mankind, probably took its rise. The alluvial grazing plain of western Babylonia, at the southern end of the valley, was formerly called Edin. The author remembers hearing George Lansbury, British Member of Parliament and Christian

---

[2]Akkad lay north of Sumer, but south of what was later to be Assyria. Thus, Babylon, located in Akkad, was north of Ur but considerably south of Nineveh and Assur.

saint, remark whimsically years ago of British interests in Iraq, "Adam and Eve had a perfect right to be there—but does that give *us* any right to be there?"

2. The Cycle of History

a. *Babylonia and its predecessors.* The earliest civilization in this area—the Sumerian—dates from a period somewhat before the third millennium B.C. Unlike most of the later inhabitants of whom we shall speak, the Sumerians were a non-Semitic people. Where they came from, if they came from anywhere outside of this region, is not known. Excavations at Ur, Nippur, Lagash and other southern cities lying in the great plain between the lower parts of the two rivers reveal early evidences of a fairly advanced society in which agriculture, cattle-breeding and the weaving of woolen goods from the produce of the flocks were the chief occupations, but also with metals—copper, bronze, gold, silver and lead—in common use. This Sumerian civilization emerged in the low flat country which had better be called at the beginning of the story the Plain of Shinar, as it is called in the Bible, but which later was to be known as Babylonia.

Since there is a dearth of building stone in southern Mesopotamia, there could be no such imperishable monuments as the Egyptians built. The houses were of sun-dried brick and when one fell down, the ground was leveled off and another built over it. Thus, it is necessary to dig through layer after layer to get down to the Sumerian relics. Among them, however, are found evidences not only of the economic pursuits just mentioned, but of trade by caravan with the other countries adjacent to them, possibly extending west to the Mediterranean and as far east as the Indus Valley;[3] of the beginnings of cuneiform (wedge-shaped) writing by picture signs

[3]Excavations reveal a very similar civilization in the Indus Valley dating back to at least 2500 B.C.

made by a stylus or sharp-cornered reed on soft clay, and baked in the sun; of temple towers, nearly cube-shaped but getting smaller toward the top, and often terraced in layers, in which dwelt their gods and near which the people offered as sacrifices tribute from their fields and flocks.

The intermingling of religion and economics is evident in the existence already of a wealthy priesthood, who were also the town bankers loaning and collecting money in the name of their god. The Sumerians had both a decimal and a sexagesimal system, and the basic unit of measure was the *mina*, or pound, which still survives in our pound weight as things are weighed up at the corner grocery. A little later under the Babylonians this was to become the basis of a silver currency, with sixty shekels making a pound, sixty pounds a talent.

The pound is not the only thing we have inherited from the Sumerians. Among their folk-lore was the story of a great flood which the god had once sent to devastate the land. One may read the Hebrew version of it in Genesis, chapters six through nine. Also, in the tower temples of the Sumerians lie the beginnings of the story of a Tower of Babel (Babylon) that men tried to make reach up to heaven (Gen. 11:1–9). Also to beset the path of Hebrew religion but to be rejected by it, are traces of human sacrifice and of a cow-goddess to be worshiped by those who wanted their herds to increase and prosperity thus to be enhanced.

The Sumerian era appears to have been relatively peaceful, though punctuated occasionally by raids and squabbles between neighboring city-kingdoms. In the twenty-sixth century B.C., this was radically changed by the conquest of the Sumerian territory and much beyond it by Sargon, the Akkadian, who was the first great Semitic leader and the first builder of empire in western Asia. His dominion stretched from Elam on the east to the Mediterranean on the west, and far up the Mesopotamian Valley to the north and west.

The Semites as they came in took over much of the Sumerian culture. They gave up their nomadic life and began to live in houses of sun-dried brick, some of them quite palatial. Since the American tourist today tends to measure culture by plumbing, it may be of interest to note that the royal palaces of this period had bathrooms and sewage systems! More important architecturally is the arched doorway, which was destined to make its way into Roman and then into Christian church architecture. The Akkadians adapted the Sumerian use of metals to the fashioning of copper helmets and took over the wedge-shaped signs to write their Semitic language.

We are in the habit of calling this mixture of Sumerian and Semitic civilization Babylonian. Strictly speaking, Babylonia had not emerged yet, though it was in the making. The line of Sargon the Great lasted for a century and a half; then the dynasty collapsed through internal intrigue. Soon after 2300 B.C. the Sumerian cities of the south again regained control, and the nation which ensued was called the kingdom of Sumer and Akkad. It was Ur, not Babylon, that was the center of power and prestige. During this time a great commercial civilization developed, at which we must presently look as we examine some of the features of Babylonian religion and morals, but Babylon as a city was as yet of minor importance.

What lifted Babylon to power was the invasion of Akkad by the Amorites. One of the Amorite chieftains about the middle of the twenty-first century B.C. established his capital at Babylon in Akkad, north of Ur, and extended his power over all this territory in the southland between the rivers. The Amorite rulers who held sway there for the next three hundred years greatly enhanced the status of Babylon and laid the foundations for the glories which were to become the symbol of luxury, opulence and power.

It was Hammurabi, the sixth in the line of these Amorite kings, who, near the beginning of the second millennium B.C.,[4]

[4]The date is in dispute. It is estimated from the twenty-first to the

established conclusively the Amorite power over this entire territory. But more than that, he issued the famous code of laws which bears his name. Hammurabi was a great conqueror, as Sargon had been, but he was also a great civilian ruler. This is not only attested by the monument bearing his laws, in which he is represented as receiving them from the Sun-god Shamash, but by a sizable collection of his letters which have survived. They show him as sending orders to and receiving reports from the local governors throughout his realm, keeping his hand on everything, executing justice with firmness but also with fairness. His code of laws was not entirely original with him, but was a systematic and selective codification of existing laws and usages with such changes as he desired to make.

Under Hammurabi's patronage and the protection of his standing army, trade was extended far and wide. With it went the Babylonian cuneiform writing and the Babylonian gods. At the head of the procession was Marduk, a Semitic deity who transcended without replacing the old Sumerian gods of the people, while the chief goddess was Ishtar, who was to plague the Hebrews as Ashtoreth and pass over into the Greek pantheon as Aphrodite.

The splendor of Hammurabi's rule barely survived him. Soon after his death the Kassites invaded from the east and the Hittites, ancestors of the present Armenians, from the northwest. The Hittites came and went with their plunder, but the Kassites stayed and brought the once glorious empire to a state of stagnation from which it did not emerge until the rise of the Chaldean, or neo-Babylonian, empire in the seventh century B.C. The next epoch in the course of empire has its scene laid in the north, with Assyria as the chief figure in the drama of contest for power.

---

eighteenth centuries. Breasted dates his reign as 1948–1905 B.C. Jack Finegan in *Light from the Ancient Past*, p. 47, puts it as late as 1728–1686 B.C.

For the next few centuries there were ups and downs of power, sometimes the south being in control, sometimes the north, but neither in undisputed dominance. After about 1300 B.C. when a famous line of Assyrian kings beginning with Shalmaneser I seized control, the scales of empire were decidedly tipped in favor of the north.

b. *Assyria.* Assyria lay somewhat to the northwest of Babylonia, its chief cities, Assur and Nineveh, being located on the upper part of the Tigris. Several geographical features marked it out for a different destiny. It was highland country rather than plain, with a much more invigorating climate than the low, flat Babylonian plain. Numerous streams from the adjacent mountains cut valleys which, being very fertile, permitted agricultural wealth to develop while the hillsides made excellent grazing lands. More distinctive, however, was a plentiful supply of building stone, which furthered the erection of more permanent buildings and monuments.

And finally, it was much nearer to Asia Minor, to Syria on the Mediterranean, and to Palestine south of Syria. The Babylonians, though their caravans managed to press westward, were both protected and cut off from these areas by the Arabian Desert. The Assyrians, being nearer and less impeded, did not only more trading but more fighting with these neighbors. Though on the map, Egypt looks a long way off, the location of Palestine, as a buffer state in war and a great caravan route in peace, made it possible for Assyria to look with eager eyes in that direction.

The early Assyrians were a mixed-breed but mainly Semitic people. They spoke a Semitic language similar to that used at Akkad to the south of them, used cuneiform writing, and adopted much of the Sumerian art and architecture. That they were influenced from the south is not surprising, for while they had periods of independence they repeatedly fell under the control of Sargon, the kings of Ur, Hammurabi, or some other Babylonian ruler. But not only did they have to contest control from the south; the Hittites from the highlands to the northwest again and again got after them. From the Hittites they learned the use of metals, particularly iron, and the art of carving in alabaster, thus being enabled to fashion chariots for war and to celebrate their military exploits in elaborate and often ferocious looking bas-reliefs.

Two major activities mark the Assyrian genius: commerce and war. Then as now, these pursuits were not unrelated. A trail of clay tablets with cuneiform writing dug up in the excavations, for the most part business records, show that the Assyrian merchants got as far west as the silver-mines of Cilicia in southeastern Asia Minor and had settlements—probably trading-posts—in Cappadocia. Silver was made into money and replaced grain as a medium of exchange. The city of Assur on the Tigris, named for the god Assur, early became a great commercial center in the trade between the nearby mountain peoples and the "far west."

But not all was plain sailing—or more accurately, trekking. Besides the Babylonians to the south and the Hittites on the northwest to dispute their power, the Assyrians had to contend with the Mitanni, their nearest neighbors on the northwest and a long-dead people who left a great reputation as horse-breeders; with the Phoenicians on the Mediterranean coast; after about 1000 B.C. with the Hebrews in Palestine; and the Arameans. The Arameans, centered in Syria but spread out over a wide territory, were a particularly virile people who had absorbed much of both the Hittite and the Egyptian civilization. It is to the Arameans that we owe the alphabet which, with Egyptian pen and ink replacing the Babylonian cuneiform writing, was to be carried by the Phoenicians to the rest of the Mediterranean world. The Arameans were a great commercial people who outlasted the Assyrian military power, and the Aramaic language came to be used so generally throughout the Fertile Crescent that it was the vernacular of the people in Palestine in the first century A.D. and therefore was spoken by Jesus.

But to return to the Assyrians. While there were minor spurts of conquest and defense for many centuries, with an eager coveting of a foothold on the Mediterranean and the control of east-west caravan routes, the Assyrians did not really start on a rampage until the ninth century B.C. This precipitated coalitions and blocs among the western nations to stave off the powerful invader, for power politics and attempts at a "balance of power" are not new in the world's history. However, Damascus, the most important city of the west and the oldest city still in existence, fell before Tiglath-pileser in 732 A.D. His successor, Shalmaneser V, besieged Samaria for three years and in 722 it fell before the Assyrians, though probably his son Sargon II was the actual conqueror.[5] Sargon then deported the people throughout his vast domain, thus bringing to a permanent end the Hebrew Northern Kingdom. To this day people speculate about the migrations of the "ten lost tribes," the Anglo-Israelites claiming descent from them, but they were so scattered that they cannot be traced.

This begins a sequence of four powerful Assyrian conquerors: Sargon II (722–705 B.C.); Sennacherib (705–681); Esarhaddon (681–668; Assurbanipal (658–626). Sargon II built himself a vast palace covering twenty-five acres near Nineveh, and had it elaborately adorned to display his prowess. In spite of revolt after revolt throughout the empire he managed to hold it together. In 701 Sennacherib, regardless of having accepted tribute money from Judah, besieged Jerusalem and all but conquered it. The siege was suddenly raised, the Bible says

---

[5]The brief account in the Old Testament, II Kgs. 17:5 f.; 18:9 f., reads as if it all happened under Shalmaneser. However, Sargon II's records claim the credit for him.

because "the angel of the Lord went forth, and slew a hundred and eighty-five thousand in the camp of the Assyrians" (II Kgs. 19:35). Herodotus says that Sennacherib's army was smitten with a plague at the borders of Egypt. Doubtless the two stories are connected. In any case, he went back home. Babylon did not fare so well, for Sennacherib annihilated what was left of the old Babylon and turned a canal over its ruins. Meanwhile he enlarged and developed the capital at Nineveh and built the first aqueduct in history to bring in its water supply.

We need not follow the details of Assyrian history under Esarhaddon and Assurbanipal, though in general they were of milder temperament. Egypt was conquered. Judah accepted the overlordship of Assyria, and by paying tribute, maintained relative security. The matter of primary interest from our standpoint is not conquest, but the building up of Assurbanipal's great library, 22,000 clay tablets of which are now in the British Museum. Much of what is known of the religious, scientific and literary development of this period has been gleaned from them. Likewise, the art treasures from the walls of the great palace of Nineveh reveal a high degree of skill in carving in alabaster, and none have ever surpassed the Assyrians in animal sculpture.

The end of the Assyrian Empire came with great rapidity when it came. The Kaldi, or Chaldeans, from the vicinity of the Persian Gulf took Babylon in 616 B.C. Then the Medes invaded from the east and took Assur in 614. They formed a coalition and Nineveh fell in 612. Much rich booty was carried off, and the city turned into "ruined mounds." The Assyrian army fled and disintegrated. Assyrian speech gave way presently to Aramaic. Xenophon two centuries later found nothing but rubble where once the proud and glorious city had stood.

What caused Assyria's rapid dissolution? The answer is

easy, and ought to point a moral for our times. Assyria over-extended her military might. People were taken from agriculture, industry and commerce—the pursuits of peace—to serve in the mammoth army, and the country's internal strength declined. Plunder impoverished the outposts of empire. Ferocity, even to the literal "skinning alive" of rebellious kings, prevented the building up of any sense of loyalty in subject states. When revolts broke out, as they were bound to, subjects were forced to serve in the Assyrian army against their own people, and "the underground" was everywhere undermining Assyrian might. When the final crisis came, chariots and battering-rams gave no support against the forces of inner decay. The Assyrian Empire, which as a Great Power lasted only about a century and a half, ought to teach us something about the futility of military strength unsupported by the power of the spirit.

c. *The Chaldeans and the neo-Babylonian Empire.* The third great epoch in the history of development between the rivers was even briefer, and the telling of its story need not delay us long. However, it was during this period that a crucial event in the history of the Hebrews occurred, destined to have a permanent influence on their faith and their legacy to posterity.

After a coalition of the Medes under Cyaxeres and the Chaldeans under Nabopolassar had taken Nineveh, the Chaldeans gained the ascendancy. At the battle of Carchemish in 605 the Chaldeans under Nebuchadnezzar defeated the remnant of the Assyrian together with the allied Egyptian army, and thus became undisputed masters of the Fertile Crescent. During Nebuchadnezzar's reign occurred the capture and destruction of Jerusalem in 597 and 586, and the deportation to Babylon which constituted the Hebrew exile. Of this we shall have more to say in a later chapter.

Nebuchadnezzar had a long reign of forty years. During

this period, Babylon was not only restored to its ancient greatness, but from the standpoint of building and external achievement was carried far beyond it. Nebuchadnezzar had a great palace built with luxurious roof-gardens one above another which, as the Hanging Gardens of Babylon, became noted as one of the seven wonders of the world. He had the temples of the early Babylonian deities rebuilt, with the famous Ishtar gate and a great tower-temple to Marduk which was a real Tower of Babel. The city itself was greatly extended, with immense fortified walls which required a vast amount of human labor to construct. At Nebuchadnezzar's order the first major bridge in history was built across the Euphrates. Commerce and business flourished, while in art and architecture, forms of writing and even of speech, there was a "conscious archaism" in the attempt to recover and imitate the Babylonia of Hammurabi.

More important than this new splendor and this attempt at recovery of the past were real advances in the science of astronomy. This was mixed with astrology, but after the superstitions connected with the attempt to read the human future by the stars are discounted, it still remains true that the Chaldeans kept remarkably accurate records and made remarkably accurate predictions. About 500 B.C., on the basis of 250 years of such records, the Chaldean astronomer Nabu-rimannu predicted the annual movements of the sun and moon with only a ten-second inaccuracy, while a century later another astronomer Kidinnu reduced the margin of error to one second. The sun and moon and five planets that were then known (Mars, Mercury, Jupiter, Venus and Saturn) under the names of Babylonian divinities gave their names to the days of the week, and by the route of the corresponding Roman and Teutonic deities have come down to us. Thus, we cannot even say what day of the week it is without an unconscious debt to this ancient Babylonian culture!

Nevertheless, this Chaldean, or neo-Babylonian, era was destined also to pass. The Chaldean astronomers remained active long after Babylon fell. Politically, this empire was one of the shortest in history. Cyrus, the Persian king from the east, swept across the Fertile Crescent to Asia Minor, seized Lydia which was the main center of resistance, turned eastwar again, and easily took Babylon from the crown prince Belshazzar. How the dissolute Belshazzar saw the "handwriting on the wall" is known to everybody who has looked into the Book of Daniel. Apparently Nebuchadnezzar's great walls were no protection, and the city surrendered without resistance in 539 B.C. Thus, after only seventy-four years of glory, the great Chaldean Empire was no more.

The rule of the Persians under Cyrus, and even more under Darius the Great who presently succeeded him, was on the whole just, humane and beneficent. It was, to be sure, a "benevolent despotism," for democracy was no characteristic of the peoples of the East and in this part of the world it had not yet been dreamed of. Democracy was rising in Greece, which was soon to be so gravely imperiled by Darius' son, Xerxes. But that is another story. We must now leave the history of this Mesopotamian valley, and look at its religion and morals.

3. Babylonian Religion

From this point on we shall speak of the culture and moral development of this area by the name usually applied to it; namely, the Babylonian. Where necessary, we shall distinguish between the Babylonian and Assyrian characteristics, and between the Babylon of Hammurabi's time and the neo-Babylonian or Chaldean Empire. For the most part, however, the term "Babylonian" will say accurately enough what is meant, for two reasons. First, the Sumerian-Akkadian culture came to its height under the Amorite Babylonian kings and most of what is to be mentioned dates from that period; second, what developed under the Assyrian and Chaldean empires, except for exploits of military conquest and great building enterprises, added little to trends already long established.

We have noted how the exposed position of the Tigris-Euphrates valley meant constant invasions and then retaliatory attacks. The result was a more warlike and less homogenous people than the Egyptians. War retarded both cultural and moral progress, though as we see when we examine the Code of Hammurabi, an advanced civilization early developed in spite of it. The commercial pursuits of the people promoted social interplay, caused an early development of individualism, called forth precise legal codifications, and made the people more materialistic than religious in their interests.

Religion was important to the Babylonians, though relatively less so than to either the Egyptians or the Hebrews. The priests and kings, instead of being united in one institution as in Egypt, were often in rivalry and conflict, and this severing of power and sanctity tended toward less stability and internal order. The antidote was an early codification of laws to mark out with exactness the civil relations and accepted procedures among those of different orders of society.

Babylonia, like Egypt, had a somewhat confused polytheism, with gods which represented both forces of nature and city states. The nature deities signified elements vital to human affairs. At the head of the pantheon were Anu, the Sky-god high over all, and Enlil, the Storm-god who symbolizes force —often a violently destructive force. Less prominent were the earth goddess bearing various names, prototype of Mother Earth, and Enki, whose name means "lord of the earth" but whose restless creativity led him to be associated with water.[6]

[6]For a very suggestive analysis of the significance of these four deities see the essay, "The Cosmos as a State," by Thorkild Jacobsen in *The Intellectual Adventure of Ancient Man,* H. and H. A. Frankfort *et al.*

Important also were Sin, the Moon-god, whose transcendence and power over the state were celebrated in poems which have come down to us and Shamash, the Sun-god, who like Re in Egypt was conceived to be the guardian of right and justice, shedding light upon all. Ishtar, or Astarte, was goddess of fertility and sex. Assur was the patron deity of Assyria, Marduk of Babylonia. A henotheism developed in which Marduk was exalted to chief place and reinforced by union with Bel, or Baal, who was the male counterpart of Ishtar. How Baal and Astarte crept into Hebrew worship and corrupted it, calling forth the vigorous protests of the prophets, is familiar to all students of the Old Testament. The gods like the people had their quarrels, and in the fact that Shamash, god of righteousness, became arrayed against the great god Marduk, there are intimations of a conflict which crops out often, even in Christian monotheism, between the religious sanctification of goodness and of national power.

Early Babylonian-Assyrian religion seems to have been largely non-ethical. There were, as in all primitive cultures, good and evil spirits to be propitiated by incantations and magical rites. There was demonism in Babylonian thought, but this was not, as among the Chinese, turned into a constructive moral influence, since the spirits were not thought of as avengers of wrong but simply as nuisances to be averted.[7] The nature myths preserved in Babylonian literature tell of a great struggle between the gods of light and powers of darkness; but these were never moralized as were the Egyptian myths of Osiris and Set, or as the Iranian myth of Ahura Mazda and Ahriman which became the fundamental note of Zoroastrianism and through it injected dualism into Christian thought.

The most important of these nature myths was that of the Creation, significant by way of comparison with the Hebrew story which it doubtless influenced. According to the Baby-

[7]P. V. N. Myers, *History as Past Ethics,* p. 46 n.

lonian tale, Bel-Marduk had a great contest with Tiamat the dragon-goddess of chaos, and cleaving her asunder, he formed heaven out of one half of her body and the earth out of the other. He then set the sun, moon and stars in order, giving them indissoluble laws, formed the plants and animals, and finally man. It is clearly on a lower level, both of art and ethical responsibility, than the Genesis account.

Comparison with Hebrew thought is again invited by the Epic of Gilgamesh, composed about the time of Hammurabi. Its theme is the attempted conquest of death. Gilgamesh, ruler of Uruk, and his intrepid friend Enkidu perform great exploits, but when Enlil decrees the death of Enkidu, Gilgamesh mourns him with a pathos suggestive of *Lycidas* or *In Memoriam*. Determined to find everlasting life, Gilgamesh gains passage over the waters of death and comes to the presence of Utnapishtim who, when Enlil had once sent a great flood to destroy mankind, had built a big boat and taken into it himself, his wife, and pairs of all living things. He then had been rewarded by Enlil with eternal life. On Utnapishtim's tip, Gilgamesh gets from the bottom of the sea a precious plant which rejuvenates anyone who eats it, only to lose it to a serpent who carries it off as he goes swimming. So death remains unconquered.

The Babylonians had a concept of the after-life, but it lacked the moral implications of the Egyptian belief in immortality. There was continuance of existence in the after-life, but no retribution, and no differentiation of status in the future life according to character or conduct in the present. Like the Hebrew Sheol, the Babylonian place of departed spirits was a vague and shadowy place beneath the earth. There the dead, without moral distinction, led a miserable existence of inactivity amid gloom and dust.

The Babylonians, again like the Hebrews who were undoubtedly influenced by them, put their rewards and punishments in the present life. Though in general religion and morals were not closely connected, there are suggestions in Babylonian literature that "piety pays." It was believed that Shamash, as the god of justice, would see to it that honesty is the best policy. In a hymn to Shamash, too long to quote in full, this is made clear:

O Shamash, out of thy net no evil-doer escapes,
Out of thy snare no sinner flees. . . .
Thy broad net is spread out for the evil-doer,
Who lifted up his eyes to the wife of his companion . . .
The unjust judge thou makest behold shackles,
As for him who takes a bribe and bends the right,
Him dost thou burden with punishment.
He who does not take a bribe, who espouses the cause of the
    weak,
Is well pleasing to Shamash: he will live long.
The careful judge, who renders a just judgment,
Prepares himself a palace, a princely residence is his dwelling.[8]

The poem continues, in characteristic Oriental fashion, to predict that the good man will have a long line of descendants while "as for them who do evil, their seed hath no permanence."

Some aspects of Babylonian religion were positively deleterious to morals. The gods were conceived as self-centered, having created man that they might be served through temples and ritualistic acts; they were thought of as being sentimentally moved to pity by mere entreaty; they engaged in sexual union which, by the substitution of priest for god, became a basis of temple prostitution.

In spite of these facts, among the Babylonian penitential psalms are some of the purest expressions of ethical religion to be found in any literature. Through them breathes a sense of personal contrition and divine dependence akin to the spirit of the Hebrew psalms. They lack, to be sure, a sense of having

[8]Quoted by J. H. Breasted in *The Dawn of Conscience*, p. 341.

sinned against society, and in this are inferior to the best Hebrew or Christian devotional literature. Yet the note of personal moral abasement before deity is clear. For example,

O lord, thy servant, cast me not down.
In the miry waters take me by the hand.
The sin that I have committed change to favour.
The misdeed I have done, let the wind bear it away!
Rend in twain my wickedness like a garment!

My god—goddess, known and unknown god, known and un-
    known goddess, my sins are seven times seven.
Forgive my sins!
Forgive my sins!
I will bow humbly before thee.
May thy heart like the heart of a mother be glad:
Like the heart of a father to whom a child is born,
May thy heart be glad![9]

Furthermore, in an incantation text suggestive of the Egyptian Negative Confession appears a catalogue of sins which indicates high moral insight. It must be remembered that magic never disappeared, but both religion and morals as they developed were intermingled with it. Thus, it is not as surprising as it might appear at first glance to find one of the purest moral expressions of this culture in an incantation text. To a person appearing before a god or goddess, such questions as these were to be put:

Has he pointed the finger at (any one); has he spoken that which is forbidden; has he spoken evil; has he spoken that which is unclean; has he caused unrighteousness to be spoken; has he nullified the decision of a judge; has he trodden down the fallen; has he oppressed the weak; has he separated son from father, father from son, daughter from mother, mother from daughter, daughter-in-law from mother-in-law, mother-in-law from daughter-in-law,

[9]From G. F. Moore, *History of Religions*, Vol. I, p. 226. It is there printed in prose form.

brother from brother, friend from friend, neighbor from neighbor? . . . Used false weights, received dishonest gold, refused honest gold? Has he removed a faithful son; established an unfaithful? . . . Has he removed a boundary, a border, or a boundary-stone? Has he entered the house of his neighbor, approached his neighbor's wife, shed his neighbor's blood, stolen his neighbor's garment? Through his fault has he destroyed a noble man, forced a brave man from his family, separated a united kin, unto an overseer delivered them? Was he in mouth upright, but in heart untrue? In his mouth this; in his heart that? . . .[10]

The last query is a quaint and pointed statement of the duplicity present in every age![11] Expressions like the above, found amid a welter of magical formulas and incantations, suggest that the religious spirit is so indigenously ethical that nothing can wholly overlay its moral vitality.

4. Morality by Law

Besides these evidences of an emerging personal morality, there were sporadic attempts to secure social justice through the agency of reformer-kings. There were several in the third millennium b.c.—probably three before the great Hammurabi. Little that is authentic is known of them, and such records as we have paint a picture so roseate as to be hardly trustworthy. There are tales of defense of the poor against the rich, of a pacifism so complete that nobody struck another, of a temple reform so thorough that no evil remained, of divine deliverance from injustice through an incarnation of Shamash. These suggest a combination of a golden age of innocence (such as is found in most early literature) with a backward-looking glorification of an idealized messiah.

[10]Quoted in *The Evolution of Ethics,* ed. E. H. Sneath, p. 80.
[11]Also rendered:
"Was his mouth full of yea
His heart full of nay?"

Arriving at Hammurabi, we are on safer historical ground. There seems no doubt that he was a great administrator and law-giver, a king with a conscience. Humility was not among his virtues, and he boldly announced himself as the perfect king, giving laws to the people that come to him from Shamash. A little bombast can be forgiven in a person so genuinely great!

The Code of Hammurabi is the oldest known law-code. Like any other body of law, it represents not what was actually done by the people but what was expected of them. Given by the king to weld together his empire, it not only reflects his judgment but apparently reveals existing standards in great detail. He could scarcely have prescribed such laws as these had they not at least partially been already in accepted usage.

A great many of the provisions of the Code have to do with property. They reveal a relatively advanced state of economic development and a thoroughly stratified society. Punishments vary greatly according to the social status of the offender, and with more honesty than we have about this same situation, this fact is so stated. There seem to have been four main strata; the "god or palace," the man (which apparently means the patrician), the common man, and the slave. Offenses against them are ranked in seriousness, with penalties correspondingly lessened, in a descending scale.

Ownership was by a sort of theocratic and feudalistic communism within which there was private property. The king owned the land in the name of God and granted it to the warriors and priests, who in turn let the farmers live on it for a share of the produce. Only one who tilled it continuously and well could keep it—a significant recognition of social function. The right of testation—always a mark of the development of property—reached the point at which one could disinherit a son for unfilial conduct by consent of the court. For sales of land, titles must be proved through documents or the oath of witnesses; for the extension of credit, bonds were given; receipts were required in commercial transactions.

There are many complex provisions about contracts, temple tithes, rents, wages, stewardships, partnerships, bankruptcies, physicians' charges, (adjusted to the social status of the man being treated), responsibility for stolen goods and even for careless workmanship. Severe penalties were to be inflicted on the man who left his dykes open and flooded his neighbor's land. If a builder put up a house so flimsy that it fell and killed the owner's son, his own son was to be put to death—a curious example of the *lex talionis*. The surgeon who caused the loss of life or limb was to have his hand cut off. Such provisions, though not always in accord with present concepts of justice, indicate great precision in the attempt to protect the individual from the dishonesty or carelessness of other individuals. Since people are not made honest by law, it is not to be supposed that they were in every case consistent with the actual conduct of the people, or that they were always meticulously enforced.

Even more striking are the family mores suggested by the Code. Monogamous marriage is presupposed, though if a wife does not present a man with children he may take a concubine. The latter, however, is not to take precedence over the wife. Marriage was by contract, and women had more rights than in any other ancient civilization—in fact, more rights than in the Occident until a century or two ago. A woman could inherit property. She could divorce her husband, though not so easily as the husband could divorce her, and could divorce him for cruelty or neglect as well as for infidelity if she could prove herself to have been a good wife. If she failed, she was drowned. Adultery was a capital offense for either sex, but a woman raped against her will was to go free. A man could divorce his wife at will, but must return her dowry and provide for the support of her children. As in other early societies, marriages were arranged by parents for a bride-price, but a woman's dowry remained her own to be inherited by her children. Not even a concubine who had borne children could be put away without support for herself and her children. Legal provisions were made for the adoption of children. Such laws idealize the facts—but there they stand as a protest against male dominance. Assyrian women, who must go veiled upon the street unless they were hierodoules[12] or prostitutes, were apparently given less freedom than those of Babylonia.

Slavery was an accepted institution, slaves being constantly recruited by war, purchase, debt, or punishment for crime. However, slaves, like women, had more rights than in most early cultures. A slave could acquire property, and might marry a free-woman whose children then were free. There was a fugitive slave law which made the harboring of a runaway slave punishable by death. Much as in this country less than a century ago, the accepted moral attitude toward the slave was not to regard him as a person, but as a piece of property to whom kindness should be shown. It is an open question whether in personal attitudes toward those of other races in the present we have gone much farther.

Was this elaborate provision for human social relations religiously motivated? The long, self-glorifying prologue in which Hammurabi claims to rule by the appointment of Marduk and receive these laws from Shamash might so indicate. However, deity is mentioned in the body of the text only in two relationships, and these practices and beliefs have persisted to our day. In cases of theft, accusations of adultery, or other such infractions, one must "take an oath in the name of God," or witnesses must "declare what they know in the presence of God." Furthermore, a sharp distinction as to re-

---

[12]Sacred harlots serving in the temples. There is an echo of this Oriental distinction regarding the veil in Paul's injunction to the Corinthian women not to pray or prophesy with their heads uncovered. I Cor. 11:5, 13.

sponsibility is drawn between the flooding of a field as an "act of God" (Adad the Storm-god), and human carelessness in letting the water of one's irrigation ditch destroy his neighbor's crops.

5. Conclusion

Before bringing this chapter to a close, there are two questions we must ask and at least tentatively answer. How has this long-buried culture made its impact on the Western world? What general principles can be deduced, or trends observed, in this story of the rise and fall of empires one upon another?

It is primarily through the Hebrews that the effects of this Sumerian and then Semitic culture has been felt. In the next chapter we shall note in more detail how this came about. The general outlines are evident and may be stated here.

In the first place, the original Canaanitic civilization which the Hebrews encountered when they entered Palestine after the exodus and wilderness periods was already permeated with elements from the east. For centuries this area had been a part of these eastern empires, with commercial as well as political ties causing infiltration. It was an agricultural society far more advanced than the Hebrew nomadic culture; its religion was a mixture of primitive polytheism with a vigorous worship of Baal and Ishtar (as Astarte); its morals show the influence of Babylonian law, though to what extent the Code of Hammurabi was a direct influence is in dispute. Since the Hebrews not only displaced but absorbed this Canaanite culture, they absorbed with it much that was the common heritage of the empires of the east.

A second influence, more indirect but potent, was the "challenge and response"[13] developed in the Hebrews through the danger of political conquest, and the interweaving of Yahweh worship with national security. Not only did this make of their

---

[13]A basic phrase and category in Toynbee's *A Study of History*.

deity a "god of battles"; the prophetic insight that approaching political doom was divine judgment and Assyria the rod of chastisement in the hands of an all-righteous deity, affected not a little the course of Israel's faith.

The major watershed in Hebrew religion is the exile in Babylon. This event made a vast difference, partly through what was absorbed in Babylon, but more because of what was not. The Hebrews discovered through the practice of their faith in a strange land and the insights of their prophets that they worshiped a God universal in His protection and power; inner stamina was generated to keep the worship of Yahweh from being submerged in paganism and lost in a Babylonian cult.

A fourth major influence stems from the dualism of good and evil, and the personifying of dualism in Ahura-Mazda and Ahriman, that is at the center of Persian Zoroastrianism. It is significant that Satan emerges late in Old Testament thought and is distinctly a post-exilic concept. Without such contact with the east the Hebrews would undoubtedly have developed an ethical monotheism with God at the center of faith and devotion; it is unlikely that the devil would have taken the place he has held in New Testament and subsequent Christian thought.

When we ask the question as to what "this story teaches—," what currents of development or dissolution we observe in this great but transient Mesopotamian civilization, the answer is of course complex. Historic forces are seldom, if ever, so unmixed that unchallengeable inferences can be drawn. Some things, however, seem here to stand out with a large amount of clarity.

The first is that it is possible to have an advanced civilization, highly individualized in functional relations and highly socialized in the interplay of parts, and still have little democracy. Whether the Mesopotamian cultures were demo-

cratic at all is a moot question. There were city-states before
the days of empire, and possibly a form of primitive democracy.[14] The Babylon of Hammurabi had not only officers of
the king but judges and courts. However, if democracy means
free elections and self-expression on the part of the people,
there is slight evidence of its existence. The picture is mainly
totalitarian. Such a government makes for strength, even for
great exploits, but not for stability or permanence.

A second observation is the relative lack of creativity in a
religion that is more non-moral than moral. Compared with
Egypt and still more with the Hebrew stream of development,
Babylonian and Assyrian religion was sterile. It produced no
great ethical system, not even any high mythology. Its legacy
at this point would be for the most part forgotten, had not
the Hebrews transformed its myths into something of high
spiritual import and preserved their own faith by fighting the
worship of Baal and Ishtar.

A third deduction to be drawn is the impossibility of pursuing at the same time and to a high degree the enterprises
of war and the arts of peace. To be sure, we have been observing the coincidence of both a military and a commercial
civilization. Conquest paved the way for commercial expansion. But it also paved the way to dissolution through over-
expansion and the undermining of the inner foundations of
the nation. It is impossible to say just how much more economic advancement would have taken place if material resources had not been dissipated in war; it is possible to observe that this culture produced little in the way of enduring
art or literature.

The final observation is with regard to the futility of empire
as a whole. Not only is it true that "power corrupts"; power

[14]Jacobsen (*op. cit.*, pp. 128 f., 135, 149, 181) makes much of this
primitive democracy and deduces from it that the pantheon of the gods
was a democratic derivative. This seems to me to overstate the case with
regard both to gods and men.

when it is overextended destroys itself. Though it is presumptuous ever to try to say with precision what might have been, there is a good likelihood that any one of these empires could have lasted longer if it had not spread itself so thin. And even if conquered, a people with a higher vision than political conquest might, like the Hebrews, have given an enduring legacy to posterity.

To the Hebrews, who accomplished what the Babylonians and Assyrians could not and who still live as a consequence, we now direct attention.

CHAPTER FIVE

EARLY HEBREW MORALITY

Hear, O Israel: The Lord our God is one Lord; and you shall love the Lord your God with all your heart, and with all your soul, and with all your might. And these words which I command you this day shall be upon your heart; and you shall teach them diligently to your children, and shall talk of them when you sit in your house, and when you walk by the way, and when you lie down, and when you rise. And you shall bind them as a sign upon your hand, and they shall be as frontlets between your eyes. And you shall write them on the doorposts of your house and on your gates.[1]

FEW words have ever been spoken which have had a more profound influence on the history of morals. These words of the *Shema*, in Deuteronomy 6:4–9, have been to the Hebrews through the ages what the simple Moslem affirmation, "There is no God but Allah and Mohammed is the prophet of Allah," has been to the Mohammedans—a rallying cry and a creed. The Hebrews were a literal-minded folk, and the more pious

[1]Deut. 6:4–9. R.S.V.

of their leaders placed these words in little boxes to bind upon the hand or forehead. To this day one may find upon the doorpost of an orthodox Jewish home a *mezuzah* containing a scroll bearing these words. But far more significantly, the Jews wrote them in their hearts, and taught them to the children, and made them the guiding force in their destiny. So the Jewish religion and the Jewish people lived, and we have the record of "that strange people who would not die."[2]

For several reasons a knowledge of Hebrew ethics is indispensable if one wishes to get a clear view of the pageant of morality. The Hebrew Scriptures have had a profound influence upon the moral development of the entire Occidental world; in part through the direct influence of the Jews, persisting with marvelous tenacity in spite of persecution, and still more through the incorporation of the Old Testament into the Christian Bible and its acceptance as an inspired body of moral doctrine. For many centuries everything from Genesis through Revelation was regarded as the unequivocal and infallible Word of God, spoken with the authority of "Thus saith the Lord." While sometimes it happened that moral practices rooted in human impulse or social custom, such as slaughtering enemies or suppressing feminism, were reinforced by quoting the Bible, this respect for its authority had likewise the effect of modifying—very often softening and purifying—the otherwise perverse tendencies of human nature. One finds in the Old Testament the vengeance and cruelty of an undeveloped patriarchal society, but one finds there also the majestic devotional literature of the Psalms and the soul-stirring calls to social justice voiced by the prophets. Without the influence of the Hebrew Scriptures the moral development of the Occident would have lacked one of its most potent strains.

In the second place, the ethical teachings of Jesus are firmly imbedded in a Hebrew setting. It is impossible to understand

[2]Lewis Browne, *Stranger Than Fiction*, p. 7.

his message apart from the background of religious formalism and political aspiration in the midst of which he lived. Both the continuity and the novelty in the Christian gospel become evident when one views the long process of moral growth which culminated in the insights of the prophet of Nazareth. The two great commandments enjoining love to God and love to neighbor are both found in the Old Testament, yet to both Jesus gave fresh meaning.[3] His mission, he said, was not to destroy but to fulfill the Law, and this he did by bringing to fruition in his own life the moral trends which had been working their way upward through centuries of Hebrew history.

Furthermore, one must study Hebrew ethics if he would get a clear idea of the growing pains of any primitive people. Written by many people over many hundred years, the Old Testament was never intended as a textbook, and much misunderstanding has arisen from the attempt to wrest from it science and history it does not contain. Yet it is the most valuable collection of source materials on early society ever brought together. The conditions typical of a patriarchal society, processes of transition from a nomadic to agricultural and from a tribal to monarchical system, the emergence of reflective morality through the voices of great leaders, the growth of individualism, the deepening and widening of a sense of social responsibility—all are clearly and naturally stated.

Finally, the blending of religion with ethics in Hebrew history makes the Old Testament a unique source of moral insight. The uniqueness does not lie in the fact that the Hebrews gave religion a central place in their culture, for other societies have done this, but in the nature of their deity and what they conceived to be His relation to them. So intertwined were religion and morality in their thinking that in this chapter and

[3]Deut. 6:4 and Lev. 19:18, 34. One of the old rabbinical stories tells of a man who boasted that he could repeat the whole of the Law while standing on one foot, whereupon he repeated Lev. 19:18, "Thou shalt love thy neighbor as thyself."

the next, we shall for the most part have to trace the development of their religion in order to get at their moral ideals. No religion has ever been completely divorced from the demands of moral living; yet in no other historical record do we find so clearly the story of a growing people's struggle to bring to maturity its concept of God and the good life. This is because there was in the Yahweh concept something not found elsewhere—an impelling force which seemed to speak unequivocally in moral terms and which would not let the people rest until they strove to do the will of their God.

1. God and Hebrew Morals

The concept of Yahweh[4] was a powerful force in Hebrew moral development because it was firmly rooted in three important formative factors: historical events, the covenant relation, and allegiance to the Law.

The historical events which bound the Hebrews most closely to Yahweh with ties of gratitudes were the exodus from Egypt, the wilderness wanderings, the conquest of the Promised Land, and later the sense of God's sustaining presence during the Babylonian captivity. One of the psalmists sings of these events in an outburst of praise:

> O give thanks unto the Lord, for he is good: for his mercy endureth forever.
>
> Let the redeemed of the Lord say so, whom he hath redeemed from the hand of the enemy; and gathered them out of the lands, from the east, and from the west, from the north and from the south.
>
> They wandered in the wilderness in a solitary way; they

---

[4]Also, Jahweh or Jehovah. So called because the early Hebrews, holding the name of their deity too sacred to speak, wrote the consonants YHWH and said Adonai (Lord). The vowels of the latter were later placed in these consonants to make a hybrid term. We shall use the term Yahweh unless the context calls for the more familiar Jehovah.

found no city to dwell in. Hungry and thirsty, their soul fainted in them.

Then they cried unto the Lord in their trouble, and he delivered them out of their distresses. And he led them forth by the right way, that they might go to a city of habitation.

Oh, that men would praise the Lord for his goodness, and for his wonderful works to the children of men![5]

Throughout their whole history the people kept giving expression to their gratitude, and the thought of Yahweh's protecting care, even when they hungered in the wilderness or sat in distress by the waters of Babylon, kept alive their faith in themselves and their future, and instilled in them a great sense of moral devotion.

The concept of the Covenant is closely related. This was thought of as a mutual relation entered into voluntarily between the people and Yahweh, whereby God promised to protect them and make them a mighty nation, while they in turn promised obedience and supreme allegiance to him before all other gods. It took the place of a blood tie between the people and the gods found in most primitive societies, and it gave Yahweh an aloofness, along with his protectiveness, which kept the Hebrews from getting too familiar with their deity. The covenant was entered into at Mount Sinai and reaffirmed again and again. There are many references to it in the Old Testament. Of these we shall cite but one, the passage which introduces the Exodus account of the giving of the Decalogue:

And Moses went up to God, and the Lord called him out of the mountain, saying, "Thus you shall say to the house of Jacob, and tell the people of Israel: You have seen what I did to the Egyptians, and how I bore you on eagles' wings and brought you to myself. Now, therefore, if you

[5]Ps. 107:1–8. The King James version is cited here because of its greater familiarity and poetic beauty.

will obey my voice and keep my covenant, you shall be
my own possession among all peoples; for all the earth is
mine, and you shall be to me a kingdom of priests and
a holy nation. These are the words which you shall speak
to the children of Israel."[6]

Such a sense of being chosen for an holy nation to receive
the special favor of God may be explained, if one likes, as
a sort of national superiority complex, akin to the idea of
the Nazis in Germany as to their God-given supremacy.
But to see only this side of the picture is to overlook an important matter. The Hebrews believed that their God gave
them not only special favors but special *duties*. The covenant
was a two-sided arrangement, and the sense of the duty they
owed to Yahweh was an impelling moral force. It might reinforce current custom but it was to them much more than
an affirmation of custom, and sometimes, as in the flaming
utterances of the prophets, it tore custom asunder.

A third foundation of Hebrew morality was allegiance to
what they conceived to be a divinely revealed Law. One need
not accept literally the story of the giving of the Decalogue
amid thunder and lightning, trumpets and smoke, or of Jehovah's writing with his own finger upon tablets of stone, to
believe that the Ten Commandments expressed to His people
the will of God. By the surest test of inspiration—the power to
inspire—this code was divinely given even though its provisions emerged out of the growing experience of the people. Its
Mosaic authorship is in dispute, though probably in its sim-
plest form of the original "ten words" it dates back to the time
of Moses. More important than its historical origin is the fact
that the people firmly believed that the Ten Commandments
and subsequent codes gave them an unequivocal statement of

[6]Exod. 19:3–6. R.S.V. The story of God's covenant with Abraham in
Gen. 17, though stated as if earlier, probably reflects a later writer's
conception of the covenant's origin.

the will of God, and this they accepted as their moral duty. These codes, though partly ceremonial in nature, had a large ethical content and were a potent force in the direction of social justice.

What, then, was the result of this devotion to Yahweh? The people became monolatrists,[7] and worshiped an anthropomorphic (man-form) tribal deity. He had unaccountable moods like their own, and could harden Pharaoh's heart against the Hebrews, inspire them to steal from the Egyptians at their departure, and put to death the innocent first-born. He could require that cities be "devoted" to himself by the massacre of all the inhabitants, and in a fit of petulance send a pestilence upon the people because David obeyed instructions and took a census. But this is not the real God of the Old Testament, and to represent Yahweh in these terms is to caricature Him. The deity who was the permanent, guiding force of the Hebrew people was a righteous God, before whom Abraham could cry, "Shall not the judge of all the earth do right?"[8] Yahweh was conceived as supreme, not only in power but in *goodness,* and the root reason why He was a "jealous" God, demanding that none be esteemed before Him, was the conviction of the people that His demands must not be cheapened by the worship of foreign deities. This conviction, often enough disregarded in practice, was never completely lost.

The tragedy of the literal, dead-level interpretation of the Bible which was current for centuries and still is often accepted is the failure to see, in Yahweh's cruelty and petulance, the reflection of the traits of an undeveloped people who conceived their God in their own image. Sermons of hate have been preached from the imprecatory Psalms, and all manner of cruelty has been justified by quoting texts.[9] But fortunately,

[7]Worshiping one god, but believing in the existence of others.

[8]Gen. 18:25.

[9]Calvin thought that the children whom Jehovah commanded through

the concept of *a good God demanding goodness* prevailed both in Hebrew culture and in Biblical interpretation, and Jehovah's moral qualities have through the centuries evoked morality in men.

2. *Periods of Hebrew History*

To understand the development of Hebrew morals we must pass in rapid review the principal events of Hebrew history. The early Genesis stories are best conceived, not as literal history, but as a primitive attempt to solve the mystery of creation, the coming of toil and sin into the world, the presence of many languages. So regarded, they are seen to have affinities with other early stories of creation and of a great flood (particularly the Babylonian), but to be superior in both moral and aesthetic qualities. They reflect the Hebrews' conception of man's destiny as the crowning work of divine creation, and the supreme duty of obeying the will of the deity.

In the patriarchal stories of Abraham, Isaac and Jacob we find a clear picture of early nomadic society. It is full of theft, trickery, rape, and petty ambition, yet softened by domestic affection, strong loyalties, and the ever-present Oriental virtue of hospitality. Though the Biblical accounts of the doings of these racial ancestors may perhaps be as legendary as the story of George Washington's cherry tree, they serve, like the latter, a useful purpose and tell between the lines a true story. In them one finds a picturesque, ingenuous account of early Semitic life and many evidences of what their national heritage meant to the Hebrews as a call to fulfillment of a great destiny.

Whatever may be the authenticity of the Joseph stories as an account of the migrations of the sons of Jacob to Egypt, it is probable that some of the Hebrews were in bondage there for a time, while others remained in Palestine, and that those in subjection to the Egyptian Pharaoh were delivered, with

---

Moses to be slain must already have been predestined for damnation, else God would not have visited upon them such a fate.

considerable chicanery as well as courage, under the leadership of a great statesman and prophet by the name of Moses. Under Moses, Hebrew national history begins, for while they were not to be united under one monarch for some centuries, he organized their religious institutions, laid the foundations of their legal system, and instilled in them a great faith in the future of their race.

The people at this time, it must be remembered, were not monotheists but monolatrists or henotheists, believing in the existence of many gods but worshiping one as supreme. They lived as nomads for a considerable time in the Arabian desert (the forty traditional years of wilderness wandering is not to be taken too literally), and at Mt. Sinai they believed that their deity Yahweh himself wrote the Ten Commandments of the Law upon two tables of stone for their instruction. These tablets were carried in their subsequent travels in a little box called the Ark of the Covenant.

Moving from place to place to find pasturage for their flocks, these Semites came to Moab, east of the Jordan, where Moses died. According to the dramatic Biblical narrative the people crossed the river under the leadership of Joshua, captured Jericho, and began to contest with the Canaanites the possession of the land. It is probable that this migration was gradual, and that tribes kept invading Palestine from the east at intervals during the fourteenth and thirteenth centuries B.C. Soon after that a sea-going people, the Philistines, invaded from the Aegean region, especially Crete, and settled on the western border. These were destined to have many battles with the Hebrews, in which the Philistines were never completely subjugated, and to give their name to the land we call Palestine.

The Hebrews found the land of Canaan bristling with enemies who had adopted a more-or-less settled agricultural life, and who did not take kindly to the idea of having their possession disputed by these nomadic tribes from the east. Numerous battles took place in which the Hebrews, knit together by the kinship bond of supposing themselves to be descended from the twelve sons of Jacob, gradually wrested the land from the Canaanites. In conquering them, they massacred, enslaved, or drove out their enemies, yet intermarried with them and adopted many of their customs. This attempt at extermination of the Canaanites was sanctioned, and, they thought, encouraged by the war-god Yahweh, though the latter expressed much displeasure at their setting up of "high places" in which to honor deities other than Himself. Meanwhile the people, desiring to gain protection from whatever source they might find it, took over the agricultural life and the gods of their victims and called upon Baal, the god of fertility, to bless their economic ventures as Yahweh their military activities.

For a time the people were ruled by local chieftains whom they called judges. These were mainly military heroes, though they were thought to rule by divine favor. Among them were Gideon, who shrewdly chose his soldiers by observing their watchfulness in drinking at a stream; Samson, famed both for his physical strength and inability to resist his wife's coaxing; Jephthah, who sacrificed his daughter's life rather than break a vow made to Yahweh; Deborah, the intrepid woman leader who, with Barak as first lieutenant, smote and put to flight the armies of Sisera. There was little of organized political life during this period, but the force of collective responsibility was very strong and the story of the war with the Benjamites told in Chapter Two belongs in this setting.

The period of the judges is followed by the establishment of the kingdom, with Saul, anointed by the prophet Samuel and accepted by the people, as the first king. This marks a decisive forward step, for it indicates that the people had achieved sufficient national consciousness to realize that their welfare demanded joint action under a single head. The choice, however, in spite of divine sanction did not prove very fortunate. Saul was subject to severe attacks of melancholia, from which he found relief in the music of the shepherd lad David, and was given to violent fits of anger in one of which he tried to kill David. This drove David from the court and made him Saul's enemy. After many encounters, during which the Philistines defeated the army of Israel and slew three of Saul's sons, Saul fell either by his own hand or by that of an Amalekite. David was proclaimed as king of Judah, and after further fighting, of Israel also. He established a brilliant court at Jerusalem. His numerous marital adventures, which included causing the death of Uriah that he might marry Uriah's widow, Bathsheba, stain the record of his later years, as the rebellion of his son Absalom saddens it.

Upon David's death the kingdom passed to his son Solomon, reputed for his great wisdom but in reality a very foolish monarch. The account of his having seven hundred wives and three hundred concubines, though perhaps exaggerated, gives evidence that he established a harem of extended proportions. He built a magnificent temple at Jerusalem, probably actuated in part by religious devotion and in part by a desire to exalt his own name, and in order to carry through this project he laid extremely heavy burdens of taxation upon the people. Their hopes of relief upon his death were dashed by the announcement of his son, Rehoboam, that he expected to treat them still more rigorously. Thereupon the ten northern tribes, under the leadership of Jeroboam, revolted and established a separate kingdom, leaving only Judah to be ruled by Rehoboam.[10] Henceforth, the history of the Hebrews diverges into two interlacing strands, the Northern Kingdom, or Israel, having its capital at Samaria, and the Southern Kingdom, called Judah from its larger division, centering in Jerusalem. The

[10]The traditional twelve tribes are accounted for by the fact that the tribe of Levi, constituting the priesthood, was divided according to the area where they lived.

period of the United Kingdom lasted almost a hundred years, from approximately 1015 to 931 B.C.

The political history of Israel and Judah after the division is largely a record of turmoil and conflict, with the two kingdoms fighting sometimes each other and sometimes their enemies to the east and southwest. Palestine lay between two powerful states, Assyria and Egypt, and its possession was eagerly coveted by both. Repeatedly the little kingdoms were on the verge of collapse but preserved themselves through favorable alliances or the payment of tribute money. Finally the pressure became too strong, and the Northern Kingdom fell before the Assyrians in 722 B.C. Its people were carried into exile and their national identity never restored. They are often referred to as the "ten lost tribes of Israel." The Southern Kingdom, smaller, but more easily guarded because of the rocky, elevated location of Jerusalem, lasted nearly a century and a half longer. An Assyrian army under Sennacherib in 701 devastated Judah and endangered Jerusalem but suddenly withdrew. Finally Jerusalem fell in 586 before the attack of Nebuchadnezzar's soldiers. The most vigorous of the people were carried off into exile in Babylon in 597 and 586.

This period of the divided kingdom, sordid though it was in political history, is illumined by the appearance of one of the greatest moral forces of all time, the work of the prophets. These were not primarily foretellers of events, though they often had enough keenness of insight to foresee what was likely to happen, but they were *forth*tellers, spokesmen of Yahweh. They had a great sense of moral indignation against the greed, injustice, extravagance, drunkenness, and other evils of the time, and with supreme courage denounced these vices and called the people to repentance in the name of their God. Elijah and Elisha who lived in the earlier part of the period did not write their messages, but in the eighth century appeared the "literary" or "writing" prophets, Amos, Hosea,

Micah and the first Isaiah. These were followed a century later by Jeremiah, during the exile by Ezekiel and the second Isaiah, and later by others of lesser importance.

The period of the exile lasted until 538 B.C., when Cyrus, king of Persia, who had captured Babylon allowed the Hebrews to return. The exile was one of the most significant experiences of their history, for they found that they could worship Yahweh even in tribulation and in a strange land, and monolatry passed over into monotheism. Out of their suffering they caught through the eyes of the second Isaiah a glimpse of Israel's mission as the suffering servant of all mankind. Upon their return they restored the temple, and unfortunately reverted to the religious formalism against which the prophets had repeatedly protested, substituting ritualistic correctness for social righteousness. A great book of devotional literature, the Psalms, was compiled in this post-exilic period, as were also some important books of philosophy or "wisdom" literature—Job, Proverbs, Ecclesiastes and Ecclesiasticus.

Palestine was conquered by Alexander the Great in 332 B.C. Upon his death it was juggled back and forth between the Seleucids of Syria and Ptolemies of Egypt. Many Jews left Palestine to go to Alexandria, and commercial interests came into prominence. This period is often called the *diaspora* or dispersion. When Antiochus Epiphanes infuriated the Jews by riding roughshod over their cherished traditions and setting himself up as God, a fiery revolt led by Judas Maccabeus and his four brothers re-established temporarily Jewish independence. The Temple was cleansed of defilement and the Temple service reinstituted with great rejoicing in 165 B.C., thus giving rise to the Jewish festival of Hanukkah still celebrated near Christmas. However, the war dragged on until it was 143 before the Maccabean leaders entirely threw off the Seleucid yoke. Jewish independence then lasted until 63 B.C. when Jerusalem and its environs were swept under the Roman power by Pompey's legions.

It was as a Roman outpost of empire that the events recorded in the New Testament took place. In 70 A.D. the Temple and much of Jerusalem were destroyed by Titus, an event commemorated by the Arch of Titus which still stands near the entrance of the Roman Forum. The Jews lingered and made out as best they could until, after the abortive Bar-Cochba rebellion of 132–135 A.D., they were scattered over the earth to make a home for themselves in every country. Not until the Zionist Movement of the twentieth century and the establishment of the State of Israel did they again find a center of political independence and a national home.

3. Pre-prophetic Morality

It is not to be supposed that Hebrew morals prior to the preaching of the great prophets were all of one piece. In the transition which took place from a nomadic culture with no settled home to a relatively well established agricultural society, changes were bound to take place. There were probably Hebrews in Palestine as early as the fourteenth century B.C. under the suzerainty of Egypt, as the references to the plundering activities of the "Habiri" in the Tell el-Amarna letters indicate. It is certain that there was a period of bondage in Egypt, a period of nomadic life in the Arabian peninsula, and an entrance—or re-entrance—into Canaan from the east, and that there they found a culture saturated with Babylonian influence and much more advanced than their own.

As was noted in Chapter Three, Egypt in the Age of Empire after the conquest of Thutmose III held sway over the territory as far east as the Euphrates. This control lasted at least nominally for several centuries, and accounts for the large number of Egyptian artifacts unearthed in Palestine. However, the direct influences of Egyptian upon Hebrew literature appear to be mainly post-exilic, and the main patterns of Hebrew life and thought in the formative stages show surprisingly little Egyptian influence. This may be due in part to the fact that as serfs in bondage the Hebrews had little connection with the main stream of Egyptian life, while in the wilderness the mores of primitivism were dominant. After they entered Canaan, the dominant influences were those of challenge and response to the culture they found there.

With due concern not to overstress the resemblances, there is enough similarity to permit an inclusive survey of the ethical characteristics of the patriarchal, Egyptian, wilderness, conquest, and united kingdom periods. Our knowledge is derived chiefly from the stories of the interwoven J and E documents, and from the Covenant Code (a part of the E document) which amplifies the Ten Commandments and is found in Exodus 20:23–23:33 directly after the Exodus Decalogue.

For those not familiar with J, E, D and P, a word of explanation may be in order. About the middle of the ninth century B.C. a writer in the Southern Kingdom with a remarkable gift for vivid narration either wrote out for the first time or compiled a collection of stories about the early history of his people. There is a double reason for calling him "J", since his name for God is YHWH (Yahweh,[11] Jehovah) and he wrote in the kingdom of Judah. Fifty to a hundred years later another story-teller, with a somewhat more developed ethical sense and a more spiritual conception of God, wrote in the Northern Kingdom. Since up to Exodus 3:15 he calls God by the generic term *El* or *Elohim,* we call this writer "E." J and E were woven together to form a consecutive narrative; then merged with D. D is in the main the Book of Deuteronomy, the "second giving of the law," and dates from 621 B.C. or shortly before. When found in repairing the Temple it was used by King Josiah as the basis of a great reformation. After the exile a fourth unknown writer, whom we call "P" because of the priestly slant in his writings, retold the story of his people

[11]First so called from the German rendering of YHWH as Jahve.

from the creation of the world. Thus it happens that the first chapter of Genesis is from P, while a second creation story from the J narrative immediately follows it.

Let us look now at the morals of the J and E stories and the legal provisions of the Covenant Code. Events stated as happening several centuries earlier, long handed down in the oral tradition, but seen through the eyes of a ninth- or eighth-century writer were bound to be colored by the prevalent concepts of that period. This circumstance, added to the fact that cultures normally change slowly, explains why there is so little evidence of moral growth throughout the early part of Hebrew history. We shall treat this pre-prophetic morality topically.

a. *Enemies, foreigners and strangers.* Tribal solidarity drew a sharp line of cleavage between enemy and kin. In the conquest of Palestine the Israelites massacred, exiled and enslaved their foes with no moral scruples against cruelty. Enslavement rather than exile seems to have been the usual course. "When Israel grew strong, they put the Canaanites to forced labor, but did not utterly drive them out" (Judges 1:28). In thus allowing the Canaanites to remain among them they may at least in part have made a virtue of necessity, for we are told that "the Lord was with Judah, and he took possession of the hill country, but he could not drive out the inhabitants of the plain, because they had chariots of iron " (Judges 1:19).

The oldest extant Hebrew poem, the Song of Deborah in the fifth chapter of Judges, expresses a fierce exultation at the downfall of the enemy and calls Jael "most blessed of women" for her assassination of Sisera. The observation that "the stars from their courses fought against Sisera" is typical of a note that permeates Old Testament morals—and, in fact, the morals of every age including our own. This is the identification of the nation's enemies with God's enemies, with the corresponding belief that a victory won is achieved by the aid of the

Almighty who supports the cause of the exultant victors. It is this union of religion with patriotism which gives war its most horrible aspect, for under guise of devotion to God and high morality the most fiendish cruelty can be engaged in with an approving conscience.

This fact, plus the natural impulse to vengeance character-istic of human nature in a relatively uncurbed society, made those "crude and cruel days." Human flesh was cheap. There is, for example, the bloody story (Numbers 31) of a great victory over the Midianites which resulted in the command by Moses to slaughter every male, including all the male children, of the enemy, saving alive only the virgin women who were to be taken as prey. The enemy's cities and encampments were burned; thirty-two thousand virgins, with an immense amount of booty in cattle and jewelry, were seized; and a portion of all the loot given as an offering to Yahweh. Then to make sure that everything was done fittingly, there was a great puri-fication of the men of war, their captives and the spoil.

The book of Judges opens with a vivid sketch which, be-tween the lines, tells much of current custom. When Judah and his brother Simeon (probably not individuals, but tribes that bore these names) went up together against the Canaanites, Jehovah delivered the enemy into their hand and they smote in Bezek ten thousand men. But the ruler, Adoni-bezek, was elusive. The story runs:

> Adoni-bezek fled; but they pursued him, and caught him, and cut off his thumbs and his great toes. And Adoni-bezek said, "Seventy kings with their thumbs and their great toes cut off used to pick up scraps under my table; as I have done, so God has requited me." And they brought him to Jerusalem, and he died there.[12]

If the record of such mutilation and slaughter affronts a more sophisticated moral sense, two reflections are in order.

[12]Judges 1:6–8. R. S. V.

The first is that it is an evidence of genuine moral progress that in general we feel revulsion at wanton cruelty. The second is that atrocities far worse than this have occurred in our own day, and in terms of gross injuries to human beings the bombs dropped on Dresden or Hamburg, Hiroshima or Nagasaki make what was done to and by Adoni-bezek seem like a minor circumstance.

Whether or not there was an overt state of war, conflict was generally in the offing, fostered by treachery and theft. David with no provocation invaded the country of the Geshurites, Girzites, and Amalekites (tribes friendly to Philistines), put to death all the inhabitants, seized their property, and returned to lie brazenly to Achish, king of the Philistines, as to where he had been (I Sam. 27:8–12). Yet this follows close upon his act of magnanimity in sparing the life of Saul in the cave of Ziph (I Sam. 26:1–12). Saul, though an enemy, was the Lord's anointed: the Philistine communities lay outside the pale.

The alien in peace times had some rights. The "stranger that is within the gates" was to rest on the Sabbath. The Covenant Code twice forbids the Hebrews to oppress the sojourner, with an injunction to remember that they themselves were sojourners in the land of Egypt (Exod. 22:21; 23:9). The uncircumcised sojourner was forbidden to eat the passover, but might submit to the Jewish rite and acquire this privilege (Exod. 12:45–49). These facts indicate a persisting tendency to grant rights to aliens which automatically become cancelled in war or economic conflict. Despite the fact that it was written, "There shall be one law for the native and for the stranger who sojourns among you" (Exod. 12:49), there is no nation yet where this is actually the case. We still have a long way to go before "foreigner" will cease to be a term of division and derision.

One of the most redeeming virtues was hospitality. No sojourner in need could be turned away. So binding was this

obligation that, as we noted, the old man of Gibeah who gave
shelter to the Levite and his concubine placed the protection
of his guest above the chastity of his daughter (Judges 19:16–
24). It was strong enough to span tribal lines and we find
David leaving his parents with the King of Moab when he
began his contest with Saul (I Sam. 22:3, 4), and receiving
succor himself from the Ammonites when in conflict with his
son Absalom (II Sam. 17:27–29). Yet if a clash occurred between hospitality and tribal loyalty, nationalism won. Jael
shamelessly lured Sisera into her tent, gave him food and
drink, put him to bed—and drove a tent-pin through his temple!
(Judges 4:17–22). Nor does the incident stop there, for the
"Song of Deborah" which recounts the event was doubtless
sung again and again in exultation and belligerent passion to
urge men to battle under its cry.

> So perish all thine enemies, O Lord!
> But thy friends be like the sun as he rises in his might.[13]

Strong as were these tribal and national cleavages and
clashes, they sometimes faded under the impact of propinquity,
much as religious or racial lines of division get overcome today
by sex attraction or by economic interest. The result was that
the Hebrews, instead of exterminating or driving out all the
original settlers of Canaan, intermarried with them and took
over their gods. The following is succinct and typical:

> So the people of Israel dwelt among the Canaanites, the
> Hittites, the Amorites, the Perizzites, the Hivites, and the
> Jebusites; and they took their daughters to themselves for
> wives, and their own daughters they gave to their sons;
> and they served their gods.

> And the people of Israel did what was evil in the sight
> of the Lord, forgetting the Lord their God, and serving
> the Baals and the Asheroth![14]

[13]Judges 5:31. R. S. V.
[14]Judges 3:5–7. R. S. V.

Whereupon the anger of Yahweh was kindled against them, and He delivered them into the hand of the enemy. Again and again this happened, each defeat being interpreted as divine displeasure at their apostasy, and every success as a sign of the restoration of Yahweh's favor. Yet they kept on intermarrying with the Canaanitish women, partly because they liked them, partly because such alliances enhanced their own security against external pressures. And in spite of the obvious differences between Yahweh and the many local Baals they kept on worshiping the Baals, partly because of the influence of the surrounding social environment, partly because they thought the Baals could give their fields fertility. As with most people, practice fell short of precept.

b. *Attitude toward women.* The story of early Israel's attitude toward woman is full of lights and shadows, ranging from the sordid story of the rape of Tamar by her half-brother Amnon (II Sam. 13) to the fine picture of Elkanah's love for Hannah, the mother of Samuel (I Sam. 1:4-8). In certain individual cases we find evidence of a higher position than is accorded to women in other early societies; for example, the acceptance of Deborah's leadership as judge; the loyalty shown by Jacob's fourteen years of service to win Rachel; the exquisite story of Hannah's making for Samuel a little coat and bringing it each year to the temple. Yet an objective reading of the record as a whole can scarcely leave one with the impression that women were accorded a very high position. Polygamy and concubinage were the accepted order of the day. Abraham and Jacob were polygamous. Elkanah had two wives who did not agree (I Sam. 1:6). David had eight wives mentioned by name and there is a blanket reference to "more concubines and wives from Jerusalem" (II Sam. 5:13). Solomon's marital adventures are world-famous—the reference to his wives and concubines in round numbers probably meaning that for political and personal reasons he made *liasons* too numerous to mention.

In the Covenant Code, a slight attempt is made to protect the chastity of women. If a virgin were seduced, the seducer must pay a dowry and marry her, or if the girl's father refused marriage, he must make a money payment in any case (Exodus 22:16–17). In the seventh commandment adultery is forbidden.[15] Yet in practice this prohibition seems to have been taken somewhat lightly. Rahab the harlot is honored for her protection of the spies rather than condemned for her profession, and the men receive no censure for their visit (Joshua 2:1). There is an equally matter-of-fact statement of Samson's visit to the harlot at Gaza (Judges 16:1). David's adultery with Bathsheba is condemned, but chiefly for his sin against Uriah (II Samuel 11).

Women in Israel, as in other patriarchal societies, were the property of their husbands and father—sometimes loved, but always possessed. Their chastity was prized when a violation of it would decrease their marriage value or dishonor their husbands, but there is little evidence of chivalry. Some fine instances of domestic affection do shine out from a welter of unlovely incidents, but not all Hebrew women were given the romantic devotion reflected in the stories of Rachel and Ruth.

It was not as wives, but as mothers, that women received their fullest recognition. As in every patriarchal society, sons were greatly desired and the woman who could bear them was greatly esteemed. In the injunction, "Honor thy father *and thy mother*," there is an important reflection of maternal respect, the significance of which is easily missed because we take it for granted. Daughters had a less privileged place than sons, but there is no suggestion in the Bible of the female infanticide found in some primitive societies.

Religion is no guarantor of sex equality. It was not among

[15]In the later codes (Deut. 22:13–29 and Lev. 20:10–14) the death penalty is imposed. It is not unusual for religious advance to be marked by increased rigor in regard to sex morals.

the Hebrews; it is not yet. Jesus broke sharply with his Hebrew background in treating women as persons—to be talked
with, healed in body and soul, treated as friends and equals.
The Christian gospel through the years has been the chief
force in lifting the general status of women, and within the
past century in freeing women from many former limitations
as to vocational choices, educational opportunities, participation in political and other community activities. Yet the Christian Church, as was noted in Chapter Two, has resisted more
resolutely than any other major institution the admission of
women to its leadership on terms of parity with men. (The
author hopes that it is not bad manners to continue to point
out this fact!)

c. *Slavery*. Slavery was a well-accepted Old Testament practice. Attempts were made to mitigate its cruelties, but it seems
to have occurred to no one that there was anything wrong
about the institution itself. The Hebrews had served as slaves
in Egypt, and when they got the chance, they enslaved others
as a matter of course. In fact, to enslave their captives rather
than slaughter them marks an humanitarian advance.

Slaves became such by being born into servitude, by capture
in war, by seizure for debt, or being sold by parents. Slavery
was of two types in early times: the heavy unrequited toil
exacted by kings for carrying on great building operations, and
the milder agricultural or domestic servitude of the patriarchal
household, the latter prevailing among the Hebrews. The absence, in general, of a wage-earning class made slavery inevitable. The nearest approximation to a wage system at this
period was found in the practice of offering one's labor to a
landed Hebrew in return for a living, a wife, or a share of the
produce, as in Jacob's service to Laban, but this form of service
was far less common than slavery.

The Covenant Code gives numerous and quite explicit provisions for the protection of Hebrew slaves (Exodus 21:2–11, 16, 20, 21, 32). Nothing is said of the rights of alien slaves— probably because they had none worth speaking of, though the provision for a day of rest upon the Sabbath appears to apply to them as well as others (Exodus 23:12). Hebrew men, often enslaved for debt, were to be released at the end of six years, taking their wives with them if married at the time of entering servitude but not otherwise. Whether through love of master or reluctance to leave his own family behind, the slave could, if he wished, refuse manumission, in which case his ear was bored through with an awl as a symbol of perpetual servitude. A girl who became a slave by being sold into servitude by her father could be "redeemed" (probably bought back by a relative) if she no longer pleased her master, but he was forbidden to sell her to a foreigner. If taken into his own family as his wife or son's wife, she must be well treated. Women were denied the general manumission privilege accorded to Hebrew men, probably because of a desire to keep the children as hereditary slaves.

A master could beat his slave, but not to death. Here is an interesting conjunction of the rights of personality and property. If the victim of such a scourging died on the spot the master could be punished; if he lived a day or two, the master was to go free, "for the slave is his money." The master who seriously mutilated a slave forfeited his ownership. And in this there was no sex discrimination! The provision reads quaintly:

> When a man strikes the eye of his slave, male or female, and destroys it, he shall let the slave go free for the eye's sake. If he knocks out the tooth of his slave, male or female, he shall let the slave go free for the tooth's sake.[16]

How much was a slave worth? To avoid dodging responsibility in case of loss a blanket figure was set by the law. If a slave were gored to death by an ox, thirty shekels of silver

[16]Exod. 21:26, 27. R. S. V.

were to be given in restitution, whether for man-servant or maid (Exod. 21:32). Slaves were sufficiently valuable property to be worth stealing, and their theft was a capital offense (Exod. 21:16).

It is apparent from these provisions that by the time of the kingdom, not only was slavery a well-established practice, but there was an emerging humanitarianism with regard to it. Slaves were chattels, but they were also in some measure persons. So important was this that a provision for their rest was written into the Decalogue. The evils of Hebrew slavery were no more serious—in fact, probably there was less general suffering under it—than in the economic insecurity of great numbers of persons in our time.

d. *Property rights.* An abundance of provisions, not applicable to the nomadic period but relevant to an agricultural society, are found in the Covenant Code. Stealing from the outsider, whether of goods or wives, was the accepted practice, but one could not steal from another Hebrew with impunity. The Decalogue says bluntly, "Thou shalt not steal." This is elaborated in the Covenant Code to require restitution four- or fivefold for the theft of a sheep or ox—twofold if found still alive in the thief's possession (Exod. 22:1–4). If a man carelessly let his beasts eat up another's crops, or set a fire that burned them, or left a pit uncovered for his neighbor's cattle to fall into (Exod. 21:33–34, 22:5, 6), such acts of negligence must be atoned for by restitution. If one man's ox gored another's to death they shared alike in the loss—unless the owner knew it to have goring tendencies and let it run wild, in which case he must make full restitution. Similarly, for the goring of a man or woman to death, the dangerous animal must be stoned; but if its owner let it out knowing it to be dangerous, he must pay for such criminal negligence by his own life or a heavy fine (Exod. 21:28–32, 35–36). Other provisions are stated regarding the degree of responsibility involved for theft or damage occurring to property borrowed or intrusted to one's charge (Exod. 22:7–15). Such detailed stipulations give evidence of a highly developed sense of honesty—probably not always observed, but at least sufficiently recognized to win a major place in the formulation of the Code.

Certain other provisions give evidence of an humanitarian attitude toward the poor. The land was to lie fallow in the seventh year that the poor might eat, as work was to cease on the seventh day that servants, cattle and sojourners might rest (Exod. 22:26, 27). It is perhaps unnecessary to point out that not only the Christian Sabbath, but the academic sabbatical of the present stems from this provision. Another provision of great historic influence was the specification that no interest was to be charged for money lent to a poor Hebrew (Exod. 22:25). This grew into a prohibition of "usury" which in a Christian culture made Jews the chief money-lenders and therefore objects of hatred and persecution; retarded the advance of trade as the European economy moved from feudalism to capitalism; assisted in a marriage of capitalism with Protestantism when John Calvin lifted the ban on interest-taking among Christians.

Other provisions indicating an emerging social conscience on matters of perennial importance appear in the Covenant Code. The widows and the fatherless were not to be afflicted (Exod. 22:22–24). The poor man was promised justice without sentimental favor in the courts (Exod. 23:3, 6). Bribery was flatly forbidden as blinding the sight and perverting the words of the righteous (Exod. 23:8). A provision primitive in its setting, permanent in principle, states that if a neighbor's garment were taken in pledge for debt it should be returned to him before sun-down, that he might have it to cover himself as he slept (Exod. 23:8). Such provisions suggest the giving of religious sanction to an unsophisticated but genuine sense of responsibility to one's brother.

Yet if we may judge by the offenses against which Amos
and the other great prophets of the eighth century felt impelled
to protest, and whose messages we shall examine in the next
chapter, many of these regulations seem to have been more
honored in the breach than the observance. This, of course, is
not new in the world's history. The laws of a people always
represent a level which is above that of common practice, else
no law would be necessary, but at the same time below that
of the persons of greatest discernment and moral wisdom. Except under conditions of divine fiat or human dictatorship, the
laws move upward as the people respond to the dual challenge
of observed injustices and prophetic insight.

In the early communistic nomadic days, there was little
disparity of wealth. With the assumption of agricultural life
with its greater measure of private ownership, inequalities developed which became increasingly accentuated. There was
never among the Hebrews, as in Babylon and Rome, a distinct separation between patrician and plebeian classes. The
implicit equalitarianism of their Covenant relation to Yahweh
was a safeguard against such stratification. Yet from two directions—the power of the kings and the power of wealthy land-
owners—economic disparities of great proportions with economic injustices appeared.

We have noted how Solomon's heavy burdens of taxation,
transmitted to his son Rehoboam, was the factor that split the
kingdom. The rich seem flagrantly to have annexed the small
ancestral estates of their neighbors, as in Ahab's seizure of
Naboth's vineyard (I Kings 21) and the Shunamite woman's
loss of her land (II Kings 8:1–6). Crop failures, taxes, exac-
tions for war, and the ordinary losses due to bad luck or bad
management forced the poor into debt, and from debt into
slavery, somewhat as happens now with the piling up of mort-
gages and their foreclosure. Once down, no amount of legis-
lation could guarantee justice to the poor. So the rich got

richer and the poor got poorer, until there came warning
voices—and finally a crash.

e. *Administration of justice.* In the Judges period the most
common means of dealing with major offenses, or what were
so regarded, was by fighting the matter out under the principles of collective responsibility and blood revenge. When the
tribes, or the members of a tribe, became "knit together as
one man," an immense amount of coercive power was available. This very often fell far short of real justice, but it was
a rude approximation of it.

Nevertheless, courts then existed, the origins of which may
go back to Moses (Exod. 18:13–26), and with the establishment of the kingdom the greater political stability thus acquired led to their more extended use. Cases were tried before
the elders at the city gates, or by the priests at the sacred
shrine. The latter used the Urim and Thummin—sacred lots
which were supposed to reveal the will of God, but which
doubtless settled many things by chance, except as they were
manipulated by the priest. A particularly perplexing case might
be brought to the ruler for settlement (*e.g.,* II Sam. 15, 2–6;
I Kings 3:16–28).

The Covenant Code reaffirms the *lex talionis* (Exod. 21:24,
25) to set limits upon vengeance, but reaches a higher moral
level than this in its injunctions against perjury, bribery, the
slaying of the innocent, the oppression of the sojourner, and
other perversions of justice (Exod. 23:1–9). There is a call to
a high degree of magnanimity in the requirement that if one
find his enemy's ox or ass gone astray or caught under its pack,
he must, instead of leaving it there, do all he can to restore
it to its owner (Exod. 23:4–5). No direct reference is made
in the Code to courts, but a person guilty of criminal negligence is to pay as a ransom for his life "whatsoever is laid upon
him" (Exod. 21:30), and in a case of theft that cannot be
easily decided "the cause of both parties shall come before

God" (Exod. 22:9)—which probably means that the matter is to be settled by the sacred lots.

Capital punishment was employed, but the list of capital offenses at this time is surprisingly brief.[17] One forfeited his life for deliberate murder, especially murder of a parent, but not for accidental homicide; for letting his vicious ox kill a person; for kidnapping; for cursing his father or mother; for sorcery; for lying with a beast; for sacrificing to strange gods (Exod. 21:12–17, 29; 22:18–19). The seriousness of the parental curse suggests the binding obligation to filial reverence in a patriarchal society, as the penalty attached to the worship of other deities suggests how vital was the preservation of the pure worship of Yahweh.

f. *Duties owed to Yahweh.* In a sense all the social requirements that have been enumerated were religious duties, for all were conceived to be imposed by divine authority. Yahweh raised up judges and gave them His spirit[18] (Judges 2:18); He chose, anointed, and dethroned kings (I Sam. 10:1–8). Through the word of priests and rulers, through signs and wonders, dreams and voices, sacred lots and angel visitants, He made known His will. So permeated was popular thought with the thought of Yahweh and His requirements that it occurred to no one to make a separation between the duties imposed by God and by man.

However, certain duties were owed to Yahweh directly. The primary of these are stated in the first table of the Ten Commandments, and are elaborated in the Covenant Code. Yahweh alone is to be worshiped and offered sacrifice: idolatry, blasphemy and Sabbath-profanation[19] are not to be countenanced. Yahweh must have the first-fruits of the flocks and the harvest (Exod. 22:29, 30; 23:19) and sacred festivals must be observed

17As we shall note, they increased in number in later codes.
18Akin to the *mana* concept.
19The motive for Sabbath keeping was in part humanitarian (Exod. 23:12). This becomes clearer in the Deuteronomic version of the Decalogue.

in his honor (Exod. 23:14–17). An elaborate ritual grew up, the correct observance of which was a religious duty, and thus the foundation was laid for the barren ritualism which had to be denounced with such vigor in later years.

Another very binding religious duty was the keeping of a vow. A promise made to Yahweh was to be kept at all hazards. The most dramatic example of this is the rash vow of Jephthah made in the heat of a battle, and its tragic denouement in the voluntary death of his only daughter (Judges 11:34–40). Another oath which came near having equally fatal consequences was Saul's injunction, broken unwittingly by Jonathan, that the people eat no food till evening on the day of battle. When the lot pointed to Jonathan as the offender, Saul would have forfeited his son's life had not the demand of the people spared him (I Samuel 14:24–46). This release gives evidence that the people's spontaneous sense of justice was sometimes stronger than the formal requirement. A curse in the name of Yahweh was as binding as a vow (Judges 21:18), and this is one reason why it was so serious a matter to curse one's parents.

Besides all these matters, the record shows a complex set of moral tendencies which root in human nature rather than in the mores of any special age. David sang an exquisite hymn of lamentation over the death of his enemy Saul and his friend Jonathan (II Samuel 1:17–27), and mourned the death of his rebellious son Absalom with a grief that shows no trace of bitterness (II Samuel 19:1–4). On his death-bed he charged Solomon to pay off an old grudge against Joab and "let not his hoar head go down to Sheol in peace"; and in the next breath he enjoined kindness to the sons of Barzillai the Gileadite for giving him succor when he fled from Absalom (I Kings 2:5–9). Such lights and shadows in the life of Israel's greatest king are typical of the times. There was bitter enmity and loyal friendship (I Sam. 18:1–9); retaliation and gratitude (I Sam. 31:11–13); treachery and magnanimity (II Sam. 15).

It was a crude and cruel age, but one from which shines moral beauty.

The total impression gathered from a study of the pre-prophetic law and the revealing incidents of the narrative is that the Hebrew faith both reinforced and challenged tribal morals. There is the fiercely drawn cleavage between the in-group and the out-group, inferior status of women, sanctioning of slavery, economic inequality, and cruelty under the guise of retribution which every conquering, agrarian society displays. Much of the good in the moral standards we have just been canvassing, as well as much of the evil in the practices, was already present in the Canaanitic culture. It is a mistake to say either that the relatively high provisions of the Covenant Code were wholly original with the Hebrews, or that they were simply a replica of Canaanite standards which in turn were derived from the Code of Hammurabi. The blending is so complex that the separation of the strands is possible only through the most extensive Biblical scholarship—and then only with much tentativeness.

Nevertheless, within and above the nomadic and Canaanitic elements in the emerging moral consciousness of the Hebrews there is discernible a growing sense of justice and an intuition, however dimly grasped, that self-restraint for the social good is ordained of God. It was not the idea of Yahweh, as an idea, that gripped them; it was the conviction that Yahweh was their God and they were His people, and that Yahweh demanded of them righteousness. They might sin against Him; they could not escape from Him. This relationship, so crucial to their very existence, was the matrix from which the prophets' clearer apprehension of both the judgment and the mercy of God was soon to appear.

To the degree that the Hebrews' relation to Yahweh could be moralized and socialized, vast possibilities lay within it. We must next examine how the prophets cleansed it and made great winds of justice blow through it.

CHAPTER SIX

ISRAEL'S PROPHETS

AND SAGES

The major task of the prophets was to declare the will of God and call people to its observance. They were not fortune-tellers. Yet their messages were predictive, for they could read the signs of the times from a religious frame of reference. The prophet is a foreteller of a unique type. Since Yahweh is Lord of history, known by and through His mighty acts within the human scene, the prophet announced what Yahweh would do and why He would do it.

With keen insight and a vigor that has seldom been equalled in human utterance, the prophets of Israel denounced social oppression and apostasy, and foretold the doom that would fall upon the people if they did not change their ways. With variations according to temperament and their times, they rang the changes on four insistent themes: supreme allegiance to Yahweh, economic justice for all, the placing of righteousness above ritualistic correctness, and the inevitable doom which a long-suffering but just God will send on the unrepentant.

A complex set of forces brought the prophets into being. They represent the protest of the old nomadic equality against agrarian inequality; the common people against corrupt landowners and kings; the lay worshiper against the priest. In general, theirs is the voice of democracy, without a political democratic structure, against entrenched feudalism. But it is to miss their most distinctive message to try to explain them mainly in terms of economic or political developments. A sense of God's holiness and righteousness underlies the entire prophetic demand for justice. Without it, they might have raised their voices in protest, as the author of "The Eloquent Peasant" did centuries earlier in Egypt or the poet Hesiod—their unknown contemporary—did in eighth-century Greece. But without this sense of God's holiness and righteousness, the Hebrew prophets would not have spoken as they did or made the indelible contribution that they made on all subsequent Hebrew-Christian thought.

A protest against inequality to be effective must rest on one or the other of two foundations: great coercive power, or a dynamic faith that transcendent, even cosmic, forces are on the side of such a protest. The first of these the prophets obviously could not have. The political rulers who had it, and who not infrequently tried to silence the prophets, have long since passed into oblivion, while the prophets still are living figures. The second requirement they had in abundant measure, and it gave them their power. It is the lack of it which has accounted for the relative lack of effectiveness in both political socialism and the preaching of a moralistic social gospel in our day, while it is its presence in powerful though perverted form that gives Communism its demonic strength.

This combination of a dynamic religious faith with insight brought to bear on economic and political matters is seen in the work of all the principal prophets. They demanded in the name of the Lord the eradication of exploitation—particularly in the acquiring of land and in shady commercial dealings, and a putting away of the idleness, luxury and debauchery which were corrupting the rich and leading to further injustices. But such protests against social acquisitiveness and pride are so intertwined with indictments of spiritual pride that the two must be understood together. A few illustrations chosen from innumerable passages will make this clear:

> Woe to the proud crown of the drunkards of Ephraim,
>   and to the fading flower of its glorious beauty,
>   which is on the head of the rich valley of those overcome with wine!
> Behold, the Lord has one who is mighty and strong;
>   like a storm of hail, a destroying tempest,
>   like a storm of mighty, overflowing waters,
>   he will cast down to the earth with violence.[1]

❖   ❖   ❖   ❖   ❖

> Woe to those who go down to Egypt for help
>   and rely on horses,
> Who trust in chariots because they are many
>   and in horsemen because they are very strong,
> but do not look to the Holy One of Israel
>   or consult the Lord! . . .
> The Egyptians are men, and not God;
>   and their horses are flesh, and not spirit.[2]

❖   ❖   ❖   ❖   ❖

> Be appalled, O heavens, at this,
>   be shocked, be utterly desolate, says the Lord,
> for my people have committed two evils:
>   they have forsaken me,
> the fountain of living waters,
>   and hewed out cisterns for themselves,
> broken cisterns,
>   that can hold no water.[3]

[1] Is. 28:1, 2. R. S. V.
[2] Is. 31:1, 3. R. S. V.
[3] Jer. 2:12, 13. R. S. V.

As interpreters of the processes of history, the prophets saw the sure judgment of God upon evil-doers, even upon His chosen people. To the familiar question of why the wicked prosper, their answer was that judgment might be delayed, but only by repentance could it be averted. This message they preached without deviation, apparently not greatly expecting it to be heeded. There is deep pessimism as to the prospect of change in such a passage as this:

> Can the Ethiopian change his skin
>   or the leopard his spots?
> Then also you can do good
>   who are accustomed to do evil.[4]

Yet the prophets, on the whole, were not pessimists. They believed too firmly in the ways of God to despair. All deep optimism is rooted in a clear awareness of the world's evil, and the prophets saw both the judgment and the mercy of God. The note of hope in their message was grounded in the faith that God would not permit His people to be utterly blotted out; a saving remnant would repent and return to Him; God would send a messiah to be their saviour. God's chosen people must be refined by suffering to become the servants of all and spread to the Gentiles the light of His saving grace.

These high insights were not attained all at once. We must now trace rapidly, but more consecutively, the growth of prophetic thought.

1. Before the Exile

a. *The earlier prophets.* The period of prophecy is often reckoned as beginning with Amos in the eighth century, for he was the first to write his message, and he spoke for social justice with a vigor unequalled by his predecessors. However, among the forerunners of the prophets are to be reckoned the

4Jer. 13:23. R. S. V.

statesman Moses; also Samuel, a lesser leader who organized the national consciousness of the people, showed them their need of a king and found the man. During the united kingdom there was no great prophetic figure, though Nathan with tact and courage rebuked David for the killing of Uriah (II Sam. 12:1–15). After the division, during the ninth century, appeared Elijah and his successor Elisha. They yearned for the morality of the early simpler nomadic life, and Elijah, at great personal danger, denounced corruption and infidelity in high places. When King Ahab coveted Naboth's ancestral vineyard and Jezebel connived to kill its owner and seize it, Elijah denounced their sin and foretold their ignoble death (I Kings 21). He protested with much vigor against the current Baalism. His contest on Mount Carmel with the four hundred and fifty prophets of Baal and their subsequent slaughter (I Kings 18:16–40) reveals a fierce and fanatical but rugged loyalty to Yahweh—a sort of over-accentuated Puritanism. Beside him Elisha, with his wonder-working power to heal leprosy and raise the dead (II Kings 4:17–37; 5:1–19) seems a kindly but rather anemic figure, though it is true that he opposed the invading king of Syria at the risk of his life (II Kings 6) and in the sequel to the story of the healing of Naaman his indignation flames out against the avarice of Gehazi in a manner akin to that of Elijah (II Kings 5:20–27).

b. *Amos.* This protest against corruption came to full vigor in the words of Amos, formerly reckoned a minor prophet but now recognized as one of the greatest figures of all time. This herdsman of Tekoa, which was twelve miles from the important city and shrine of Bethel in the northern kingdom, appeared suddenly one day in the midst of a religious festival and began to talk. With consummate strategy he first won the attention and assent of his hearers by picturing the judgments of Yahweh upon their neighbors:

Thus says the Lord:
"For three transgressions of Damascus,
and for four, I will not revoke the punishment;
because they have threshed Gilead
with threshing sledges of iron. . . ."[5]

And so Gaza, and Tyre, and Edom, and Ammon, and Moab.
The worshipers gathered at Bethel must have been getting
nervous by that time. Finally, with a sledge-hammer blow the
condemnation fell squarely upon their own heads:

Thus says the Lord:
"For three transgressions of Israel,
and for four, I will not revoke the punishment;
because they sell the righteous for silver,
and the needy for a pair of shoes—
they that trample the head of the poor
into the dust of the earth,
and turn aside the way of the afflicted;
a man and his father go in to the same maiden,
so that my holy name is profaned;
they lay themselves down beside every altar
upon garments taken in pledge;
and in the house of their God they drink
the wine of those who have been fined."[6]

In this succinct statement Amos enumerates the characteristic offenses of any corrupt, wealthy, class-divided civilization
—economic exploitation, sexual looseness, irreverence, selfishness, drunkenness. Elsewhere he charges the capitalists of his
day with cheating the poor man with false balances and sell-
ing him the refuse of the wheat (8:5, 6); of afflicting the innocent, bribing judges and perverting justice in the courts (5:12);
of suppressing any who might wish to speak for the underprivileged (5:10, 13). The women, too, (cows of Bashan, he
calls them!) are guilty, for they entice their husbands to op-

[5]Amos 1:3, R. S. V. "I" refers to Yahweh, as whose mouthpiece the
prophet speaks.
[6]Amos 2:6–8. R. S. V.

pression that they may have luxury and drink (4:1). He was
portraying the Israel of the reign of Jeroboam II, but he might
equally well have been describing Rome in its period of decadence—or America in our own day.

Amos saw that internal corruption was threatening Israel's
national security, and impelled by a sense of divine mission
he said so. He must have startled these "chosen" people when
he declared that special privilege would not save them; rather,
it laid upon them the heavier obligation!

You only have I known
   of all the families of the earth;
therefore I will punish you
   for all your iniquities . . .[7]

Furthermore, though they be the chosen people, they are not
the only recipients of divine favor:

"Are you not like the Ethiopians to me,
   O people of Israel?" says the Lord.
"Did I not bring up Israel from the land of Egypt,
   and the Philistines from Caphtor and the Syrians from Kir?"[8]

The great day of the Lord for which they have been looking will be darkness, and not light, as one fleeing from a lion
meets a bear, or going into a house for security is bitten by
a serpent (5:18–20). One way only of escape is open, "Seek
good, and not evil, that you may live" (5:14). No ceremony
will avail. In fact, it is the substitution of ritual for righteousness that has brought them to this pass, and Yahweh will have
no more of it:

I hate, I despise your feasts,
   and I take no delight in your solemn assemblies.
Even though you offer me your burnt offerings
      and cereal offerings,

[7]Amos 3:2. R. S. V.   [8]Amos 9:7. R. S. V.

I will not accept them,
and the peace offerings of your fatted beasts
    I will not look upon.
Take away from me the noise of your songs;
    to the melody of your harps I will not listen.
But let justice roll down like waters,
    and righteousness like an ever-flowing stream.[9]

This forthright statement of the superiority of justice to
ceremonial observance marks a watershed in moral development, for while there had been calls to justice and righteousness before, there had never been so sharp an assertion that
religious ceremonies are valueless without moral living. It was
as if God were emphatically saying through Amos that He
would not be pleased with praying or church-going if one
were enriching himself at the expense of another's life.

c. *Hosea.* As Amos is often called the prophet of justice, so
his younger contemporary Hosea is termed the prophet of
love. He, too, laments the wickedness of the people, but he
speaks in a gentler strain. The setting is his own domestic
affliction. Though the story is obscure, the common interpretation is that he married a woman by the name of Gomer who,
becoming unfaithful, fell into sin and finally sank into slavery.
Hosea, loving her still, bought her back and restored her to
her former place by his side. Whether or not this is Hosea's
own experience, the major note of the book is Yahweh's love
for Israel (often personified as Ephraim) in spite of the apostasy of His wayward people. The book abounds in striking
images. Israel has behaved like a stubborn heifer but will be
fed by Yahweh like a lamb (4:16); Israel is like a heated oven
and the king a careless baker (7:4–7); Ephraim is a cake not
turned (7:8); it is like a silly dove, without understanding
calling to Egypt or Assyria for help (7:11); Israel has sown

9Amos 5:21–24. R. S. V.

the wind and shall reap the whirlwind (8:7); yet it is like grapes in the wilderness (9:10) or a luxuriant vine (10:1). A particularly beautiful figure is that in which Yahweh compares Israel to a child whom He has taken in His arms and taught to walk (11:1–4).

Like Amos, Hosea condemns the practice of making ceremonial worship do duty for righteousness, and there is nowhere a more direct statement of the supremacy of moral demands than in his declaration spoken as the word of Yahweh,

> For I desire steadfast love and not sacrifice,
>   the knowledge of God, rather than burnt offerings.[10]

Hosea's primary emphasis, however, is not on social justice but on the duty of fidelity to Yahweh in return for God's consummate love. The people are destroyed for lack of knowledge (4:6); they have played the harlot (4:12); they must suffer for their sin—but Yahweh stands ready to heal their backsliding and to love them freely (14:4).

Not long after the preaching of Amos and Hosea in the northern kingdom, the doom which they had been predicting fell. In 722 Samaria was forced to surrender before the Assyrian armies. The scene shifts to the southern kingdom.

d. *Isaiah.* Here lived a great prophetic statesman, the first Isaiah. We say "the first Isaiah" because the sixty-six chapters of the book bearing that name are certainly the work of at least two men, possibly three. The author of the greater part of chapters 1–39 lived in the latter half of the eighth century, preaching from the time of the death of King Uzziah about 740 B.C. until after the invasion of Sennacherib's army in 701. The message of the second, called Deutero-Isaiah, is from the setting of the exile about two centuries later.

The story of the first Isaiah's call to be a prophet (Is. 6)

[10]Hosea 6:6.

is one of the most beautiful and dramatic passages in the Bible. Praying one day in the temple in the year that King Uzziah died, and thinking undoubtedly about the internal corruption and external danger that beset the land, he saw a vision of the majesty and glory of God in contrast with his own impurity and that of his people. Feeling the touch of divine forgiveness upon his lips, he heard a voice speaking from the smoke which filled the temple. "Whom shall I send, and who will go for us?" it asked; and Isaiah answered, "Here I am; send me."

Isaiah's social message is much like that of Amos, for he lived in similar conditions. Unlike the herdsman Amos, he belonged to the Jerusalem nobility, but this did not stop him from denouncing corruption in high places. He attacked land monopolies—the wrestling of their patrimony from the poor (5:8); the perversion of the courts (5:23); bribery (1:23); drunken reveling 5:11, 22); deception (5:20) and self-righteousness (5:21) in terms which left no doubt of his meaning. These familiar charges are intertwined in every age.

Isaiah was as stern as Amos in his denunciation of ceremonialism as a substitute for human kindness, as gentle as Hosea in portraying God's forgiving love. He states majestically his conception of Yahweh's moral demands and proffered salvation:

> Your new moons and your appointed feasts
>   my soul hates;
> they have become a burden to me,
>   I am weary of bearing them.
> When you spread forth your hands,
>   I will hide my eyes from you;
> even though you make many prayers,
>   I will not listen;
>   Your hands are full of blood.
> Wash yourselves; make yourselves clean;
>   remove the evil of your doings
>   from before my eyes;

cease to do evil,
    learn to do good;
seek justice,
    correct oppression;
defend the fatherless,
    plead for the widow.

Come now, let us reason together,
    says the Lord:
though your sins are like scarlet,
    they shall be as white as snow;
though they are red like crimson,
    they shall become like wool.
If you are willing and obedient,
    you shall eat the good of the land;
But if you refuse and rebel,
    you shall be devoured by the sword;
    for the mouth of the Lord has spoken.[11]

Isaiah's political message was summed up in his repeated advice to kings to avoid entangling alliances. We cannot here go into the events of his long period of prophecy, but by word and object lesson[12] he tried to make the rulers see that there was more safety to be had through trust in God than through alliances with Egypt or Assyria.

In Isaiah we get the first clear expression of a very important doctrine—that "a remnant will return."[13] The prophets, with all their thundering against sin, never thought the situation hopeless. A few would remain faithful; God in His abundant mercy would save His people from utter annihilation. There are anticipations of this in the patriarchal stories of Noah's deliverance by the ark and of Abraham's intercession for Sodom and Gomorrah. It appears repeatedly in Hebrew thought to inject a note of confidence and challenge. In the

[11]Isaiah 1:14–20. R. S. V.
[12]He named his sons Maher-shahal-hash-baz (hasty booty-speedy prey) and Shearjashub (a remnant shall return); and walked barefoot three years to foreshadow impending disaster.
[13]Isaiah 1:9; 10:21; 11:11. Note also Amos 5:15.

exile it became literalized to apply to the return of a remnant to Jerusalem, but its major meaning was never geographical. It reaches its highest expression in Jesus' teaching of the leaven, the grain of mustard seed, the salt of the earth, the city set on a hill. This hope has given tenacity under persecution, pain and loss to both Jews and Christians through the centuries.

An insight in the book of Isaiah so far ahead of the times that the vision is still unfulfilled is the prophecy, repeated in Micah, of a world without war. In the latter days, when the mountain of the house of the Lord shall be established above all and many peoples shall seek to learn of His ways and walk in His paths, then

> He shall judge between the nations,
>   and shall decide for many peoples;
> and they shall beat their swords into plowshares,
>   and their spears into pruning hooks;
> nation shall not lift up sword against nation,
>   neither shall they learn war any more.[14]

This is one of the most remarkable passages in the Old Testament because it is one of the few in which the will of Yahweh is clearly at variance with strife. It is a plea for international peace but it is more than that; it is a vision of the truth that a common exaltation of God is the basic requirement for good will among men.

e. *Micah.* The last of the great eighth-century reformers was Micah, who probably lived about the time of Sennacherib's invasion, toward the end of Isaiah's period of prophecy. Isaiah was of the nobility; Micah was a poor man speaking for the poor—yet they saw the same vision of a just and peaceful world. Micah was a lesser figure than his predecessors and said little that had not already been said, but it was a message

[14]Isaiah 2:4.

which requires repetition. He protested again at the oppression of the poor and the turning aside of justice from the weak, and restated Isaiah's vision of a warless world in words so similar that they may not be his own (4:1–5). But even if one copied from the other or a later hand inserted them in the text, credit is due for recognizing that they were magnificent words!

Micah strikes a new note, however, in his condemnation of the clergy—priests and false prophets who for their own gain condone the evil deeds of the rulers and rely, in false security, on the presence of the Lord (3:9–12). Apparently some religious leaders then as now were reluctant to mix in social issues or offend the influential. Micah saw clearly the stultifying effect of such complacency. His greatest utterance, often since misquoted as a cloak for indifference to those social issues which stirred him so deeply, is his definition of true religion:

> He has showed you, O man, what is good;
>   and what does the Lord require of you
> but to do justice, and to love kindness,
>   and to walk humbly with your God?[15]

f. *Minor pre-exilic prophets.* The seventh century produced only one great prophet, Jeremiah. Within it falls probably the preaching of three strongly nationalistic figures, Zephaniah, Nahum, and Habakkuk. Zephaniah predicts destruction both to Judah and her enemies but promises restoration and security to a faithful remnant. Nahum exults at the prospect of the overthrow of Nineveh. Habakkuk pronounces woes upon the Chaldeans for being even more wicked than the Hebrews. The narrowness of outlook manifested here is redeemed in the last chapter of Habakkuk by a beautiful hymn of confidence in God in the midst of disaster. It ends thus:

> Though the fig tree do not blossom,
>   nor fruit be on the vines,

15Micah 6:8. R. S. V.

the produce of the olive fail
and the fields yield no food,
the flock be cut off from the fold
and there be no herd in the stalls,
yet I will rejoice in the Lord,
I will joy in the God of my salvation.
God, the Lord, is my strength;
he makes my feet like hinds' feet,
he makes me tread upon my high places.[16]

So different is this from the usual Hebrew idea that it may be a psalm of post-exilic date.

g. *Jeremiah.* Jeremiah, like Isaiah, lived a long life in close connection with the court, and the fifty-two chapters of his prophecy are full of political turmoil. He was drawn into it not only by his denunciation of the social corruption of the times but by his determined insistence that the wisest political move was to yield to Babylon. He saw the futility of resistance, and emphasizing personal religion more than any of his predecessors, he believed that the worship of Yahweh and His protection could survive even national extinction. For this he was misunderstood. So unpopular was he that his life was jeopardized. The people of Anathoth, his native town, tried to murder him (11:18–23); he was put in the stocks (20:1, 2); he was charged with blasphemy and escaped death only by his courageous and forthright defense (26:8–19); he was imprisoned in a dungeon and thrown into a miry cistern to die (37:16–38:13). His writings were publicly burned by King Jehoikim, whereupon he promptly rewrote them (36:20–32). A very human character, he denounced his oppressors (22:10–30), and he became so discouraged at times that he cursed the day of his birth (20:14–18). But he kept on speaking his mind.

Jeremiah himself was a victim of the crisis in national affairs that he saw approaching. Imprisoned for steadily counsel-

[16]Habakkuk 3:17–19. R. S. V.

ing submission after the first exile, he remained in custody until the capture of the city in 586. He then threw in his lot with the new governor Gedaliah, and after the latter was assassinated, Jeremiah's frightened countrymen carried him to Egypt. There, tradition says, he opposed their idolatry and met death at their hands. To the end he battled sublimely for his ideals.

In Jeremiah's message is found Amos' passion for social justice, Hosea's conception of God's tender yearning love, Isaiah's sublime faith in God and hope of a saving remnant. Yet there is more here than a mere restatement. In his life and public utterances, and when these were silenced, in his writings, he preached a spiritual conception of religion which is more intimate and personal than that of any of his predecessors. He gave up the old Semitic idea which identified religion with the State and proclaimed a religion of the heart which was not dependent on political security or temple ritual.[17] This was very vital advice, though they dimly comprehended it, to a people about to be exiled.

Jeremiah's conception of religion as a personal relation between each man and God is summed up in his doctrine of the new covenant, written not on tables of stone but in the heart, and in it he almost attains to a monotheistic and universal faith:

> Behold, the days are coming, says the Lord, when I will make a new covenant with the house of Israel and the house of Judah, not like the covenant which I made with their fathers when I took them by the hand to bring them out of the land of Egypt, my covenant which they broke, though I was their husband, says the Lord. But this is the covenant which I will make with the house of Israel after those days, says the Lord: I will put my law within them, and I will write it upon their hearts; and I will be their God, and they shall be my people. And no longer shall each man teach his neighbor and each his brother, say-

[17]Jeremiah 24:4-7.

ing, "Know the Lord," for they shall all know me, from the least of them to the greatest, says the Lord; for I will forgive their iniquity, and I will remember their sin no more.[18]

Jeremiah glimpsed a great idea, but it remained for the Isaiah of the exile to affirm a clear-cut monotheism. In the meantime, forces were in operation which gave the people something easier to grasp than Jeremiah's sublimely difficult message of a new covenant written in the hearts of men.

2. The Great Reformation

Before plunging into the story of the exile we must go back to a very important event which occurred in the earlier years of Jeremiah's ministry. This was the great cleansing under King Josiah in 621 B.C.

The events of the reformation form a dramatic interlude in the nation's history.[19] The good king Josiah had probably in his youth come under the influence of the prophet Zephaniah; in any case he was concerned for the religious welfare of his people. The temple having fallen into neglect, he gave orders that it be repaired. In the process a strange scroll was found which was recognized as a book of the law. Upon hearing it read, Josiah was deeply disturbed at his people's apostasy and determined to make amends. He summoned at the temple a great mass meeting of all the people of Israel, in whose presence the new code was read, and in their name the king made a solemn covenant to obey its injunctions.

Then followed a great house-cleaning! (II Kings 23:4–14.) From the house of God were brought and burned the vessels polluted by the worship of Baal and the pagan deities of the sky, for offerings had been made not only to the god of fer-

18Jeremiah 31:31–34. R. S. V.
19II Kings 22:3, 23: 27.

tility but to the sun, moon, planets and "host of heaven." The idolatrous priests were deposed; the mediums and wizards ejected; the sacred prostitutes driven from the temple of God. The idols and the asheim (sacred poles and pillars taken over from Canaanitic worship) were burned and the ashes beaten in the dust. "All the abominations that were seen in the land of Judah" were put away.

Not only in Jerusalem, but in the surrounding towns iconoclasm seized the reformers. The local shrines were torn down, even to the ancient shrine at Bethel in the north, and the people were forbidden henceforth to worship anywhere except at the Jerusalem sanctuary. Never had the Hebrews witnessed so thorough a cleansing. At its close the feast of the passover was celebrated at Jerusalem, and the people turned their faces with new zeal to the keeping of the law.

One wonders perhaps why the prophets had anything more to do after this outburst! It is evident, however, that the cleansing was much more ceremonial than moral. It bears more resemblance to image-smashing in Roman Catholic churches and monasteries in the early Reformation than to the ringing calls to social justice which the prophets from Elijah to Jeremiah had been uttering.

The book which caused this turmoil is found in our Bibles as part of Deuteronomy. This code (Deut. 12–26) which used to be thought the work of Moses, was almost certainly written under prophetic influence shortly before the great reformation, and was very likely placed in the temple to be found—a dramatic device for getting it before the people. It repeats many of the social provisions of the Covenant Code, but with a decided emphasis on ritualistic correctness. This indicates that the people had grasped but dimly the message of the prophets. Stirred by them to feel that something must be done if the nation were to survive, the writers moved toward purifying the Yahweh worship by driving in deeper that very ritualism against which every one of the great prophets had protested. This is characteristic of the human tendency to take refuge in the familiar and the traditional to escape the pain of change when life is challenged at its foundations.

The Deuteronomic Code represents a composite of priestly and prophetic morals and is both more ritualistic and more socialized than the Covenant Code. It repeats and makes explicit the provisions for eradication of idolatry by destruction of the images and altars to strange gods, and for the keeping of the feast days—the Passover in the spring and the Feast of Weeks and of Tabernacles at harvest time (16:1–17). It enjoins the offering of the temple sacrifices of the first-born of the flocks without blemish (15:19–22) and draws a distinction between clean and unclean animals—from which grew the Jew's aversion to pork (14:6–8) and his custom of eating bloodless Kosher (12:23, 24). Far more drastic than these were the injunctions to destroy utterly not only idols, but *idolaters* and all worshipers of strange gods, even though the blow might fall on one's own brother, wife, or closest friend (13:6–11). An apostate city was to be put to the edge of the sword and completely "devoted" to Yahweh, and thus the faithful would find favor in His eyes (13:12–18).

Such a return to ritualism not only helped to undo the work of the prophets, but it laid the basis for a wall of Jewish separatism which after the exile grew higher and higher. But probably its worst consequences were not among the Jews themselves, for these meticulous requirements helped to keep the Jews distinct from other peoples when otherwise they might have lost their identity with the loss of their nation. More serious consequences came when these provisions were taken over by Christians as the literal word of God, and were quoted to support a fanatical intolerance against those of another faith. Under the injunction to destroy idolaters and the worshipers of strange gods, Calvin had Servetus burned at the stake, the Inquisition hounded heretics, and Europe ran with blood. Under the obligation to wipe out Yahweh's enemies a fierce war ethic found divine sanction, and we have not yet seen the last of it.

Yet side by side with these requirements stand provisions in the code which evidence a growing humanitarian sense. Various points of progress over the Covenant Code are visible. The Hebrew poor are to be aided by having their debts remitted every seventh year (15:1–3) and one's millstone—a necessity of life in an agricultural society—is not to be taken in pledge (24:6). The fields, vineyards, and olive trees are not to be too carefully gleaned: the remainder is for the sojourner, the fatherless and the widow (24:19–22). One is forbidden to use false weights and measures (25:13–16) or to remove his neighbor's landmark (19:14; 27:17)—a protest against two evils often on the tongues of the prophets. A hired servant, whether Hebrew or stranger, is not to be oppressed, and wages must be paid at the close of day (24:14, 15). This is one of the earliest suggestions of a wage system.

Women fare somewhat better than in the Covenant Code. Women slaves as well as men are to be released every seventh year and sent out with a store of the necessities liberally provided (15:12–15). A man may divorce his wife, but only through a written bill of divorcement, and she may remarry (24:1–2). Adultery becomes a capital offense for both parties (22:22–29). For forcible seduction of a betrothed maiden the man pays with his life; if she is unbetrothed, he pays her father fifty shekels and must marry her (22:25–29). The Levirate marriage is instituted—a curious provision by which if a man die childless, his brother is obligated to marry the widow and raise up sons to the dead brother's name. If he refuse, the woman may report him to the elders and spit in his face! (25:5–10).

Impartial justice in the courts is again insisted upon (10:17,

18; 16:18–20). Though the *lex talionis* still holds, an attempt is made to mitigate the law of blood revenge by the provision of cities of refuge to which one guilty of accidental homicide may flee (19:1–10). Deliberate murder is still a capital offense, as is the worshiping of strange gods, but only on the testimony of two or more witnesses may the penalty be imposed (19:15; 17:6).

Thus we find in the Deuteronomic Code the blending of two elements, priestly separatism and the prophetic sense of social justice. When Jerusalem fell before Nebuchadnezzar's armies and the most virile of the people were carried to Babylon, they took with them both strains.

3. The Exile

The exile is a watershed in Hebrew history, for it marks the destruction of the Hebrew state, which though restored was never so strong again, and it caused some very important changes in Hebrew religion.

The exile split the people into three parts. The least vigorous of them stayed in Palestine, to be harassed by hostile neighbors and lose their national and religious identity. Their pitiable lot is mourned in the Book of Lamentations. Another group fled to Egypt, where they prospered and established a sizable colony at Elephantine. A temple of Yahu (Yahweh) erected there shows some effort to preserve the ancestral faith, but many went over to heathen gods. The destinies of Israel were in the keeping of the little group that was carried to Babylon.

The Jews took up commercial activity—the beginning of a process not yet ended—and many of them achieved wealth and prominence. They were given considerable self-government and outwardly were well off. Many of them began to worship

Bel instead of Yahweh, and thought the exile had not been a bad thing for them.

But not all. In a vigorous minority there was a divine discontent, and these sat down by the waters of Babylon and wept. They were far from Jerusalem, where alone they could offer sacrifice according to the Deuteronomic Code, and the next best substitute for the temple ritual was to meet on the Sabbath in synagogues (literally "meeting-houses") where they fasted and prayed with their faces toward Jerusalem, and yearned for deliverance.

In this setting came an intensification of both the priestly and the prophetic spirit. To the priests it seemed essential to get back to Jerusalem and its temple ritual lest their religion perish, and since they could not go physically in the present they let their minds run to the past and future. They collected many narratives of Israel's past glory, and this priestly or P document is interwoven in our Bible with J (Jahvist) and E (Elohist) documents of the ninth or eighth century and with the D document of the book of Deuteronomy. Looking forward, they conceived a glorious kingdom in which a Messiah should deliver them from bondage and set up their nation and its temple again in greater splendor than before.

But to others came a different outlook. Led by the thought of the second Isaiah, they conceived the idea that their God was the God of all the earth—the *only* God—who could watch over them as well in Babylon as Jerusalem, and who had laid upon them through their very sufferings the divine task of spreading his worship to all mankind. This thought of ethical monotheism and their own mission as the suffering servant of Yahweh was almost too much for them, but a few of them grasped it. These concepts were developed through the preaching of the two great prophets of the exile, Ezekiel and Deutero-Isaiah.

a. *Ezekiel.* Ezekiel was a prophet who was the son of a priest, and he had in him both strains. He is the prophet of individual responsibility and the progenitor of priestly Judaism.

Ezekiel was carried to Babylon in the first deportation of 597, and the letters which he wrote back to his struggling countrymen are full of the call to repentance and the prospect of doom. Why does Israel suffer? Not because Yahweh cannot help them, but because He is just. Jerusalem is like a useless vine, to be cast into the fire for fuel (15:1–8; 19:10–14). Her king is a caged lion (19:1–9). Jerusalem is a rusty caldron which is being cleansed of its filth by fire (24:6–14). Babylon is the sword of Yahweh to smite the people for their sins (21: 8–17).

After the final blow fell, the mood of the prophet changed. His message was no longer one of lashing but healing. His vision of the valley of dry bones gives a graphic picture of a nation revivified by the inbreathing of the spirit of God (37:1–14); while his description of Yahweh as the divine shepherd leading his people again to safety and good pasturage is unsurpassed—save in the Shepherd Psalm which it much resembles (34:11–16; *cf.* Psalm 23). Through such imagery the prophet assured the people that all was not lost, but their God would lead them to glorious restoration. But here enters the priestly element, for the last nine chapters of his message form a sort of constitution for a messianic state and consist of explicit directions for the rebuilding of the temple and the establishment of its ordinances when this restoration should come to pass.

The most distinctive ethical contribution of Ezekiel is his doctrine that the individual himself, and no one else, is responsible for his sins. "The soul that sinneth, it shall die"—not his son or father (18:20). The current proverb, "The fathers have eaten sour grapes and the children's teeth are set on edge," is all wrong, says Ezekiel. Rather, the righteous man shall live and the sinner shall die, whatever his fathers have done. Throughout the eighteenth chapter this point—so directly opposed to collective responsibility and kinship blood revenge—is driven home. This statement is important, not because it indicates an entirely new idea, for it is suggested in Jeremiah (Jer. 31:29, 31) and the two great codes had implicitly recognized it, but because it gives explicit and forceful criticism of a waning concept.

b. *Deutero-Isaiah.* The prophet whose insights were the deepest of all was the second Isaiah. He probably lived toward the closing years of the exile, and his message is found mainly in Isaiah 40–55. From his pen in the fifty-third chapter are words so sublime that they have often been taken as a prophecy of Christ, but they doubtless refer to Israel's mission as the suffering servant of Yahweh.

Starting from the background of the old Hebraic idea that prosperity was a reward of piety and calamity a punishment for sin, Isaiah saw that this concept must be broadened if his people were to continue to worship Yahweh in a land where the faithless prospered and the faithful foresaw no deliverance. The answer to his problem came as a clear-cut monotheism in which he declared that Yahweh was not weaker than the gods of Babylon—mere idols made by men—but He was the creator of all the earth, the only God, who held Babylon like Judah in His hand. Isaiah could cry "Comfort ye, comfort ye my people," for

> . . . the everlasting God, the Lord, the Creator of the ends of the earth, fainteth not, neither is weary. . . .
> Thus saith the Lord the King of Israel, and his Redeemer the Lord of hosts: I am the first, and I am the last; and besides me there is no god.[20]

But with this assurance that they were in the care of this all-powerful, only God came the further insight that God was calling His stricken people to be "a light to the Gentiles." Isaiah states this majestically:

[20]Isaiah 40:28; 44:6. *Cf.* also 46:9.

Thus saith God the Lord, he that created the heavens, and stretched them out; he that spread forth the earth, and that which cometh out of it; he that giveth breath unto the people upon it, and spirit to them that walk therein:

I the Lord have called thee in righteousness, and will hold thine hand, and will keep thee, and give thee for a covenant of the people, for a light of the Gentiles; to open the blind eyes, to bring out the prisoners from the prison, and them that sit in darkness out of the prison house.[21]

And for this task of opening the eyes of the blind their own afflictions have prepared them! Isaiah proclaims this in four "servant songs" which are too long to be quoted here, but which are among the world's great literature. The first, in 42:1–13, is the servant's commission; 49:1–23 renews Israel's charge to be a light to the Gentiles and promises salvation to Jews and Gentiles alike who wait upon the Lord; 50:4–9 promises Yahweh's help to Israel; and chapter 53 poignantly describes the servant—"despised and rejected of men; a man of sorrows and acquainted with grief" through whose vicarious love and suffering the great task is brought to fruition.

Thus Isaiah set forth his insight that Israel's sufferings were redemptive and not merely punitive—that the nation was suffering for the sins of others as members of a great world family whose darkness they might help to lighten. It was a message so close to the meaning of the cross that it is not surprising that later generations of Christians read in it a portrayal of the death of Jesus for the sins of men.

It was a sublime thought, and later when people could understand it better it was to bear much fruit—though there are many yet, both Jews and Christians, who do not understand what it means by their own suffering to open the eyes of the blind and bring release to the captives. Jesus did: he read Isaiah's words and lived by them. But the people could under-

[21] Isaiah 42:5–7. *Cf.* 61:1–3.

stand Ezekiel's provisions for their own temple ritual a great deal more clearly than Isaiah's call to the service of the Gentiles. So when they got back to Palestine, ritualism again outran moral devotion.

4. The Rise of Judaism

In 539 B.C. Cyrus of Persia captured Babylon, and the next year let the exiles return. Not all went back, for many had become too much at home in Babylon to want to leave it. Those who returned found the land so in ruin that it was almost twenty years before they were able to set themselves to the task of rebuilding the temple. Perhaps they would not have done so then except for the preaching of Haggai and Zechariah, who told them that God was punishing them with poor crops and hard times for neglecting His house while they built comfortable homes for themselves. This message urged the people on to restore the sanctuary, though they could not bring back the glory of Solomon's temple. About seventy-five years later, a Jewish governor, Nehemiah, came up from Babylon and under his vigorous and watchful leadership they rebuilt the wall around the city. Once again they were a nation, impoverished but *Jewish*.

Another wall, much more divisive, was being reared by the priests out of intangible attitudes. To its building Nehemiah the governor and later Ezra the scribe gave a great impulse. Babylonian Judaism was more exclusive than Palestinian because the Jews in exile were a minority group who had had to preserve their existence by their separateness. It was through Ezra that the people were led to accept the Holiness Code of Leviticus 17–26.[22] This reads much like the Deuteronomic Code, but with many more provisions for ceremonial cleansing and the correct observance of ritualistic acts. It is a mixture

[22] The story is given in Nehemiah 8–10.

of great provisions for social justice with a host of petty regulations. For example:

> You shall not eat any flesh with the blood in it. You shall not practice augury or witchcraft. You shall not round off the hair on your temples or mar the edges of your beard. You shall not make any cuttings in your flesh on account of the dead or tattoo any marks upon you: I am the Lord.
>
> Do not profane your daughter by making her a harlot, lest the land fall into harlotry and the land become full of wickedness. You shall keep my sabbaths and reverence my sanctuary: I am the Lord.
>
> Do not turn to mediums or wizards; do not seek them out, to be defiled by them: I am the Lord your God.
>
> You shall rise up before the hoary head, and honor the face of an old man, and you shall fear your God: I am the Lord.
>
> When a stranger sojourns with you in your land, you shall not do him wrong. The stranger who sojourns with you shall be to you as the native among you, and you shall love him as yourself; for you were strangers in the land of Egypt: I am the Lord your God.[23]

It is not to be supposed that this last provision means racial or religious equality. In spite of what prophets or codes might say, Jews were Jews—God's people! And Gentiles were not. They might eat all the blood they liked and do what they pleased with their beards.

This attitude of Jewish separateness and ceremonialism which developed during and after the exile is known as Judaism.[24] Its main characteristics were (1) a type of nationalism which envisaged a coming messianic kingdom as a triumphant Jewish world; and (2) an emphasis on observance

[23]Lev. 19:26–34. R. S. V.

[24]The term Judaism has also a broader meaning, connoting in general any conformity to Jewish rites and customs.

of the minutiae of the temple law which often overshadowed
the requirements of human justice. We find the former reflected
in many of the "imprecatory" Psalms which invoke destruction
upon their (and Yahweh's) enemies (*e.g.*, Ps. 58, 69, 109, 137:
8, 9); the latter was the chief offense of the "scribes and Pharisees, hypocrites" whom Jesus condemned for tithing mint and
anise and cummin and leaving undone the weightier matters
of the law—justice, mercy and faith (Matt. 23:23).

Post-exilic Judaism was accompanied by an increased use
not only of the temple but of the synagogue, where the holy
writings were read and expounded on the sabbath, and a little
later of the synagogue schools where instruction in the Law
was given by the rabbis. The people's thirst for education
seemed to increase in this period after the exile, and there
came into being one of the most persistent traits of the Jewish
people—the quest of knowledge. In the later years when Alexander's conquest and their own "dispersion" had brought them
in close contact with Greek culture they took to secular learning—particularly philosophy—with a good deal of eagerness.
But the Jew was insatiably religious, and religious disputation
remained his chief delight. Because the rabbis studied the
Torah,[25] and commented upon it, and then commented upon
the comments, the Talmud came into being, though it did not
assume its present form until some centuries after the time of
Christ. Because of disagreements about the correct interpretation of the Law, the Pharisees arose who gave much time to
such disputations, and their interpretations weakened the
power of the priests. And because the priests objected to any
infringement of their power, the Sadducees—priestly aristocrats and religious politicians—opposed the Pharisees. It was
in such a setting of controversy that Jesus did his work.

[25]The Pentateuch, or first five books of the Bible, often called the Law.

5. *Post-exilic Literature*

Under Judaistic influence new types of literature emerged: apocalyptic and eschatological, legendary and allegorical, side by side with philosophical wisdom, prophesy and the majestic poetry of the Psalms. Some of this literature is very Jewish; some of it reveals a spirit of internationalism which contradicts the narrowly nationalistic outlook of priestly Judaism and shows that the message of the Isaiah of the exile had at least been dimly understood.

a. *Apocalypse.* Apocalyptic literature expresses through visions and symbols a revelation, or apocalypse, of the future—usually of a great day when present sorrows shall give way to triumphant victory. The best example of it is the book of Revelation in the New Testament, but there is a strongly apocalyptic element in the latter part of Ezekiel, particularly in the great contest with Gog and Magog (Ezek. 39) which symbolizes Yahweh's conquest of His enemies. The last six chapters of Daniel are apocalyptic, as are the apocryphal books of Enoch, Baruch and II Esdras.[26]

With apocalypse is generally found eschatology—the doctrine of the "last things," man's final destiny beyond this world. Although Amos' idea of the coming Day of the Lord (5:16–20) is eschatological, the Hebrews did not have a very strong eschatological sense before the exile. The expectancy of divine judgment within history and the hope of deliverance through the coming of the messiah took its place, and the continuance of the individual beyond death was thought of only vaguely

[26]The Apocrypha is the literature dealing with the events between the Testaments. It consists of the books included in the Greek Septuagint (and taken over from it into the Roman Catholic Bible through St. Jerome's translation), but excluded from the Jewish and Protestant Christian canons.

KANS SCHOOL OF RELIGION
UNIVERSITY OF KANSAS
1300 OREAD AVENUE
LAWRENCE, KANSAS 66044

as existence in Sheol—a shadowy place of departed spirits. When during the exile the Jews came in contact with the Persian dualistic religion of Zoroaster, they took over from it the belief in the devil contending with God for the soul of man and a cataclysmic Last Judgment with heaven and hell as places of moral reward and punishment. This belief, perhaps augmented by a quest for cosmic justice as their fortunes declined, kept getting stronger in the period between the Testaments and in the New Testament it appears full grown.

b. *Short stories.* The post-exilic stories throw light on racial and national attitudes. The book of Esther has for its setting the clash between Jew and Persian, with a Jewish heroine and Jewish victory. The story of Ruth, the Moabite maid, on the other hand, is a protest against the ultra-Jewishness which forbade intermarriage with a foreigner. Likewise, the book of Jonah proclaims a message of the universality of God's love and mercy, even to the distant people of Nineveh—a missionary message which has been tragically obscured by petty bickerings over the literal accuracy of the story.

c. *Philosophy.* The philosophy, or wisdom literature, of the post-exilic period has a richness which merits more extended treatment than can here be given it. Its greatest book is Job, a drama of doubt which tackles squarely the age-old problem, "Why do the righteous suffer?" Rejecting the old Semitic idea that prosperity is the reward of goodness and calamity the punishment for sin, its unknown author portrays Job as the subject of a celestial contest between Jehovah and Satan, who claims that man will not "serve God for naught." Job suffers in quick succession the loss of his possessions, his sons and daughter, his wife's confidence, his health, and emerges, after an intense soul-struggle and much platitudinous cold comfort from his friends, to a firmer faith in God. Its climax comes, not in the restoration of Job's possessions—an addition by a later hand which shows failure to grasp the true import of the story— but when God speaks in majesty from the whirlwind, not answering arguments but declaring unanswerably the divine greatness. Humbled, silenced and illumined, Job replies:

> I know that thou canst do all things,
>   and that no purpose of thine can be thwarted. . . .
> Therefore I have uttered what I did not understand,
>   things too wonderful for me, which I did not know . . .
> I had heard of thee by the hearing of the ear,
>   but now my eye sees thee.[27]

To feel its grandeur one must read for himself this magnificent statement of the power of suffering to cleanse the spirit and uncover hidden depths within the soul.

Ecclesiastes is much less majestic, and about its interpretation there is difference of opinion. It reflects Greek influence and was almost certainly written by a man who had been captured by the Epicurean philosophy of hedonism, and who tried to mix two strains not naturally compatible. As we shall note in Chapter Eight, Epicurus believed that the way to happiness lay, not in riotous living, but in simple and unstrenuous living. In Ecclesiastes, Koheleth (the Preacher) reflects much of this spirit. His attitude is one of sophistication without moral tension. There is a time for everything; life has in it glimpses of eternity (3:1–15). But a living dog is better than a dead lion (9:4). With the advice not to work too hard for riches or wisdom stand observations on the futility of life. "All is vanity and a striving after wind" (1:14). What is crooked cannot be made straight, and he that increases knowledge increases sorrow (1:15–18); prosperity is no mark of God's favor, for the righteous suffer the same fate as the wicked (6:1–2; 8:14, 9:2, 3). This strain has caused Koheleth to be read as a pessimist or "gentle cynic," but probably a better interpretation is that

[27]Job 42:2–5. R. S. V.

he was a rather easy-going optimist who objected to any single-track striving for great objectives.

The book of Proverbs, not as formerly supposed the work of Solomon but of composite authorship, consists of concise practical maxims on all sorts of domestic, legal and social issues. Its fundamental tenets are that religion is the basis of all true wisdom and that piety pays. It is almost wholly moral rather than ceremonial in emphasis, and repeats the teachings of the social prophets in less spirited form, with a message directed mainly to the individual rather than the nation. It abounds in injunctions to pity the poor and underprivileged and to avoid oppression, bribery, perjury and every other form of false dealing. "Give me neither poverty nor riches" (30:8), is the economic ideal. God is honored by human justice:

> A false balance is an abomination to the Lord,
> but a just weight is his delight.[28]

Unchastity, family brawling, slander, hot-headedness, drunkenness and all such personal excesses are condemned and their corresponding virtues lauded. One finds here an excellent compendium of what was considered to be one's duty to one's neighbor at about the third century B.C. Its finest passages are those in praise of wisdom (3:13–18; 4:7–9) and the concluding chapter which describes the ideal woman (31:10–31).

Another book of wisdom literature, unfortunately relegated to the Apocrypha and therefore not much read, is Ecclesiasticus. This is an essay with an optimistic tone, similar to Proverbs in content, which was probably written in Alexandria about 200 B.C. Its author is Jesus ben-Sirach (son of Sirach) and he sets forth much homely wisdom about how to live what would now be called a "well-adjusted" life. It has some choice flashes of humor, as, for example, an observation about gossip:

> Hast thou heard anything? Let it die with thee;

[28]Prov. 11:1. R. S. V.

Be of good courage, it will not burst thee![29]

In the author's scale of values he ranks as highest wisdom, true love between men and women, purity of speech, a discreet wife, righteousness, good counsel and the fear of God. Man is free to choose his destiny (15:14–17), and he who strives for the right will be rewarded of the Lord (4:28).

This idea that piety pays in material terms, so deeply Hebraic that only Koheleth and the author of Job break clearly with it, is reflected in the work of the last great prophet Malachi. He arraigns the priests for neglect of temple ritual, scores the people for robbing Jehovah of His tithes, and promises prosperity to generous givers (3:8–12)—an inducement too often still re-echoed.

d. *Worship and praise.* The book of Psalms has been called "the hymn-book of the second temple." It grew out of the worship experience of the people, and its authorship ranges in date probably from a few psalms written by David in the tenth century up till as late as the Maccabean period (the second century). The content is not primarily moral or philosophical, but deeply devotional. One finds here the outreach of the soul for God.

The psalms deal with a wide range of themes. There are general hymns of praise, and hymns of lamentation, both national and personal. There is a liturgy of entrance into the temple, while others are festal hymns for use at the passover and other special occasions. The hymns of Zion reflect the devotion of the people to Jerusalem and its temple; the prophetic hymns proclaim the triumph of God and His righteousness. The psalms contain some of the most beautiful nature poems ever written. The psalms of history look backward, while others glorify the revelation of God in the Law. There

---

[29]Ecclus. 19:10.

are hymns in praise of wisdom, and prayers for protection in trouble. The psalmist, like Job, wrestles with the problem of cosmic justice; he cries out for cleansing from sin and affirms his devotion and trust. Among the most numerous are the songs of thanksgiving.

The affirmative social morality of the Psalms is perhaps seen at its best in the description of the ideal citizen of Zion:

> O Lord, who shall sojourn in thy tent?
> Who shall dwell on thy holy hill?
>
> He who walks blamelessly, and does what is right,
>   and speaks truth from his heart;
> who does not slander with his tongue,
>   and does no evil to his friend,
>   nor takes up a reproach against his neighbor;
> in whose eyes a reprobate is despised,
>   but who honors those who fear the Lord;
> who swears to his own hurt and does not change;
> who does not put out his money at interest,
>   and does not take a bribe against the innocent.
>
> He who does these things shall never be moved.[30]

The imprecatory psalms, some of them rather bloodthirsty in tone, heap woes upon the people's (and, by identification, Yahweh's) enemies, and call for their destruction. There is a less serious moral problem here than a literal reading suggests, for these expressions simply reflect a union of natural human pugnacity with an intensely Jewish nationalism which could brook no triumph of Yahweh's enemies in the wicked Gentile world. Such passages reflect also the current assumption of a necessary connection between goodness and material welfare, which in the absence of a grasp of the message of Job and of Jesus is not to be wondered at. Here justice is unseasoned with mercy.

[30]Ps. 15. R. S. V.

Yet in spite of the presence of calls to vengeance and stern insistence that "the wicked shall be cut off," the major trend of the psalms is on the side of righteousness. So interwoven is the Hebrew concept of God with goodness that there is not a page in this hymn-book which does not in some way call the worshipers to better living.

6. Contributions to Morality

What, then, have been the major gifts of the Hebrews to the development of morals? Some of these were suggested earlier, and we may now canvass the situation in retrospect.

At the apex stands the idea of a righteous God demanding righteousness in His worshipers. This we have seen developing from polytheism through monolatry to ethical monotheism; from crude anthropomorphism to a God of justice and love. The motive of morality is primarily God-centered, and in the emergence of codes, in the teachings of the great prophets, and in the post-exilic literature concern for human good is made emphatically a divine duty. The Hebrew desire to serve jointly both God and man is nowhere better incarnated than in the greatest of all codes, the Ten Commandments.

The priestly side of Judaism, with its ritual, sometimes worked against the growth of social morality by pre-empting its field; yet in spite of abuses the organizational side of the Jewish faith kept the religion alive, and by providing a body in which a spirit could grow it helped to pass on the moral heritage of the race. The prophets moralized the popular religion; the priests popularized the prophetic religion.

The relation between goodness and material blessings remains to the end primarily a utilitarian conception; yet in the courageous living of heroic figures—pre-eminently Jeremiah, in Habakkuk's great affirmation, in Deutero-Isaiah's conception of the Suffering Servant, and in the drama of Job we find a more spiritual and disinterested conception of the call to moral idealism.

The social solidarity of the people passes, in the course of the Old Testament, from an unreflective collective responsibility typical of primitive peoples to the reflective social sympathy of the eighth-century prophets, the individual responsibility affirmed by Jeremiah and Ezekiel, and the redemptive world vision of Deutero-Isaiah.

The lines of division grew from tribe to nation, and in some luminous passages, though never in the practice of the people, to an international outlook. In Isaiah and Micah is the vision of a world without war; Jeremiah placed the worship of God above national or territorial bounds; the second Isaiah would have the Jews a light to the Gentiles; the authors of the stories of Jonah and Ruth saw beyond walls of Jewish separatism. The Hebrews kept their Jewishness and suffered persecution for it, yet they have contributed richly to the world's internationalism.

Could we follow here the story of the Jews after they lost their national identity, we should find much more to learn from "the international Jew," who through centuries of persecution has kept alive his loyalty to the heritage of the past. In observance of religious duties, in eagerness for knowledge in every field, in filial reverence, in courage under difficulties, the Jewish people have revealed the potency of their devotion to Yahweh and the Law. If in commercial enterprise, shrewdness has sometimes passed over into aggressive acquisitiveness, this fact should not be allowed to overcloud weightier matters. "As a rule, the love of the Lord and of his Law has been spiritual and sublime."[31] For a Christian to dislike a Jew simply because he is a Jew is a very unchristian—and a very unintelligent—attitude.

[31]W. K. Wright: *General Introduction to Ethics*, p. 87.

CHAPTER SEVEN

THE GREEK IDEAL

1. Hebrew versus Greek

THAT there was a difference between the Hebrew and the Greek spirit must have been recognized very early. When the prophet Zechariah says, "I will stir up thy sons, O Zion, against thy sons, O Greece" (Zech. 9:13), he is probably using the terms in a political sense, but figuratively his prophecy has been many times fulfilled in opposition of the religious to the artistic and reflective spirit.

There is a clear difference between the two peoples in the place which religion played in morals. The Greeks were religious but in a much more casual way. They had an anthropomorphic polytheism, attractive in many respects, but with a bevy of gods so much like men that it was impossible to stand very much in awe of them. The greater deities lived on Mount Olympus, but they came down freely to mingle with men—to play with them, trick them, frighten them, fall in love with them, intermarry with them and beget half-divine children. The gods had some moral influence; Zeus and Apollo were guardians of righteousness and Nemesis had the particular function of causing the miscreant's wrong-doing to come back upon his own head. The tragic dramatists, particularly Aeschylus, had a highly spiritualized conception of the gods' moral demands. But there is little in the Greek's attitude toward his gods which is comparable with the Hebrew "fear of the Lord." Yahweh inspired awe, reverence and moral obedience; the Greek gods inspired affection, conflict, and judicious respect.

We have seen how Yahweh, in the minds of the Hebrews, grew in power and in moral qualities as their development progressed. On the contrary, the Greek gods waned. This decline is probably due to the fact that they had too many human weaknesses. Familiarity breeds contempt. They were too tolerant: they let humans do too much as they pleased and made few demands in the way of suffering or sacrifice. Then, too, there were too many of them. They quarreled among themselves and could offer no single center of personal loyalty. The Olympic pantheon gave way in the minds of thinkers to philosophic monotheism, but never to one deity of compelling religious power. So the Greeks, instead of centering their moral life in their gods, offered libations to them and held festivals and revels in their honor.

This difference in the nature of deity had important consequences. To the Hebrews, membership in an elect nation standing in the covenant relation to Yahweh and therefore under obligation to obey and serve Him was a very important matter, but of citizenship in the sense of civic duties owed to the nation as such, they had little consciousness. To the Greeks, political duties were a major concern. While some of the Hebrews wrote beautiful literature and there is interest in music and song—especially in the sacred music of the psalms, the Hebrew people as a whole had no interest in art, and the prohibition against the making of graven images closed to them one of the Greeks' greatest media of expression. To the Greeks, beauty was almost identical with goodness, and to have a beautiful soul in a beautiful body was the Greek ideal.

This contrast is ingrained in the whole moral outlook of the people. To the Greek, character was more important than conduct; the building of a well-rounded personality more imperative than the doing of duties. The Hebrew prophets called sinners to righteousness; the Greek philosophers formed theories about the nature of the good life. The Greeks seem to have been almost wholly lacking in the Hebrew sense of sin, for while they believed, as any people must, that some things are wrong, they believed characteristically in the natural goodness of man, including themselves. Pindar's injunction, "Be what you are," sums up the Greek moral consciousness. Where the Hebrew religion demanded the suppression of many natural impulses as a divine command, the Greek spirit sanctioned their free expression, safeguarded by the principle of moderation. When the Greeks gave themselves to the pursuit of the good life, it was not because they felt the impulsion to love any god with all one's heart and soul and strength; it was because they felt the good life to be the appropriate and beautiful mode of expression.

If we ask why these two peoples, living only about five hundred miles apart, developed so radically different a culture and outlook upon life, we must find the answer in their whole experience. In their historical background there is the same invasion of a new land and transition from nomadic to agricultural life, but the Greeks had no such sense of mighty deliverance from bondage by the strong arm of God. Nor did they have such a sense of supernatural backing for their law; they respected Draco and Solon as great human law-givers but not as the oracles of deity.

The greater flexibility of the Greek spirit is due in part to the fact that their commerce developed early, while among the Jews contact with other peoples except in battle was a late development. Not the least of the factors in causing the difference was the physical environment. The rugged topography of Palestine made for a rugged people with a single-track de-

votion to a great idea, while the inviting bays and verdure-
clad hills of Greece lured its people to new adventures in the
quest for truth and beauty.

Biological differences have been proposed as an explanation
of their cultural differences, the Hebrews being of Semitic and
the Greeks of Indo-European stock. This does not get us far,
for unless inherent racial differences in personality are to be
asserted—a contention now largely challenged by anthropologists—the question still remains unanswered as to why the
Semites should have followed one course and the Indo-Euro-
peans another.

Beyond any differences in geographic or economic factors
or the "challenge and response" of political events, religious
differences are most definitive. The Hebrews had a mighty
faith in Yahweh which colored their whole history; the Greeks
had a faith in the natural goodness of man which generated
ethical and political reflection. And the faith of a people—
explicit or covert—is always the most powerful force in the
shaping of its destiny. But when we have said this, we have
still not said *why* the Hebrews had one kind of faith and the
Greeks another. Perhaps we had better simply say that an over-
arching Providence was marking them out for fulfilling great
but differing functions in service to mankind.

2. The Birth of Democracy

It is fruitless to ask how the Greeks came to be as they were.
The non-theocratic nature of their culture explains much, and
in turn requires to be explained. In modern Greece the same
landscape and coast-line are there, but they fail to produce the
same glory. The inhabitants of all the Greek city-states were
of a common racial stock, yet Sparta is remembered for little
more than physical bravery while Greece and Athens are
nearly synonymous terms. The Greeks borrowed most of their

intellectual materials from Egypt, Mesopotamia and Asia Minor. The route of their borrowings can be traced, but not the fact that they transformed everything they touched and gave it such universal meaning that it still sounds amazingly contemporary. Greek culture, like the great individuals who created it, is best understood as a unique entity with physical and historical connections which are instructive but not explanatory.

The Greeks were not always in Greece. About the middle of the second millennium before Christ they moved down from the north and occupied an area in which a highly developed Aegean civilization, centering in Crete and greatly influenced by Egypt, had been developed. The original population were reduced to serfdom, while the invaders built up an agricultural-urban society on the ruins of the cities they destroyed. Troy, not far from the present location of Constantinople, was the center of a Hittite empire important for its use of iron, and in spite of the uncertainty of the legends about the Trojan War, it is probable that the Greeks conquered it in the twelfth century.

The subsequent period was marked by the development of the Greek city-state. This is the most characteristic feature of Greek political life, source of its greatness as the seedbed of democracy, and of the strife which led to its dissolution. Each city-state was a little nation in its own right, with its own laws, army, courts, ruling officers and gods. Each citizen felt a patriotic duty to his city, but not to Greece as a whole. A common language with variations in dialect and a common possession of the Olympic pantheon provided a type of unity, but the city-states, of which there were hundreds with Athens and Sparta as the greatest, never were welded together to become a single nation.

The first period of Greek civilization, after the nomadic stage had given way to settled agricultural and urban life, is the Age of the Kings (*ca.* 1000–750 B.C.). During this time the city-states were established, to be ruled by a king and usually also by a council of elders who sat in the market-place and settled disputes. This is the period of the Homeric bards, whose singing of hero songs helped to intensify faith in the Greek gods who, they thought, had played so great a part in their past. Because of these ancient singers we have two of the greatest epics in all literature, though the *Iliad* and the *Odyssey* were not written down until about 700 B.C. During this period the Greeks adopted the Phoenician alphabet, with paper also from Egypt by way of the Phoenicians, and the tools were ready for the writing of a great literature.

The next period is the Age of the Nobles (*ca.* 750–650 B.C.). The nobles were for the most part wealthy land-owners, landed aristocrats (called *eupatrids*) who by hereditary economic power forced their way into political power at the expense of both kings and common people. The kings were either forced out or reduced to figurehead status. The peasants lost more and more of their lands, often being reduced by debt to serf-dom, and the Assembly which had formerly included all the free, weapon-bearing men no longer had much function. This evoked the poetry of Hesiod, the first plea for social justice on the continent of Europe, contemporary with that of Amos in Palestine.

This period of the Nobles, though on the whole a grim time for the people, is marked by great colonial expansion west-ward and at home by the beginning of the Olympic games. To this era belongs the establishment of Hellas, or Magna Graecia, throughout the Mediterranean basin except in North Africa where the Phoenicians were in power. As a consequence, a new commercial class was emerging, a "middle class" ready to dispute with the nobles their power.

The next period, the Age of the Tyrants (*ca.* 650–500) marks, strangely enough, a rise in democracy. By this time the nobles were considerably weakened by feuds among themselves; the prosperous *nouveaux riches* capitalists were contesting their power; and the people were ready to side with anybody who would champion their cause. In this juncture strong individuals seized control, kings in all but name, but with power always insecure. To this period belong the first Greek written law code, that of Draco, so severe that "draconic" has passed into our language as a symbol of austerity; the reforms of Solon, which corrected some of the worst abuses from which the people were suffering and gave them a new written constitution by which every free citizen had the right to vote; the rule of Pisistratus, who inaugurated the Panathenean festival at which the *Iliad* and *Odyssey* were to be recited, and caused the poems to be put in order and a standard text made. After the death of Pisistratus, the people refused to accept his sons as rulers, and Clisthenes, a noble friendly to the common people, put an end to the Age of the Tyrants.

Under Clisthenes, important forward steps in democracy were taken. For one thing, he instituted a democratic constitution, greatly restricting the power of the land-owning nobles by realignment of political units. For another, he introduced the practice of ostracism, by which the people could banish an unwelcome ruler when enough of them wrote his name on a piece of broken pottery (ostracon) and placed it in the voting urn. Thus another word comes into our language.

Up until 500 B.C. Greece had made considerable economic and political headway, and had given the world an enduring gift in the Homeric poems. But had it achieved no more, we should not now be stopping to study its legacy of ideals. The real Greece was that which emerged after the repulse of the Persians at Marathon and Salamis in 490 and 480, and lasted until the death of Aristotle in 322. Within these years are compressed all the greatest achievements of Greek culture. Only a fraction of the writing of that period has been preserved, and we do not know whether we have the best part. Yet what we have has influenced the entire thought life of the Western world.

It will not be profitable for our purpose to try to follow the ups and downs of political fortunes during this period. The wars of this era, though certainly important to the people involved in them, have for the most part been forgotten while the achievements of peace are immortal.

Athenian democracy was at its height during the fifth century, with the Age of Pericles (459–431 B.C.) as its most brilliant period. Large numbers of citizens had political experience through serving on the Council of Five Hundred, with many more serving as paid jurors chosen by lot. The chief elective office, that of *strategos* (or military commander), was held by Pericles year after year. He caused the Parthenon to be built, beautifully adorned by Phidias. To this period belong the great tragedians, Aeschylus, Sophocles and Euripides. The greatest physician of the time was Hippocrates, and Herodotus was inaugurating the writing of world history. In the field of education and philosophy, the Sophists, of whom we shall speak presently, were stirring people out of their old ways of thinking.

Socrates lived during the latter two-thirds of the fifth century, dying in 399 B.C. Plato and Aristotle did their work in the fourth. Yet the Athens of all three men is essentially the Athens of the Age of Pericles and the Golden Age of Greece. They and their associates lived in the midst of great works of art, architecture, sculpture, painting, drama, athletic games and religious festivals. While we are not to suppose that all of Athens was literate and cultured, literature and culture with citizen participation in government had reached surprising heights.[1]

[1]During World War II a personal letter from a friend who had been reading Thucydides brought this significant comment, "Thucydides makes

Nearly contemporary with the end of this period of cultural greatness is the end of Greek political independence. With the defeat of Athens by Philip of Macedon at Chaeronea in 338, Greece became part of the Macedonian Empire, and it remained so until the destruction of Corinth in 146 caused it to be absorbed by Rome. Long before its loss of independence, Greece had become weakened by internal strife—strife both *between* and *within* its component city-states.

It is a curious fact that a people who gave the world its first great political theory and who made much of civic loyalty were nevertheless not very successful in governing themselves. A major reason is that whether as states, as classes, or as individuals, they lacked the power of self-subordination essential to cooperative living. They were essentially a secular-minded people; and in spite of exalting patriotism as a virtue, they lacked a compelling spiritual ground of unity. As a consequence, factionalism was always ready to break out, not only between the rival city-states but within the state. We shall note presently that Greece's greatest philosophers were not very enthusiastic about democracy which we laud so highly, the reason being that it so often degenerated into mob rule. But it will not do to condemn the Greeks too severely for their lack of undergirding spiritual unity, for the secularism and dissension which undermined their strength assails us still.

3. The Greek Moral Consciousness

Greek culture is paganism at its best. The term pagan ought not to be used as an epithet of condemnation, for in the clas-

---

somewhat illuminating reading—almost as good as Sorokin or Spengler or Toynbee. I note that while Thucydides knew personally Socrates, Plato, Sophocles, Aeschylus, Euripides, Aristophanes, Phidias, Hippocrates,—he mentions none of them. His preoccupation with the war limits his vision. Something to remember when people demand that everyone be measured by his direct participation in the war effort."

sical sense it means simply non-Christian. Its derivation is suggestive. It comes from *paganus,* meaning a person in the country, presumably regarded by the city dweller as not only different but inferior! So ingrained is the tendency to think of anybody of another faith or culture as inferior that inevitably an unpleasant connotation has crept into the word.

The keynote of Greek thought is order, proportion, harmony. This idea permeates art, philosophy, literature and conduct. The Greeks excelled in architecture, sculpture, the choral dance, tragic drama and lyric verse because they took seriously the motto attributed to Solon, "Nothing in excess."

The principle of order and harmony lies at the root of the four Greek cardinal virtues: wisdom, courage, temperance and justice. The most conspicuous of these in the early literature is courage—particularly courage in battle. This means, however, not mere willingness to meet death without flinching but sacrificial devotion to one's state, and courage is closely intertwined with *aidos,* an inner sense of honor and self-respect. To restrain one's passions in war and live the balanced life in peace one must have temperance, by which the Greek meant very nearly what we mean by self-control. The ideal gentleman (*kalokagathos—*"fair and good") has a sense of proportion which makes him able to be courageous in peace and war without being foolhardy, and able to curb his appetites without crushing them.

Such a state of balanced living in individual and state roots in wisdom and culminates in justice, for only the wise man can *know* what is truly courageous, prudent or just. One must know himself in order to be one's own best self—hence "know thyself" took its place beside "nothing in excess" as succinct statements of the Greek ideal. By wisdom the Greeks meant not only mental self-culture but an expanding knowledge of everything knowable, and they became the first scientists and first philosophers—"knowers" and "lovers of wisdom." If this knowledge did not flower in what is to us a *just* social order, it is at least to their eternal credit that they examined what justice meant and strove for it according to their idea of what the good life demanded.

This ideal found its primary expression in the Greek civic consciousness. Devotion to the state meant not only courage in fighting its wars but a challenge to enhance its outward beauty and internal justice. The ephebic oath, which every Greek youth must take upon assuming the rights and duties of citizenship, is a majestic statement of this civic ideal:

> I will never disgrace these sacred arms, nor desert my companion in the ranks. I will fight for temples and public property, both alone and with many. I will transmit my fatherland, not only not less, but greater and better, than it was transmitted to me. I will obey the magistrates who may at any time be in power. I will observe both the existing laws and those which the people may unanimously hereafter make, and, if any person seek to annul the laws or to set them at naught, I will do my best to prevent him, and will defend them both alone and with many. I will honor the religion of my fathers.[2]

Such, then, were the finer elements in the Greek ideal: love of beauty in all things, courage and self-respect, moderation and balance, devotion to wisdom, a deep sense of civic responsibility. But it has a darker side. It was aristocratic, not only in the original meaning of "the rule of the best," but in the ordinary sense. Birth had so much to do with standing that Socrates had to protest against a confusion of goodness with respectability. Goodness, then as now, was often measured by the marks of outward success. The Greek spirit was as exclusive of non-Greeks, whom they called barbarians, as were the Hebrews of non-Jews, though on the basis of intellectual and cultural superiority rather than divine election. Even Aris-

[2]As quoted by E. P. Cubberley in *The History of Education,* p. 35.

totle said that it was as legitimate to hunt barbarians to get slaves as to hunt animals for food.[3] The pan-Athenaic procession, perpetuated in marble on the frieze of the Parthenon, symbolizes the triumph of Greek wisdom over barbarian darkness.

Greek society was highly stratified. A hierarchical arrangement was taken for granted, with the landed owners at the top, beneath them the tradesmen and artisans, and the slaves at the bottom. Sparta did not admit tradesmen to citizenship but in Athens, though they were held in contempt, they had the right to vote. Athens had, as we have here, a political democracy and an economic oligarchy.

Slavery was everywhere accepted, and slaves had no rights as persons, though the *mores* enjoined kindness of treatment, as one should be kind to an animal. Free-born Greeks scorned manual labor as the natural work of slaves, fearing also that it would mar the much-prized beauty of body. On the foundation of slave labor a leisure class developed whose justification must be found, if at all, in what its great figures gave to the world rather than in any concept of the intrinsic worth of persons.

The factionalism and parochialism of outlook which were the curse of Greece and finally its undoing were in part due to geographical division, but more to this internal stratification. On the one hand, religious reverence was not strong enough to be an effective instrument of social unity and cooperation. On the other, there was too much acceptance of the *status quo* with comfortable rationalizations supplied by the leisured intelligentsia—a situation which the victims of injustice sporadically burst through to cause slave revolts and other economic disturbances. Reason without religious motivation to give it dynamic is more often a socially conservative than a revolutionary force, challenging injustice in theory but accepting it in practice.

[3]*Politics,* i, 7, 8; vii, 14.

In the Greek outlook the family virtues had no exalted place. In militaristic Sparta the family almost disappeared, and Plato's ideal state would destroy family life to rear strong citizens. Exposure of infants was an accepted practice, affording the basis for the story of King Oedipus immortalized by Sophocles. The position of woman was ordinarily low. Monogamy was the domestic ideal but chastity in men was not highly esteemed —and was more esteemed than practiced. There seems to have been a more romantic conception of marriage in the Homeric period than in Greece at its height. Prostitution was then common, the *hetairai* being intellectual companions as well as sexual mates, and homosexuality was rampant.

The Greek spirit presents all the paradoxes inherent in human nature. Its interpreters reached magnificent heights from which they could proclaim a message of permanent value to the centuries ahead. The rank and file, like the common people of all ages, lived mainly by impulse and practical exigency and not by reflection. But since it is the Greece of the writings that has come down to us as *our* Greece, it is this which we must now examine further.

4. Early Greek Morality

a. *The Homeric age.* Nowhere is this clash of good and evil, of beauty and ugliness, reflected more clearly than in the *Iliad* and *Odyssey.* These date from about the ninth century B.C. and reflect the moral consciousness of that day, though the matter of Homeric authorship is an unsettled literary matter that need not concern us here. As in the patriarchal stories of the Old Testament, legend takes on life and pictures tell more than literal history in the early narratives of the siege of Troy and Odysseus' subsequent wanderings.

> The heroic age is filled with battle, murder and sudden death, but intermingled with acts of bravery, chivalry and hospitality which do much to offset the dark side of the

picture. The heroes of the Trojan War . . . followed no
Christian code of an advanced age of chivalry, yet they
had their own ten commandments of which this list has
been given: Bravery, wisdom, self-control, justice, vengeance belonging to the wronged, family affection, patriotism, generosity, magnanimity, and truth.[4]

So writes Professor Woodbridge Riley of the morals of the
Homeric era, and with some reservations imposed by the
cruder side of the story this list of virtues may be accepted.
The heroes, both Greek and Trojan, displayed much physical
courage, and if not wisdom, at least shrewdness. Self-control
appears in endurance of hardship rather than in calmness
under insult, and justice is mainly limited to friends and kin.
The Trojan War itself is a colossal example of an enterprise
undertaken to avenge a wrong, and in it the Trojans fought
valiantly to defend their wives and children. Patriotism on
both sides is clear-cut, and at least in the form of hospitality,
generosity is exemplified. But while magnanimity and truth-
fulness are lauded, examples of anger, craftiness and deceit
appear on almost every page. Odysseus' chief epithet, "the
crafty-minded," fits him admirably, for the whole tale of his
wanderings is built upon his cleverness in deception. The
"great-souled" Achilles is great in some ways and very petty
in others. He could boast foolishly, sulk in his tent like a
spoiled child, and treat Hector's body with ugly cruelty; yet
it is he whom we find saying, "Hateful to me even as the gates
of Hades is he that hideth one thing in his heart and uttereth
another."

The gods of this early age were no better than its heroes;
indeed, in some respects inferior, for there was less need to
place halos upon them to exalt the glory of the Greek name.
They were skilled in all the arts of deception. Athena could
make herself invisible and stab Ares in the abdomen with the

[4]*Men and Morals,* p. 34.

same *sang froid* with which Jael drove a tentpin into Sisera's temple. Zeus and Poseidon got angry and clashed as vigorously as did their favorites. The favor of the gods could be bought by sacrifices, and religion was largely a matter of clever bargaining, with punishment falling swiftly on him who failed to carry out his part of it. Yet back of these tales of faction and trickery lies the conviction, at least dimly sensed, that there is a destiny, or *moira*—a fate more powerful even than Zeus, which metes out to every man his due.

b. *Post-Homeric developments.* The gods of the fifth century are both better and worse than those of the tenth. Aphrodite, for example, became a more sensual deity and the Dionysian revels linked worship with indulgence of the senses in a manner not calculated to inspire worshipers either to religious reverence or to higher moral living. Yet in the work of the greater poets and philosophers the gods are increasingly moralized. Pindar portrays them on a higher plane than does Homer. Plato reproves Hesiod for telling lies about Uranus, and in his ideal educational system he would have tales of gods and heroes read by the young only in editions which leave out their immoralities.[5] His major concept was not the old polytheism at all, but an ethical monotheism based on philosophy rather than religious tradition, as was true also of Socrates and Aristotle.

The importance of the gods waned more through disregard than outright rejection. Their literary and philosophical refinement and "de-anthropomorphizing" had an influence not unlike the use of our modern historical approach to the Bible; for in the attempt to see things in their true perspective, some people were led to a more ethical and more intellectual concept of deity, while others, dissatisfied with tradition but unable to put anything in its place, fell into religious indifference

[5]*Republic,* iii, 386–392.

or atheism. Likewise, a growing materialism—both a demand for material comfort and the philosophic materialism of Democritus—tended to dethrone deity. By the fifth century Aristophanes could say, "Whirl is king, having driven out Zeus."

But the gods did not die easily, and an evidence of their vitality is found in the increasing development of the doctrine of Nemesis. This is an enlargement upon the more primitive idea of *Moira*, or fate, made explicit and given moral significance. It first comes to clear expression in Herodotus' dramatic story of the defeat of the Persians, with an interpretation which expresses not merely national exultation over victory but a conviction that ignominious defeat is the natural consequence of arrogance and pride. This idea gripped the Greeks so strongly that Phidias was asked by the Athenians to carve a statue of Nemesis as a war memorial, and it lingered with them as a dominant moral note. Its greatest portrayal is in the tragedies of Aeschylus. In *Prometheus Bound* and *Agamemnon* the dramatist pictures with consummate skill the inevitable doom which the stern goddess metes out to him who is guilty of presumption or crime. With this doctrine of retribution is woven the sublimer concept that the gods *in divine mercy* send suffering for the moral welfare of the wrong-doer. This is akin to the Hebrew concept of cosmic justice, but falls short of the insights of a Job who can suffer in innocency and find his soul cleansed with refining fire.

5. *The Sophists*

The movement which most directly paved the way for the great ethical theorists was the work of the Sophists. They, like Herodotus, Phidias and Aeschylus were products of the fifth century—the Golden Age which began with the defeat of the Persians at Plataea in 479 and lasted in its high points till the death of Pericles in 431, though its influence persisted far be-

yond that time and has not yet ceased. It was a time when
the minds of the Athenians turned from conflict to rejoicing,
from the strain of war to the adornment of their city by the
arts of peace. It was the time of the building of the Parthenon
and the age of the great dramatists, Aeschylus, Sophocles and
Euripides. It was also a time of great upheaval and reorgan-
ization in which political changes were taking place, old
standards of morals were breaking down, and the gods were
under fire. Athens was the political and intellectual center of
Greek life, and no other city has ever produced in so short
a time so many great names and so many imperishable works
of art and literature.

In this time of intellectual ferment, it was natural that the
minds of many people should have been awakened to want
more knowledge, practical as well as cultural, and it was to
supply this need that the Sophists came into prominence. They
were professional teachers who, contrary to current custom,
charged fees for their instruction, and thus called down on
their heads the disgust of the philosophers. In general, there
was no love lost between the "lovers of wisdom" and these
professional "wisemen." To Socrates, Plato and Aristotle, intellectual pursuits called for great moral earnestness, and they
did not approve of these rhetoricians and teachers of argu-
mentation who boasted that they could "make the worse cause
seem the better." In a day when vote-getting by oratory was
very important, they were in much demand as instructors in
public speaking, and there is no doubt that like many moderns
skilled in the arts of "sophistry" they sometimes misused this
power. However, among them were good teachers and serious-
minded scholars and they opened up some very important developments in thought.

Apart from these professional differences, there were two
important aspects in which the Sophists broke radically with
current philosophy. These were their insistence that learning

must be practical, and that belief must be individual. In these they were the forerunners of the pragmatists and relativists of the present day, and in general of those who believe that human experience is the only test of truth, that truth is a varying instrument of adjustment to life rather than something absolute in itself, and that morals are matters of individual opinion, or, at most, of social convention.

The philosophers before the time of the Sophists had been mainly concerned with metaphysical speculations about the ultimate nature of the universe. Thales of Miletus, the first systematic philosopher, had said that the whole could be conceived in terms of water; Anaximander after him had substituted *to apeiron,* the boundless; Anaximemes had made air the key to reality. Heraclitus thought the world was in eternal flux—all Becoming; the Eleatics had made it all eternal Being. Democritus said that the whole world was simply physical matter—not ordinary stuff that one could see, but uncuttable particles, *atoms.* All this to the Sophists was nonsense. Aristophanes has immortalized the practical man's disgust with such speculations by representing Socrates as sitting in a basket in the clouds mooning about such unearthly things, though in reality Socrates was not very much interested in this aspect of philosophy either.

It was natural, therefore, that the Sophists should try to give people the tools for material success and personal well-being. The greatest of the Sophists was Protagoras, who declared boldly that "man is the measure of all things." This was one of the most important statements ever made, for in it roots epistemological idealism—the doctrine that since we have only our own experience through which to know, the knowing process puts its stamp upon the nature of the objects we know and in a sense determines their reality. In it roots also—and this is more pertinent to our study—the pragmatic doctrine that the truth of any idea, or the goodness of any act, hinges on its value to the individual who thinks the idea or does the act. Modern pragmatism is much more inclined to introduce a criterion of *social* value than was Protagoras, but agrees with him in rejecting all absolutes and universals. It is a moot question as to just how far Protagoras meant to carry his individualism, but people understand him, at least, to mean by "man is the measure of all things" that "each man is the measure of things for himself." This is so close to skepticism—since it denies the existence of any common measure—that in the Sophist Gorgias it passed over into the denial of the possibility of any knowledge. Its more important effect from a moral standpoint was the challenging of all moral standards as being merely artificial conventions, with the consequence that the later Sophists felt justified in casting off ordinary moral restraints and living about as they pleased. If one's own sensations are the only key to knowledge so are one's senses the key to conduct, and morality becomes an egoistic, often a sensual, pleasure-seeking. Such slipperiness aroused Socrates' ire and he set himself to the reinstatement of the universals the Sophists were undermining.

The Sophist attitude is one of *subjectivism* (variation according to individual opinion) or at best of *relativism* (variation according to changing social conventions—a social subjectivism). There is both truth and error in this position. An individual's standard of judgment must always be *his* standard, and the Sophists did well to call attention to the important truth that any value judgment must be *personal*. But to say that there is no objective foundation is to defeat the quest for truth or goodness before it starts. Unless there is some real principle to be discovered, even our relative and imperfect attempts to find it become mere sprawls on shifting sands.

The practical effect of the Sophist doctrine has modern parallels. The moral laxity which brought the later Sophists into disrepute came from a popularization of the slippery individualism of their theory, and similarly in our day the tendency to reject all absolutes in religion and morals and to "live one's own life" has made for self-indulgence more often than for creative self-expression. Likewise the demand that learning be "practical," valuable as a protest against over-abstraction, becomes, when interpreted too narrowly, a negation of the intellectual life and a mere excuse for mental laziness.

The Sophists not only introduced important concepts into philosophy but they actually spread a good deal of learning, stimulated people to individual thinking, challenged entrenched conservatism. Perhaps their chief constructive function was to be the "gad-fly" which Socrates delighted to call himself.

6. Socrates

The story of Socrates—homely stone-cutter, magnificent idler, divine rebel and martyr—is the most familiar in all philosophy. Like Jesus, with whom he is often compared, he left no writings of his own, and we know him only through the words of those who knew and loved him. Xenophon in his *Memorabilia* gives us the moral philosopher, but as chief character in the dialogues of his pupil Plato, Socrates becomes a very human and lovable person. Though one can never be sure just how much is Plato and how much is Socrates, one can scarcely read the story of his trial and death in the *Apology, Crito,* and *Phaedo* without a feeling of having been face to face with one whom Plato called "the wisest, the most just and the best of men."

In proportion to its influence the life of Socrates was uneventful. We know that he was of the common people, the son of a midwife; that he was a sculptor by trade—apparently not very successful or much interested in his profession; that he served faithfully as a soldier in campaigns at Potidaea, Delium, and Amphipolis; that in his youth he visited the

Delphic oracle, where on being told by the priestess that he was the wisest man in the world, he interpreted this to mean wisdom through awareness of his own ignorance; that he spent many hours and days in conversation upon the streets with whoever would talk with him; that he had three sons and a shrewish wife, Xanthippe, who—legend says—did not like so much idling in the bread-winner. Plato makes him a philosopher even in battle, and has him say that on one occasion he stood motionless in thought for twenty-four hours on the field of Potidaea.[6]

Of his work as sculptor little is known and if, as some archaeologists think, the Chiaramonti Graces in Rome are a copy of his work, it is easy to see why he preferred philosophy.[7] His interest was not in art in the usual sense, but in straight thinking and the art of living. He possessed to a high degree the Greek virtues of wisdom, courage, temperance and justice. Though not an ascetic, his tastes were simple and he had few material wants. There is an immortal plea for inner riches in his prayer to Pan:

> Beloved Pan, and all ye other gods who haunt this place, give me beauty in the inward soul; and may the outward and the inward man be at one. May I reckon the wise to be the wealthy; and may I have such a quantity of gold as a temperate man and he only can bear and carry. Anything more? The prayer, I think, is enough for me.[8]

Conversation was his life. The street-corner interviews in which he spent his days were regarded by him always as laid upon him by an inner divine voice, a *daimon* that would not let him rest till he did his utmost to arouse his fellow Athenians to truer thinking. The Platonic dialogues give many examples of the tact and geniality with which he tangled up his oppo-

[6]*Symposium,* 220.
[7]J. M. Warbeke: *The Searching Mind of Greece,* p. 133.
[8]*Phaedrus,* 279.

nents—the famous "Socratic irony" by which, assuming himself to be ignorant, he asked questions which soon revealed
to the other that it was he who was really ignorant. His purpose, however, was not the discomfiture of his opponent but
a mutual quest for the universal truth which Socrates thought
lay buried in men's minds under the surface use of familiar
words. He constantly challenged people to define their terms,
not merely as a rhetorical device, but as a philosophic method
of getting at that basic truth which the Sophists had said did
not exist. Thus the "Socratic method" of teaching came into
being.

The events of which we have fullest knowledge are his
trial and death. Accused of corrupting the youth and intro-
ducing strange divinities—gods which were not the gods of the
city—he was brought to trial and found guilty. Asked to name
his penalty, he boldly suggested that he be given a pension
at the Prytaneum for his services to the state! This so offended
the jurors that he was promptly condemned to death. Socrates
remained undisturbed, discoursing to the jurors of the interesting possibility of finding in the after-life either sleep, or a
journey to a realm where he would find communion with great
spirits. His word about death has become a classic:

> Wherefore be of good cheer about death, and know
> of a certainty that no evil can befall a good man, either
> in life or after death.[9]

Even after the imposition of the sentence he might have
escaped, had he been willing to accept the aid of his friend
Crito who wanted to help him leave the city. But Socrates
replied that having obeyed the laws of Athens all his days,
there was no reason to disobey them in his old age. In the
interval before the execution of the penalty he discoursed
calmly with his friends. When the fatal day came he drank the

[9]*Apology*, 41.

hemlock with full composure, and died as serenely as he had lived. Plato describes his death at the end of the *Phaedo,* and no death-story in literature, save that of the crucifixion in the Gospels, gives a picture more sublime.

The charges brought against Socrates were obviously untrue. The real reason for the Athenians' dislike for him was not moral corruption or false religion but the fact that he was a disturber of the *status quo*—a prophet, like Jeremiah, who spoke ahead of his times. Added to the dissatisfaction, repeated in every age, which arises at the hearing of a new prophetic voice, were personal pique and a desire for revenge on the part of those whom he had shown to be—not only bad, but worse yet, ignorant! And back of all this was a political reason, for Socrates favored an aristocracy of capable rulers rather than the democracy then in power—a "rule by the people" which meant putting people into office by the casting of lots. So the Athenians ended his life, but they could not end his influence.

It is in the life and personality of Socrates that his moral teaching centers. His doctrine cannot be disentangled from that of Plato, but his martyrdom can. The element which emerges most clearly from the story is an heroic devotion to truth and to the state—a devotion generated by a sense of religious mission. This is epitomized when he says that if he were to be promised release on condition of inquiring and speculating no more, he would reply:

> Men of Athens, I honor and love you; but I shall obey God rather than you, and while I have life and strength I shall never cease from the practice and teaching of philosophy.[10]

In Socrates' ethical teaching, the primary principle is that virtue is achieved through knowledge. All evil is the result of

[10]*Apology,* 29.

ignorance; only the person who does not know the right fails to do it. Knowledge meant to Socrates much more than book-learning, and he was careful to emphasize the principle, characteristic of Greek thought, that *self*-knowledge is the most important kind. "Know thyself" stands beside "Knowledge is virtue" as typical Socratic doctrine. This led him to say that if one really knows and seeks his own best interest, he will serve others. And if one steadfastly lives the good life, it will lead to happiness, which is man's highest good. Note, however, that Socrates was not an egoist in any exclusive sense, for while he put the self in the center of the moral life he never glorified self-indulgence. Nor was he a hedonist in the usual meaning of the term, for he did not make happiness a goal at the expense of virtue but rather a product of "beauty in the inward soul." These distinctions will assume importance when we study the schools which emerged from his teaching.

These are important precepts, and they laid the foundation for a type of ethics, still widely held, which puts its chief trust in reason and knowledge. It is at this point that the Greek diverges most sharply from the Christian moral outlook. As much as Socrates and Jesus were alike in the manner of their dying, there is a great difference between them. Socrates in his teaching oversimplified the moral life, making it rest on wisdom, while Jesus with more discernment saw that nothing but love born of faith in God is adequate for life's strains.

Only a religiously grounded love (which Socrates exemplified more than he taught) can keep self-interest from becoming selfishness, or self-knowledge from running into self-righteousness. It is both false and dangerous to assume that, given sufficient knowledge, even including self-knowledge, right living will ensue. Much bad action comes from ignorance. An awareness of this fact is basic to moral education and the intelligent control of social living, and Socrates is to be thanked for showing the imperative necessity of knowledge to the good life. But it is to trust too far the goodness of human nature to assume that knowledge of what is right will inevitably make one *do* the right. Experience rises up to refute Socrates in this, and to say in the words of Paul, "The evil that I would not, that I do."

7. *Cyrenaics and Cynics*

It is not unusual in history for a great figure to give rise to opposing streams of thought; for a person really great is apt to have more than one side to his nature, and these strains serve as authority by which admiring followers justify their own preferences. This happened in the case of Jesus, and movements as different as militarism and pacifism, fundamentalism and religious humanism, Roman Catholicism and Christian Science still look to Jesus as leader and source. It happened with Socrates, and from his influence the Cyrenaics developed a pleasure-seeking and the Cynics a pleasure-denying philosophy.

Aristippus of Cyrene was the first clear-cut philosophical hedonist. Cyrene on the coast of Africa was a sunny spot appropriate to be the seat of a school of pleasure-loving folk, and here Aristippus drew about him a group who believed with him that ἡδονή—pleasure—is the true goal of life. Aristippus was a Sophist who greatly admired Socrates, and what he saw in him was not the martyr dying for noble ideals but the genial figure that liked to have a good time with his friends, that enjoyed the sight of dancing girls and drank wine though not to drunkenness, that made self-interest the key to the good life and happiness its product. Probably Aristippus got as much of his pleasure philosophy from the Sophists as from Socrates, but it seemed to him that the real spirit of Socrates spoke for the appropriation of the sweets of life.

Aristippus himself did not advocate a crass and unrestrained indulgence of the appetites. He placed the pleasures of body above those of mind because they are more intense, and to him as to the other Sophists sensation was a more dependable guide than reason. Yet one must be restrained by principles of moderation and a consideration for the long run, lest pleasure become master instead of servant. He was fond of saying, "I possess; I am not possessed."

But the later Cyrenaics did not live on so high a plane as Aristippus. When pleasure is put in the foreground it tends to become master, even in spite of valiant assertions that one expects only in moderation to eat, drink, or be merry. The later Cyrenaics insisted on having the pleasures of the passing moment while they could. Moral distinctions based on restraints of conscience were cancelled. Religion sank out of sight and many of the Cyrenaics were atheists. And then, paradoxically but naturally, hedonism passed over in pessimism, and we have in the words of Hegesias, the "death-persuader," the advocacy of suicide as the best means of escape from life's pain. When satiation within and thwarting without bars the door in the quest for thrills, death becomes sweeter than life.

Cyrenaic hedonism ran its course and died of its own poison, but we shall find hedonism appearing again on a higher level in Epicurus, and repeatedly through the history of morals. It cannot be wholly killed, for it is founded on an element of truth—that the good life is something to be *enjoyed*. But its fatal error lies in the "hedonistic paradox." Experience taught, and still teaches, that the way to get pleasure is not to pursue it, but to set one's life toward worthy ideals of character and service with the result that, quite unsought, happiness comes. The shallowness of much present-day living and the tendency to lose moral distinctions and religious values in the quest for a good time is a re-enactment of the Cyrenaic philosophy— satiation and suicide not omitted.

The Cynic philosophy, headed by Antisthenes who taught in the gymnasium of Cynosarges, was of a quite different type.

Antisthenes saw in Socrates the wise man who, guided by reason, lived the simple life and refused to be perturbed by the quest for material goods or the external frills of society. The Socrates who wore one garment summer and winter, who walked barefoot in the snow and exclaimed at the fair, "How many things there are I do not need!"—this Socrates set the Cynic standard. The term in the beginning did not have the connotation of bitterness which we now read into it, but it was from the start an ascetic ideal. The Cynics scorned riches, luxury, honors, learning, family life, and even the ordinary social conventions, feeling that for the health of the soul they must hold themselves aloof from such worldly entanglements. Twenty-one centuries before Rousseau, they advocated a "back to nature" movement to try to get clear of what seemed to them the corrupting artificialities of civilization.

The most famous Cynic was not Antisthenes but Diogenes, of the familiar story of the lantern and tub. Another tradition says that when Alexander asked Diogenes if he might do him any kindness, Diogenes replied, "Only to get out of my light." Still another story represents Diogenes as coming uninvited to Plato's party to trample upon the philosopher's pride, whereupon Plato merely remarked, "With greater pride, Diogenes," and let him stay. The Cynics wearing rags prided themselves on having no arrogance—a fact which prompted Socrates to say to Antisthenes, "I see your pride through the holes in your cloak." These stories are true to the spirit if not the letter of the Cynic philosophy.

But the Cynics, like the Cyrenaics, having caught a good idea warped it sadly. The legitimate supremacy of spirit over outward circumstance was distorted into a pharisaic pride at their own superiority and an anti-social renunciation of much that enriches life. They were of the type of people—fortunately growing fewer in a freer age—who gloat over their martyrdoms and wish to impose on others their own ultra-puritanical standards. There is something attractive about the moral sternness of the Cynics, as of our Puritan fathers and the medieval saints, but they were not the kind of folk whom it would have been easy to live with. They did not, like the later Cyrenaics, advocate suicide, but they committed aesthetic, intellectual, social and economic suicide.[11] Perhaps the severest condemnation (or the deepest ground for pity?) lies in the fact that their spiritual pride passed over into the bitterness of "cynicism," and they gave to our language one of its most unpleasant terms.

The Greek ideal is a tapestry woven of many threads. In it is to be read the quest for power and knowledge, for civic service and philosophic inquiry, for self-indulgence and self-abnegation. Through it all runs a pattern of moral goodness conceived as an harmoniously ordered life. This pattern, as yet not clearly marked, was to become explicit in the work of the great system-builders.

[11]J. M. Warbeke, *The Searching Mind of Greece,* p. 152.

CHAPTER EIGHT

SYSTEM BUILDERS
OF GREECE AND ROME

THE Cyrenaics and Cynics, with their extremes of pleasure-seeking and ascetism, were off the main stream of Greek moderation. In the great ethical systems there is a return to it, and an elaboration of it which incarnates its genius. Nothing save the Christian gospel, which borrowed much from Greek as well as Hebrew thought, has been so influential in subsequent development as these. Four of what Professor William DeWitt Hyde in a widely read book of a generation ago called "the five great philosophies of life"[1] were born on Greek soil, though Stoicism reached its greatest development in Rome. We must now see what is meant by Platonic harmony of soul, the Aristotelian sense of proportion, the Epicurean pursuit of pleasure, Stoic self-control.

1. Plato (427-347 B.C.)

Considering how important a person Plato was, we know comparatively little that is authentic about his life. Diogenes

[1]Also published under the title, *From Epicurus to Christ.*

Laertius has preserved some interesting tales about him as about the other ancient philosophers,[2] and we have thirteen letters purporting to have been written by Plato, but possibly spurious. His dialogues are singularly unbiographical, telling more of Socrates than himself.

According to the generally accepted tradition, Plato was born of a wealthy and aristocratic family. He was named Aristocles, but his gymnasium teacher, noting his broad shoulders, gave him the nickname he has borne ever since.[3] He was a descendant of Codrus, the last king of Athens and of Solon, the law-giver, and his family connections would have given him easy access to a political career. This was his intention until he met Socrates—but he had the spirit of poetry and philosophy in him and these led him away from temporal politics to eternal ideas. For eight years he was associated with Socrates until the death of his teacher in 399. Several years of travel culminated in an attempt at the age of forty to establish an ideal state under Dionysius of Syracuse. The attempt ended in his being thrown into prison and into slavery, but he was ransomed by an altruistic Cyrenaic, Annicerus. He returned to Athens to set up a school in his own estate which he called the Academy,[4] thus giving our language a familiar term. There he taught for forty years in a democratic fellowship in which Aristotle was his most famous pupil. Legend says that he died serenely at the age of eighty at a wedding-feast.[5]

During his long life he wrote at least twenty-four *Dialogues* —prose poems and masterpieces of classical literature which have been the fountain-head of idealistic philosophy ever since

[2]His *Lives of the Philosophers,* written about 300 B.C. is full of interesting mythology.

[3]Plato means "broad." It is a bit grotesque to think of so distinguished a philosopher's being nicknamed Fatty or Big Boy!

[4]He does not mention the Academy in the Dialogues, but his followers maintained it until it was closed by Justinian as a pagan school in 529 A.D.

[5]This chronology is untrustworthy, for the Greeks had a way of assuming that a man reached his acme at forty and died at eighty.

—and possibly others which have not survived. For the most part, his life was given uneventfully to discussion and thought, and his writings, carefully preserved by his school for their intrinsic beauty and depth of insight, entitle him to rank as probably the greatest philosopher of all time.

There is little doubt that Plato wrote these dialogues, but there is a great deal of question as to how to interpret them. He had a marvelously catholic mind which embraced so much of human thought and experience that everyone tends to find in Plato what he himself believes. Furthermore, like Shakespeare, his interests were so timeless that one seems to hear him speaking of the events of yesterday and today. These characteristics give him his greatness but make it difficult not to use his words, like those of the Bible, as proof-texts to prove a theory.

Plato was not the logician Aristotle was. His ideas come pouring out torrentially and sometimes inconsistently in the dialogues. These were, of course, never intended to be acted. Yet they form dramatic commentaries upon life, which have artistic balance rather than logical coherence. One feels that Plato is speaking through Socrates, but it is unsafe to assume that everything that Plato puts in the mouth of Socrates is his own thought. Many of his most important ideas are couched in myth, as great religious truth is apt to be. After one reads for a time, one begins to grasp intuitively Plato's major emphasis rather than find it in specific sentences.

This is the clue to the understanding of his ethics. His thought all hangs together with such unity that we cannot examine his ethics without looking also at his metaphysics, his theory of knowledge, his psychology, and his political theory. But it is the unity of the artist, the religious mystic, and the prophet rather than the logician. Plato was above all a philosopher of *theoria* which means not abstract theory but, on the contrary, *seeing, insight, vision*.

If one bears these facts in mind he finds written throughout the dialogues certain fundamental principles. Among them are that the basis of all existence is a moral order; that man's chief task is to lead the good, which is also the beautiful, life; that this is to be measured by health and harmony of soul; that the state exists for moral ends; that no morality, whether individual or social, can be attained apart from reason. We must now survey rapidly how these concepts take shape in the major Platonic doctrines.

a. *The doctrine of ideas.* The concept most often associated with Plato's name, and most influential in subsequent thought, is his theory of ideas. Plato himself says very little about it, treating it explicitly as a theory only at the beginning of the *Parmenides* where he seems to refute it. Our chief knowledge of it is from Aristotle's *Metaphysics.*[6] Yet Plato suggests it in a number of his myths, particularly those of the *Phaedrus, Phaedo* and *Meno,*[7] and what he apparently meant by it is implicit throughout the dialogues.

Its primary element is the reality of the ideal. Plato believed that beyond and above the limitations of the sense world and of our fragmentary human knowledge lies the perfect and eternal. Plato, like Socrates, protested against the relativism of the Sophists, but instead of thinking that the reality of universal concepts lay in the common elements of human thinking to be elicited by definition, he gave them an independent reality of their own. That is, justice is not something that men devise or agree to; it is something eternally real in the very structure of the universe, a reality that men must *discover* rather than create. So, too, with beauty; men may rise through human experience to a discernment of it if one has the mystic's

[6]Book Alpha, Chaps. 6 and 9.
[7]The *Phaedrus* portrays the flight of the soul to the dome of heaven, where it looks upon true being. The souls that see most come to birth as philosophers and artists. The *Phaedo* and *Meno* suggest that knowledge is recollection from a prior state of existence.

vision, but beauty itself is uncreated and eternal—*absolute.*
"[This beauty is] not fair or foul, according to the point of
view, or time, or place, but beauty absolute, apart; simple and
everlasting, without increase, decrease or any change, im-
parted to the ever-growing changeful beauties of all other
things."[8]

In the theory as it was developed and defended through the
Middle Ages, every *universal,* that is, every characteristic like
redness or roundness which is common to many things, has its
perfect and eternal archetype. Plato even suggests (though he
does not develop the idea) that concrete objects like beds and
tables have their ideal patterns according to which the sense
objects we perceive are formed.[9] Matter, a principle of limita-
tion, is a barrier to perfect embodiment of the eternal form.
As the concept of a mathematical relation like a perfect circle
exists eternally while every circle one may draw is imperfect
and transitory, so for everything else there is an eternal, un-
changing pattern which man's experience imperfectly repro-
duces. To explain man's power to grasp by thought in some
measure these eternal ideas, Plato has the doctrine of recollection, the idea that at birth the soul comes from the realm
of ideas and therefore partakes of their nature.[10]

It is not certain that Plato ever intended the eternal ideas
to be thought of as existing in a separate realm. In his own
thought there is less disjunction between the world of sense
and the world of ideas than later Platonists put into it. Yet it
is clear throughout that for Plato, the truly real is neither the
material world nor a world of human dreams. It is an eternal
and ideal goodness, truth and beauty in which man, as he
lives at his best, may participate, but which he may never fully
fathom or encompass.

[8]*Symposium,* 211. I use here the translation found in *Lyra Mystica,*
p. 7, edited by C. C. Albertson.
[9]*Republic* X, 596–598.
[10]*Cf.* Wordsworth's *Ode on the Intimations of Immortality.*

b. *The idea of the good.* The highest of all the ideas, standing at the apex and subsuming under it all others, is the idea of the Good. This Plato often (though not always) identifies with God. Thus his whole system roots in an ethical idealism which is a form of religious monotheism.[11] In his famous allegory of the cave he shows how men tend to mistake shadows for reality and shrink from the light until, enlightened by the Good, which he compares to the sun, they see things as they really are. Then, nothing but the truth can satisfy, and they must return to enlighten those in darkness. The parable concludes:

> My opinion is that in the world of knowledge the idea of good appears last of all, and is seen only with an effort; and when seen it is inferred to be the universal author of all things beautiful and right . . . the immediate source of reason and truth in the world of thought: and this is the power upon which he must have his eye fixed who would act rationally either in public or private life.[12]

To Plato, the true, the good and the beautiful were not separate values, but harmonious elements in one world of value, *i.e.,* in the Good. Here appears his most distinctive ethical contribution, the *harmony theory of value,* which links his metaphysics with his ethics. Harmony is a principle not merely of the transmundane world of ideas; it is the key to the good life in man. It was Plato's Socrates who prayed, "Give me beauty in the inward soul."

c. *Eros.* Plato's theory of the good life for the individual, rooted in this obligation to inner harmony of soul and harmony with the eternal goodness of the universe, is linked with his

[11]In the *Timaeus,* God is the Demiourgos who fashions the imperfect and chaotic world of matter into order according to principles of goodness. When Plato refers to God or the gods, he usually speaks as if deity were personal.

[12]*Republic,* VII, 517.

doctrine of *Eros*. Eros is love, but Plato means by it neither sex love nor unselfish love in the Christian sense. Rather, Eros is the impulse leading one towards the highest, a sort of divine madness driving people towards goodness, truth and beauty. Wedded to high things by such love as this, one experiences "birth in beauty." In classic words put into the mouth of the wise woman Diotima, Plato writes:

> The time process, of being led to things of love, is this— to use earth's beauty as the stair up which he mounts to other beauty, going from one to all fair forms, and from fair forms to actions fair, to fair ideas, until he comes to beauty absolute, to beauty's essence.[13]

This concept of Eros is very important, for it supplies the motive power without which Plato's ethics would have been an intellectual abstraction, largely impotent for living. While Plato, like Socrates, believed knowledge essential to the good life, he saw that knowledge must be joined with the compelling emotional force of a great attraction if there is to be any achievement of value on a high level.

d. *The nature of man.* It is necessary to keep this fact in mind as one looks at Plato's doctrine of man, for there he seems to put reason in supreme control. It is characteristic of his weaving everything together that he incorporates the four great Greek virtues into his psychology. He believed the soul to be composed of three parts: reason, spirit (by which he seems to have meant the will or emotional impulses), and the appetites. Reason, the higher part, should govern the two irrational elements for the harmony of the whole. Each part has its appropriate virtue. *Wisdom* is the rule of reason; *courage* is the subordination of spirit to reason; *temperance* is the rational subordination of the appetites. The lower elements are not to

[13]*Symposium*, 211. Albertson, *op. cit.*

be crushed but held in check to do their proper work. With each under due control, performing its appropriate function, one gets a state of *justice* in the soul.

In the doctrine that for harmonious living reason must curb the lower impulses, Plato gives expression to a form of the ethical theory called *self-realization*, which makes the good life consist in rounded development of the whole personality. This has had a great history, extending to the present, and has mingled with and sometimes arrayed itself against Christian ethics, which has as its keynote the ideal of perfect love. Plato's threefold division of man is no longer held to. But as in so many of his theories, what he was getting at is as true as ever; namely, that there can be no healthy moral personality with a "divided self," impulse or appetite running rampant over the claims of reason.

e. *The State.* The State is the man writ large. As the soul has three divisions, so the State—and it is the task of the rulers to govern the State with wisdom, of the soldiers to protect it with courage, of the artisans to support it with temperance. Then this smoothly functioning harmony of the whole would produce—so Plato thought—a condition of justice. Whether there can be real justice in so class-divided a social order is a question on which the modern mind may differ with him. It must be remembered that Plato's was a thoroughly aristocratic outlook. There is, at least, a large suggestion in his words that temperance among the workers meant an obedient keeping of their places, courage among the soldiers a single-minded devotion to military pursuits for the success of the State in war.

However, Plato had an insight into the need of social reconstruction which far outran his day. His ideal State portrayed in the *Republic* is a great Utopia, a communism so thoroughgoing that it would be impossible to put its details into operation. It is a mistake to suppose that Plato ever meant the

Republic as a blueprint for an actual State. In his old age, with less artistry, he wrote the *Laws* for this purpose. The *Republic* is a picture of what life could be like in a State where every person was fulfilling his function for the common good in a secure and ordered society. That Plato expected no such State to exist this side of heaven is suggested by his words at the end of the ninth book:

> In heaven there is laid up a pattern of it, methinks, which he who desires may behold, and beholding may set his own house in order. But whether such a one exists, or will exist in fact, is no matter; for he will live after the manner of that city, having nothing to do with any other.[14]

It is not certain that we should want to live in Plato's ideal State, though it has its attractive features. He would have all men, and women too, educated together to serve the State, with much association in the formative childhood years with music, poetry and tales of heroes, and much physical education. At twenty, the dullest were to drop out to become the workers, and at thirty another great elimination would determine the military class. But the most able were destined to be rulers, and these were to continue their education in philosophy and the practice of statecraft until at fifty they were ready to take their places as guardians of the State. But not on any self-seeking basis. They were to have their wives in common and the children were to be reared in institutions, lest family affection or ambition tempt them to rule corruptly. Marriage being an affair of the State, mating was to be eugenically determined. Plato would have complete sex equality, with women taking their places with men not only in education but in service in battle and in the highest offices of the State.

Plato realized well the corrupting power of the profit motive. The lowest artisan-farmer-trader class might be permitted

[14]*Republic*, IX, 592.

the incentive of acquiring private property, for they had no part in government; but the guarding and governing classes must forego private ownership, working only in the service of the State and supported by it. He saw as clearly as any modern social theorist the disruptive power of personal acquisitiveness and hereditary fortunes, and he set safeguards against it so drastic that his system is easily read as totalitarian. But what underlies it all is the idea that men and women through natural competence and long training must win the right to govern for the good of the whole.

The two historical systems which have most closely approximated the scheme of the *Republic* have been the medieval monastic orders and present-day Communism. It is significant that while one of these is God-centered and the other militantly atheistic, both have found their principal source of power in a dynamic faith. In both, this faith has been strong enough to curtail personal acquisitiveness and subordinate the will of the individual to rigorous group control. This is by no means to equate these systems, for monasticism with its spiritual impulse and its fruits in service both to God and society has on the whole been a constructive force, while Communism is the most dangerous foe not only of Christianity but of democracy and freedom in the world today. Yet they meet at the point of a vital commitment, strong enough to induce self-subordination over great areas of life.

Is Plato's system built also on such a faith? One may doubt it. Human nature is so rooted and grounded in feeling that men will die for a great ideal, as Socrates did and some men do today. But men will not give up their goods, their wives, or their personal pursuits for the sake of a reasoned system of justice.

What shall we make, in general, of Plato's ethical idealism?

Philosophers are not agreed as to the independent existence of universals, and theistic idealism finds it more appropriate to believe that all universals and absolutes exist in the mind of God rather than in an independent Realm of Ideas. Nevertheless, we owe to Plato the first clear formulation of the important concept of the *objectivity of values*, the belief that man's highest ideals are grounded in reality and not in mere wishful thinking, and that accordingly, truth, beauty and goodness are to be discovered and not simply devised according to our private preferences. Likewise, his concept of the Good as the supreme Idea, transcendent and cosmic, is consistent with the belief that the universe is a moral order with laws as eternal as those of physical nature and with obligations as binding upon man's mind and conduct.

Then if we ask how these objective, eternal, *real* values are to be distinguished from mere value claims—objects and purposes which attract us to wrong ends—Plato helps us to find an answer, though it is not the full answer. This lies in his criterion of harmony. We are more apt to call it coherence, or inclusiveness, but it means that that is good which makes for the widest possible range of values in a consistent whole of personality—that is, for health and harmony within the soul of the individual and in all his relationships. While Plato by his threefold division splits too much the unitary nature of personality, reason and the subordination of feeling and impulse to its control are necessary for that harmonious development of personality which every man ought to seek. This falls short of Christian *agape*, self-giving love, but is a long step forward in the direction of the good life.

Likewise, if we take from Plato's social theory his principles rather than specific procedures, there is much to command respect. We are not ready to abolish family life or private property even among the guardians of the State, but his proposals for sex equality, elimination of selfish profit-seeking and political wire-pulling, education of all the people according to their abilities and in the service of the State, and finally, his provision that only the wise and highly trained should rule— these principles if carried into effect today would make for a better society. Interpreting "philosophers" broadly to mean the wise, there is eternal truth in his utterance:

> Until philosophers are kings, or the kings and princes of this world have the spirit and power of philosophy, and political greatness and wisdom meet in one, and those commoner natures who pursue either to the exclusion of the other are compelled to stand aside, cities will never rest from their evils—no, nor the human race, as I believe, —and then only will this our State have a possibility of life and behold the light of day.[15]

Platonic thought is Greek intellectualism at its best. Its Eros (not always under this name) has been setting before men for centuries the attractive power of great ideals. There is a darker side of human nature which only salvation from sin by divine grace can touch. It remained for the Hebrew-Christian faith to minister to this. But no one can read Plato long with an eye of understanding and not feel like taking life more seriously, and living it more beautifully and richly.

2. Aristotle (384-322 B.C.)

The "great Stagirite," born at Stagira in Thrace and reared at the Macedonian court, where his father was physician to King Amyntas, was predisposed by environment to an outlook both aristocratic and scientific. In twenty years of study at the Academy with Plato, who calls him "the mind of the school," his metaphysical interests were ripened by contact with the great idealist and sharpened by conflict. Tales of personal estrangement are probably unfounded. At Plato's death, not

[15]Republic, V, 473.

liking the way Speucippus was conducting the Academy, Aristotle left to travel for twelve years. During this period he carried on extensive biological investigations, and at Assos in the Aegean where he stayed for three years he married Pythias, sister of King Hermias.

In 343 B.C. Aristotle was called to the court of Philip of Macedon to act as tutor to the young Alexander, then thirteen, who—tradition says—was more interested in taming wild horses than in self-mastery. This experience was of historic importance: to Alexander and the world because it gave the prince the respect for Greek learning which caused him to Hellenize the world of his future conquests; to Aristotle and the world because it laid the foundation for great subsidies for scientific research.

Returning to Athens, Aristotle founded a school which like the Academy placed a word in our vocabularies. In his Lyceum, so-called from its location near the temple of Apollo Lyceus, Aristotle and his Peripatetic ("walking around") philosophers engaged in intellectual conversation while political storms were raging in the state. In 338 Philip of Macedon conquered Greece. In 323 Alexander died, anti-Macedonian sentiment rose, and Aristotle—long under suspicion as a Macedonian sympathizer—withdrew to Chalcis in order, he said, "to spare the Athenians a second crime against philosophy." There he died in 322.

Dante gave Aristotle an immortal appellation when he called him "the master of those who know." Probably no other person has ever had a wider grasp of the knowledge available to his time. Aristotle had an encyclopedic mind and was the first encyclopedia-maker—for his treatises, which ran into the hundreds, discuss almost every field of scientific or philosophical inquiry. He wrote on metaphysics, physics, astronomy, botany, zoology, psychology, rhetoric, poetics, logic, ethics, politics and economics. He was the first man to do scientific research, gathering by his subsidized expeditions enormous collections of plant and animal life; he was the founder of formal logic, studied in colleges to the present day; he wrote the first systematic treatise on ethics, on politics, on the principles of literary criticism—treatises which still have pertinent value, though his science has long since been superseded. If his scientific achievements were less permanent, the wonder is that he accomplished as much as he did, for he was obliged, as Zeller puts it, "to fix time without a watch, to compare degrees of heat without a thermometer, to observe the heavens without a telescope, and the weather without a barometer."[16]

Aristotle began his intellectual life as a Platonist. He seems during his Academy period to have written dialogues, of which a few fragments have survived. When his pupil Hermias was crucified he wrote a hymn of passionate Greek patriotism. But Aristotle's was not the mind of a poet. He wrote plain prose—great because of its plainness. His style, like his manner of thought, is less seductive than Plato's. The scientific or "tough-minded" person is likely to prefer Aristotle, the person of spiritual insight turns to Plato. The history of thought since their day could largely be written in terms of the dominance of these two men.

It would be out of place in a book on the history of morals to try to survey Aristotle's total philosophy. Indeed, it is less necessary to do so than in the case of Plato, for Aristotle wrote out his ideas on the good life instead of leaving them to be gleaned from many works. It may be useful, however, to suggest his major trends of thought.

Aristotle's many writings center in four basic interests. The first of these is pure knowledge. It is suggested by the words with which his *Metaphysics* opens, "All men by nature desire to know." For him, there was not the separation we tend to make between science and philosophy. Both were attempts

16*Aristotle and the Earlier Peripatetics*, i, 264.

to *understand* the world, not to *control* it. Modern science is impregnated with a concept of utility foreign to the thinking of the ancient world. For Aristotle, the contemplative life was man's supreme pursuit, yielding a happiness which called for no extrinsic justification.

Yet this did not mean detachment from reality. Aristotle's writings are permeated with the concept of *function*. He believed that nothing (not even thought) was good unless it was good for something, and that the way to judge was to see whether it was fulfilling the function for which nature intended it. For this reason he set forth an *Organon* (instrument) for correct thinking as well as treatises on ethics, politics and poetics.

These intellectual and practical concerns meet in a third which primarily differentiates him from Plato. This is interest in the world we live in—the visible and tangible world of experience—in contrast with a world of perfect and eternal forms. Aristotle is the great forerunner of the realists in philosophy as Plato of the idealists.[17] Yet he had a place for ideals in the sense of unfulfilled possibilities. He thought that the true reality of anything lay not in what it was, but in what it might become. Though his outlook was thoroughly teleological, he shrank from the dualism he thought Plato had set up; and in his thought religion occupied a very minor place.[18]

Finally Aristotle had a keen sense of the connection between thought and language. No one before him had realized so clearly that the word (logos) is not merely an instrument of communication but of thinking. We know a thing when, with accurate distinctions, we can say what it is and why it is so. In this connection roots both Aristotle's elaboration of the

---

[17]In the Middle Ages Platonic realism, affirming the reality of universals, meant the opposite of what realism now means.

[18]When St. Thomas Aquinas in the thirteenth century made Aristotle the substructure of Catholic theology, he grafted a religious system on an essentially irreligious one.

principles of reasoning and his passion for classification. He grasped here a permanent truth, the blurring of which has been responsible for much hazy thinking and equally bad writing.

a. *His ethics.* These interests throw light on Aristotle's metaphysics, and therefore on his ethics. The keynote of his thought is the union of form and matter, joined by the principle of development. Aristotle takes Plato's eternal forms out of the realm of pure being and unites them with the immediate, everyday objects of our experience to constitute the essential nature of the latter. Everything which exists, save God, is a union of form and matter, with the form the true reality which causes matter to assume ever higher and higher stages of development. The *end,* what a thing *may become,* is its real being, as it is the oak which the acorn may grow into which makes the acorn what it is. The unhewn block of marble is more than a block: it is the work of art which the mind and hand of the sculptor may make of it. Matter is potential being: form is reality. God alone is pure form unmixed with matter—the Unmoved Mover who (or which) by *existing* rather than by personally creating causes all else to be.

Applied to ethics, this doctrine of development gave rise to the theory set forth in Aristotle's *Nichomachean Ethics,*[19] that the good life consists in perfection of function—in living as fully as possible the life of a human being, and performing the functions which as a human being and not a mere animal one ought to perform. Man's most distinctive trait is his reason; therefore, the good life must be guided by reason. Aristotle, like Socrates, believed in the natural goodness of man—a doctrine of "original sin" would have horrified him. While he, of course, believed that men sometimes do evil things, he con-

[19]Named for his son Nichomachus, the child of his second wife, Herpyllis.

sidered these acts unnatural, a deviation from man's true "form." Human nature, to Aristotle, was not an excuse for self-indulgence; it was a call to a reasoned life of virtue.

The supreme object of life, "final and self-sufficient, the end at which all actions aim,"[20] was summed up by Aristotle in the term *eudaemonia*. This word (literally well-spirit-ism) is not an easy term to translate though it is usually rendered happiness. It means the combination of well-being and enjoyment, or self-expression and self-control, of living happily and beautifully, which results when life is in its true proportion. However, Aristotle makes clear that he does not mean by it mere pleasure, and his system is usually called eudaemonism to distinguish it from the hedonism of the Cyrenaics and Epicureans. The Platonic ideal of reasoned and harmonious self-realization is much closer to it.

Reason is the guide to the life of happiness. But it, too, must be guided, and Aristotle finds his determining principle in a sense of proportion. This is his famous doctrine of the mean —or, as it has come to be commonly called, the golden mean. This is a reapplication of the familiar principle, written over the Delphic oracle and in the Greek spirit, of "nothing in excess." Courage, says Aristotle, is the mean between rashness and cowardice, temperance between insensibility to pleasure and profligacy, liberality between extravagance and stinginess,[21] high-mindedness between vanity and self-abasement. Aristotle never advocated turning the other cheek. He describes good temper—the mean between irascibility and spiritlessness —as "growing angry on the right occasion and with the right people, and also in the right manner, at the right time and for the right length of time."[22] This is in keeping with his general principle that conduct is not to be guided by fixed rules, but by the use of reason and moderation under the cir-

[20]*Nichomachean Ethics,* I, vii.
[21]*Ibid.,* II, viii.　　　　[22]*Ibid.,* IV, v.

cumstances given. Yet he does not hesitate to say that some things are always and unconditionally wrong, admitting of no mean. Among these he names malice, shamelessness and envy as wrong emotions; adultery, theft and murder as wrong acts.[23]

Aristotle drew a distinction between the activity of contemplation (dianoetic virtue) and the practical virtues. The first, to be pursued and prized for its own sake, yields the highest happiness and has in it an element of divinity. The moral virtues such as justice and courage are purely human matters, but very necessary to our social intercourse. He does not limit their number, and in addition to the usual justice, courage and temperance he stresses high-mindedness (by which he seems to mean honor or self-respect), liberality and friendship.

More clearly than any other Greek, Aristotle developed the implications of friendship. True friendship, he says, is possible only between the good whose virtues serve as a common bond.[24] Friendships based on utility or pleasure are readily dissolved, passing away when the transient relations on which they rest are altered. "The friendship of good men is the only kind that can withstand calumny,"[25] for only in such friendship is there mutual trust.

Virtue must be a settled moral habit. Goodness is no flash-in-the-pan outburst. "One swallow does not make a summer, nor does one day."[26] In this, Aristotle dissents also from the Socratic-Platonic identification of knowledge with virtue; for highly as he prized wisdom, he did not believe that the dianoetic would automatically generate the moral virtues. These must be wrought into character by the exercise of reason in the protracted strain of daily living.

---

[23]*Ibid.*, II, vi. This answers the charge sometimes made that Aristotle's middle way is simply "a mean of mediocrity."

[24]*Ibid.*, VIII, iii.

[25]*Ibid.*, iv.

[26]*Ibid.*, I, vii.

b. *Politics.* Aristotle's theory of the State is more unlike that of Plato than is his doctrine of the good life in the individual man. More individualistic and conservative than Plato, he expressly repudiated Plato's communism of goods and family as stifling private enterprise and affection. Like Plato, he believed that rulers should be educated, but he had no formal scheme either for education or government. He believed that that is the best government which is best suited to the community to be governed—a principle perhaps easier to enunciate than to carry out.

Monarchy (the rule of a single high-minded and capable man), aristocracy (the rule of a small but able and disinterested group), polity (the rule of an educated middle class) —each had its legitimate function if it did not become perverted. But if monarchy became tyranny, or aristocracy became an oligarchy of a few self-seeking demagogues, or polity became democracy—the rule of the ignorant herd, then each form lost its justification.

He drew a distinction far in advance of his times in his analysis of justice as *distributive* (a proper distribution of goods) or *corrective* (a remedial use of punishment). Yet like Adam Smith and the many who have justified free competition in a capitalistic society as automatically adjusting possession to ability, he failed to see that private profit would not guarantee distributive justice.

An element destined to have much influence was his prohibition of usury. He tried to distinguish between the natural and unnatural uses of money, and in the latter he included all taking of interest on the ground that "money does not beget money." Obviously he was mistaken as to the legitimate uses of credit. His authority, in conjunction with that of the Old Testament, held back the advance of trade in the late Middle Ages.[27] For the money-grubbing activities of shopkeepers and

[27]*Cf.* R. H. Tawney, *Religion and the Rise of Capitalism,* p. 44.

bankers he had slight respect—an attitude in which there is a curious mingling of aristocratic prejudice with an ethical aversion to absorption in money-making. Among those who have enough, this attitude toward those who have not is a persistent tendency.

The part of Aristotle's politics most foreign to the modern spirit is his justification of slavery. Slaves, to Aristotle, were instruments for the use of free men, and slavery is justified by the inherent differences in men's capacities. "From the hour of their birth some are marked out for subjection and others for rule."[28] He thought that slaves, like animals, should be kindly treated, but it probably never occurred to him that they should be treated as *persons*—as the equals of free men. Similarly, in spite of his Macedonian sympathies, he had the typical Greek spirit of superiority to all non-Greeks. The barbarian had no rights which the free-born Greek was under obligation to respect. Unlike Plato, he regarded women also as an inferior group, existing only for the bearing and rearing of children. A typical Greek aristocrat, he scorned the manual labor of mechanics and craftsmen, and seemed to assume that the poor were poor because of natural inferiority. He was a many-sided genius, yet the child of his age. And perhaps of every age—for after two thousand years of Christian emphasis on world brotherhood and the worth of every man as precious in God's sight, there is still plenty of exclusiveness and class superiority in our society without a compensating Aristotelian sense of proportion.

How shall we appraise this genius, and his moral contribution to the stream of Western thought? If we judge him for what he says, rather than for what he leaves out, it is difficult to overestimate his importance. Realistic, down to earth, rational and benign, he not only spoke to St. Thomas Aquinas in the thirteenth century, but he speaks to us today. The

[28]*Politics*, I, v.

Nichomachean Ethics is one of the most discerning ethical treatises ever written. Nevertheless, Christian ethics cannot be built upon it. It lacks the sense of sin which any true realism about human nature must include; it lacks the note of God's redeeming love and forgiving mercy. Its counsels of moderation and of "nothing in excess" make for refinement of living, but not for great self-giving in love of one's fellow-man or in pursuit of causes that demand one's all. In a word, this call to balanced and friendly living—"gracious living," we might call it today—lacks the union of tragedy with divine concern which makes the Christian ethic both difficult and grand.

3. The Epicureans

Two of Aristotle's younger contemporaries were Epicurus (341–277 A.D.) and Zeno (336–264 A.D.), founders respectively of the Epicurean and Stoic schools. The stream of influence which we have seen running through Socrates, Plato and Aristotle is here shunted off, and we see schools of ethical thought emerging more from the spirit of the times than from the influence of a single predecessor. Greece by this time was a Macedonian province, and while Greek culture was being spread through the eastern world, the tendency at its fountainhead was again to turn from speculation to practical adjustment. With the loss of civic liberties Greek ethics could no longer center in the State, and as corrupting Oriental cults crept in and materialism became more rampant, the moral quest increasingly took the form of an answer to the query, "How can I be happy in these troubled times?"

Of the events of Epicurus' life little is known. By his own statement, he was self-educated. Tradition says he was the son of a priestess—a matter which, if true, may account for his rebelling against the superstitions of the religion in which he was reared. The chief intellectual influences upon his thought were the doctrines of Aristippus and the materialist Democritus. For thirty years or more he was the presiding spirit of his garden school, gathering about him a group of congenial friends with whom he passed his days in pleasant intercourse. The atmosphere was one of retired leisure in which refinement and congeniality of interest, rather than stern devotion to serious tasks, was the order of the day. Epicurus was most decidedly not an "epicure," and the saying often attributed to him, "Eat, drink, and be merry, for tomorrow we die," is an unwarranted smirch upon his character. It characterizes some of the later Epicureans, but Epicurus himself had a taste for the simple life which finds truer expression in the words, "Give me barley-bread and water, and I will vie with Zeus in happiness."

Epicurus seems to have written a good deal, but only fragments of his work survive, for his writings offended his countrymen by attacks on the traditional polytheism, and what survived Greek censorship perished, for the most part, at the hands of Christians who believed his doctrine both irreligious and immoral. We know his doctrine best through the *De Rerum Natura* of Lucretius, Roman Epicurean of more than two centuries later (98–55 B.C.) and his only great successor.

Epicurean thought is rooted in the atomism of Democritus and the hedonism of the Cyrenaics, for the marriage of materialism with pleasure-seeking is a natural union, often repeated in the history of thought. From Democritus, Epicurus derived the idea that everything, including the soul, is made of fine material atoms whose combination as they try to fall toward the earth gives things their form. Mechanism jostles free will in his theory without much regard for consistency. But on one point he was thoroughly consistent—that man's chief good is to live without fear or worry or the torment of seeking the unattainable. This made him put the gods out in the interstellar spaces where they could do men no harm!

There, he thought, they lived in blissful unconcern, and men would do better neither to worship nor fear them. Likewise death could be robbed of its terrors if one looked on it calmly as the end of all—nothing to be afraid of now, nothing to be aware of then.

Epicurus' moral ideal is summed up in *ataraxia*, which means freedom from confusion, calmness, peace of mind. Like Gautama the Buddha, he believed that the way to happiness lies in the cutting off of desire. So he taught that men should keep themselves free from "entangling alliances" like marriage and politics! When things are bound to be full of disturbing situations, steer clear of them. Live the simple life, and do not upset tranquility by pursuing wealth, or trying to make friends with uninteresting people, or championing causes, or worrying about religion, or wrestling over-much with knotty intellectual problems. Plain fare, a few congenial friends, interesting conversation, and leisure in which to enjoy one's self—these are all one needs. This is the good life, and the true life according to nature, for the love of happiness is the one thing that is "natural" to all.

It is evident that this is hedonism on a higher plane than that of the Cyrenaics. Pleasures of the mind are to be preferred to those of the body, and the durability of a pleasure is more important than its intensity. Epicurus is even willing to admit there is a certain amount of good in pain, provided it leads to ultimate enjoyment. Yet it is hedonism still, with no real criterion of goodness save the individual's private feeling. It partakes strongly of the slippery go-as-you-please philosophy of the Sophists, and like the Sophists and Cyrenaics the Epicureans slumped in their living until the later followers of Epicurus were the epicures and sensual hedonists that he himself had refused to be.

How shall we estimate this comfortable philosophy, still so current among cultured people? There can be no doubt that

Epicurus spoke words of permanent worth in his plea for the finding of happiness through refined simplicity. Contentment, friendship, leisure, tolerance, freedom from superstition and fear—all these are good. It is true that all men do desire happiness, and all men ought to have it. If one wants to find modern Epicureanism at its best, charmingly and beautifully expressed, he should read Walter Pater's *Marius the Epicurean*.

Yet if one has a feeling for the serious side of life, he cannot be fully satisfied with Epicureanism. "Learn betimes to die, or if you like it better, to pass over to the gods," says Epicurus. "If you like it better"—there is the keynote to the weakness of the system. What Epicurus announces is a selfish individualism. It is selfish because it is parasitic. Epicurus and his friends could have leisure because others worked; he could be born and reared because others married; he could be protected in a political state because others maintained it; he could have ideas to converse with because others labored to find the truth. This affronts our sense of fair play. As Kant pointed out centuries later, any moral principle which is really right must be one that can be universalized.

Epicureanism is a one-sided philosophy. It rests on emotional preference rather than reason, for if pleasure, even refined pleasure, is the only aim of conduct, pleasant feelings are bound to vary so much that there is no rational way of deciding which feelings are best. One must fall back on the criterion of intensity, subjectively appraised. And since pleasures of the body are usually more intense than spiritual joys, we come upon a further fault: that the hedonistic outlook is unprogressive. Unguided by reason, it is often retrogressive, for "when joy and duty clash" joy will have its way to the point of exalting the flesh and crushing out hard-won spiritual values. It is not by accident that the fruitage of a refined but egoistic hedonism has so often been a callous sensualism.

4. Stoicism

Stoicism is like, yet very unlike, the Epicurean doctrine. The Stoic *apatheia,* indifference to external circumstance, gave a serenity and peace of mind akin to the Epicurean *ataraxia,* but it came through a very different channel.

Stoicism, like Epicureanism, is still a very live doctrine and it appeals to rugged natures as much as the hedonistic outlook does to those who are attracted by the joy of life. For about five hundred years (approximately 300 B.C. to 200 A.D.) it was the dominant philosophy of Greece and Rome, and it stands as a bridge between the Greek and the Christian spirit. Though born on Greek soil, it had its greater days in Rome, and gave Roman law its philosophic undergirding. It merged with Christian doctrine and directly contributed the "Logos" doctrine to the Gospel of John. Through political, religious, and literary channels it laid a permanent stamp on future thought.

The founder of Stoicism, who gave it its name, was the Greek Zeno, a contemporary of Epicurus who taught in a covered colonnade (Stoa, porch) near the Athenian agora. Having brought to birth a philosophy of resolute endurance he died by his own hand—paradoxically, it seems to us, but the Stoics believed that suicide was better than defeat. A successor was Cleanthes (304–233 B.C.), whose *Hymn to Zeus* is Miltonic in its swing, and it is probably from this that Paul quoted when he said to the Athenians on Mars Hill,

> "In him we live and more and have our being;" as even some of your poets have said, "for we are indeed his offspring."[29]

The poem is too long to quote in full, but a few lines will give one a sense of its majestic cadences.

[29]Acts 17:28. R. S. V.

O God most glorious, called by many a name,
Nature's great King, through endless years the same;
Omnipotence, who by thy just decree
Controllest all, hail, Zeus for unto thee
Behooves thy creatures in all lands to call.
We are thy children, we alone, of all
In earth's broad ways that wander to and fro,
Bearing thine image wheresoe'er we go.

*   *   *   *   *

Thy children save from error's deadly sway:
Turn thou the darkness from their souls away:
Vouchsafe that unto knowledge they attain;
For thou by knowledge art made strong to reign
O'er all, and all things rulest righteously.
So by thee honored, we will honor thee,
Praising thy works continually with songs,
As mortals should; nor higher meed belongs
E'en to the gods, than justly to adore
The universal law forevermore.[30]

Then came Chrysippus, great debater who is said to have boasted of his skill in argument to the point of saying, "Give me doctrines and I will find reasons for them." (If the English philosopher F. H. Bradley was right when he said that "metaphysics is the finding of bad reasons for what we already believe upon instinct," perhaps Chrysippus was not so unphilosophical as he sounds!) We must pass by these earlier Stoics hastily, and state Stoicism's major tenets.

The chief forebears of Stoicism are Heraclitus, Socrates, and the Cynics. Heraclitus, philosopher of Becoming, had taught that all is change; perpetual flux, lambent and flickering as fire, the symbol of change. Yet in the eternal flux of things, one element is stable, the law of change. This pervasive universal element, the Logos, gives rational unity to all. The Stoics took over this Logos doctrine, gave it a more religious significance than Heraclitus had attached to it, and made it

---

[30]Quoted in Woodbridge Riley, *Men and Morals*, p. 134.

the basis of their metaphysics and ethics. The Logos was divinity, a World Reason present everywhere even in the midst of apparent evil, determining destiny, kindling humanity with the divine spark, making all men brothers as kindred sharers in the divine flame. The world to the Stoics was mechanical —a manifestation of universal law; yet rational—filled with the living presence of God. This is pantheism, not the theistic Christian belief in a personal God, but with a sublime inconsistency which did not trouble the Stoics, they often speak of God as a personal deity caring benevolently for men. To live in harmony with the Logos is to live according to nature. And so once more, with a new turn, we find the good life to be the life "according to nature."

From Socrates and the Platonic-Aristotelian tradition, the Stoics took the idea of a union of knowledge with virtue. The Virtuous Wise Man is the moral ideal. Through reason and force of will one must not merely curb, one must root out the emotions as a disease, and with a calm indifference to outward circumstance let the will reign supreme over the kingdom of the inner life. This is not a doctrine for the many, for only the wise man can achieve this mastery, and between the wise man and the ignorant (or between the good man and the evil) there is no middle ground. Later Stoicism softened somewhat this cleavage, but there remained inherent in Stoic thought a clear sense of superiority over those lacking the knowledge and will to attain to its high demands.

The connection with Cynic philosophy is by this time apparent. The Stoics did not run away from society as the Cynics did. Though some of the early Stoics advocated eschewing domestic and political ties as corrupting to the soul, the later and greater exponents accepted the family and the state as congruent with the life of nature. They regarded all men as brothers—fellow-participants in the divine nature. They did not reject wealth, honor, social conventions or physical comfort; they regarded these as matters of indifference—so long as they did not stain the inner life. Stoic doctrine is therefore less ascetic, more natural, social and positive than the Cynic position. But there is the same emphasis on virtue as its own (and only) reward, the same moral sternness, almost the same self-righteousness. Stoicism in the words of its great exponents is sublime; Stoicism as practised has been time and again but a step removed from cynicism.

So here we have the major Stoic doctrines: divine providence at the heart of the universe, life according to man's divine nature, a serene acceptance of whatever comes from without, mastery in the inner life through reason, a cosmopolitan sense of the brotherhood of all men—a courageous, resolute, optimistic idealism. What shall we do with it?

Stoicism's merit is too apparent to require elaborate exposition or defense. But in a fair appraisal, one must consider also its self-righteousness, its abrupt cleavage between good and evil, its doctrine of acceptance rather than modification of events, its dethronement of the emotions, its exaltation of suicide, its often indiscriminate mixture of theism with pantheism. Having looked at those factors, one may conclude that with all its merits, Stoicism gave way to Christianity in the march of historical events because there was something in the latter that Stoicism lacked. But before we examine the Christian ethic, we must look at the soil on which the Stoic doctrine found its most fertile growth.

5. The Roman Temper

It will not be possible in this study to give as many pages to the Roman ideal as to the Greek. Nor is it necessary, for the Romans were borrowers, and their greatest philosophical contribution is the enrichment and transmission of Stoicism. But this borrowing and transmitting was so well done that civilization owes the Romans an incalculable debt. When "conquered Greece took captive her rude conqueror," a far-reaching political system, a common language, and a great system of roads facilitating communication made Rome the schoolmaster of the Western world. This tamer of our barbarian ancestors and tutor of the Church was the instrument through which the achievements of the Greek spirit and the Hebrew-Christian tradition became our heritage.

Almost everybody knows that Rome's chief gift to the world was a system of law. The Roman genius was *practical* rather than religious, aesthetic or speculative, and this practical trend revealed itself in great engineering feats, in a marvelously disciplined army, and most of all in skill in governing. The factionalism which weakened and finally destroyed the Greek city-states was to a large degree avoided in Rome by a form of government which in general permitted citizen-participation without mob rule or extreme autocracy. Rome held her colonies, not by military force alone, but by political assimilation of conquered territories and the granting of rights of citizenship to the conquered. The most difficult of all political tasks is to combine freedom with restraint for the common good, and while Rome's success is not to be over-glorified, she laid the foundations on which all subsequent political life in the West has built.

The Roman social outlook, like our own, displays great paradoxes. Not only is there a union politically of freedom with restraint, but there is a conspicuous juxtaposition of ideals of human brotherhood with social and economic cleavage. No early nation had greater extremes of wealth and poverty than did Rome—wealth often wrung from the poor by the extortion of provincial governors and tax-gatherers, poverty pandered to by the giving of "bread and circuses" to amuse the rabble and win votes for demagogues. Roman industry was built on slave labor, and magnificent private villas still stand as memorials of a class-divided civilization. The most original Roman literature is that which satirizes the luxuries and vices of Rome in her period of decadence. Yet the most sublime moral statements produced by the ancient world, outside of the Bible, are the writings of the Roman Stoic philosophers, and through these there breathes the spirit of world brotherhood and the spiritual equality of all men.

This cosmopolitan message, dimly sensed by the masses but not without influence in its own day, was destined later to bear much fruit. Our ideals of political liberty and civic responsibility, conceived on Greek soil and augmented by the influence which flowed forth from the life and words of a Galilean Jew, took flesh in Roman law and exist today as the product of the blending of Stoic and Christian thought.

6. Contributions of Roman Stoicism

The essential concepts of Roman Stoicism are already familiar. They have thus been compactly summarized:

> The more important of these doctrines which found expression in Roman law and thereby were handed down to modern times as elements not only of our law, but of our morals, are (1) the conception of nature as a source of universal law; (2) the conception of Reason as the essential principle of nature; (3) the conception that all men share in reason, and therefore are equal; (4) the conception that justice is the rightful source of government; (5) the conception of duty.[31]

The Roman writers express variously this union of political, religious, and moral outlook. In Cicero, long known to high school students because of the clarity and vigor of his oratory, one finds much that is Stoic, though he was not so fully repre-

[31]John Dewey and James H. Tufts, *Ethics*, revised edition, p. 137.

sentative of this school as were Seneca, Epictetus and Marcus
Aurelius. Cicero's delightful essays on *Old Age, Friendship*
and *Duties* glow with the spirit of kindliness, self-control and
rational living. He gave literary expression to the belief in a
natural law of eternal and immutable morality, derived from
God and forming the true basis of justice for men.

In Seneca, philosopher-statesman, teacher of Nero and victim of that emperor's jealous intrigue, one finds a clear statement of a principle which not even Aristotle in his breadth
of insight had grasped; namely, that differences in men are
often due, not to inborn capacity, but to fortune. On this basis
he roundly condemned slavery and declared the slave to be
the spiritual equal of his master—a declaration which must
have taken courage in a world where slavery was a universally
accepted institution. Exalting the philanthropic virtues he denounced the gladiatorial games and enjoined relief of suffering,
though with the typical Stoic fear of a sentimental yielding
to the emotions he declared that the wise man would succor
but not pity those in distress.

In Epictetus, manumitted Phrygian slave, we find a living
demonstration that slavery is no inherent mark of inferiority.
His *Discourses* cover the whole range of higher Stoic thought.
Distinguishing between the things that are in our power (our
own wills and attitude toward life), and the things that are
not in our power (health and disease, riches and poverty, and
all manner of external events), he calls us to the exercise of
freedom in the inner life and a calm acceptance of what God
in His wisdom may send as our lot. He is almost Christian in
his doctrine of the divine Providence, the rationality of a God-
directed universe, and man's duty to be grateful for divine
care. "Seek not to have things happen as you choose, but
rather choose that they should happen as they do; and you
shall live prosperously." If there is too much of resignation

here to fit in with a Christian ideal of the active conquest of evil, there is at least a much-needed emphasis on the serenity which comes through self-mastery and trust.

In the emperor Marcus Aurelius Antoninus, at the opposite end of the social scale, one finds the same benignity of spirit and calm trust in the goodness of God. He was the adopted son of M. Antoninus Pius, and his *Meditations* opens with a statement of debt to his foster-father and many others—ancestors, parents, brother, sister, teachers, friends, and to the gods who have bestowed such gifts. This is typical of the outgoing reach of his spirit. He was cosmopolitan in his outlook, and we find him saying such altruistic words as "To care for all men is according to man's nature"; and "Men exist for the sake of one another." The spirit of internationalism breathes in his declaration, "My city and country, so far as I am Antoninus, is Rome; but so far as I am a man, it is the world." He enjoins forgiveness to those who injure us, the doing of good to all men, the living of life richly and without hurry while it lasts, and the acceptance of death unafraid. We find him saying:

> Pass then through this little space of time conformably to nature, and end thy journey in content, just as an olive falls off when it is ripe, blessing nature who produced it, and thanking the tree on which it grew.[32]

In his private life the emperor seems to have lived with the serene benignity which shines through his *Meditations*. He was a good emperor, as emperors go, but his reign was torn with colonial rebellions which fanned his suspicion of anything new; and when a sect of Christians arose proclaiming a doctrine very like his own, he authorized that they be persecuted and put to death. This does not mean that he was insincere; it means only that like most men, he lacked the vision to carry

[32]*Meditations*, Bk. IV, 48.

a sublime personal ideal into its wider social relations. Jesus did—and died on a cross as his reward.

These various Stoic ideals converge in the concept of morality as grounded in the *lex naturae*—a universal moral law essentially rational in which all men participate, a law which calls to the individual to live his own life at its best and establish justice for all men. The *lex naturae* doctrine, never dead but sometimes dormant, was revised in the seventeenth century and made the philosophical basis of Grotius' attempt to formulate international law. In the meantime Christian theology had taken it over, and had identified it with the Hebrew-Christian concept of obedience to the will of God. The strands thus interlaced were never clearly separated, and the familiar eighteenth-century doctrine of natural rights has a double parentage. To this day our bills of rights and declarations that "all men are created free and equal," the emancipation of slaves, our laws for the protection of women, children and the underprivileged, our efforts for world disarmament and racial brotherhood, trace their ancestry to the marriage of the Stoic with the Christian ideal of "liberty and justice for all." But there were differences, and these we must note in the next chapter.

CHAPTER NINE

THE BEGINNINGS

OF CHRISTIAN ETHICS

1. The Meaning of Christian Ethics

THE term "Christian ethics" is a very ambiguous one. Obviously, there are wide disparities of belief as to what a Christian ought to do in concrete situations. With equal sincerity and with great devotion, Christians through the centuries have found themselves on opposite sides of complex moral issues. Furthermore, if one is concerned with ethical theory, it soon becomes evident that except for some generalizations in regard to love, Christians are by no means agreed as to the foundations on which Christian morality rests. To some, Christian ethics means self-realization, closely allied with the best in Greek thought; to others, the whole idea of self-realization is perversion. To some, Christian love requires coercion, if necessary, even to the point of global war and mass destruction by atomic or hydrogen bombs; to others, this is a diabolical affront to everything Jesus taught and the Christian faith professes.

Not only do Christians disagree as to what we ought to do and why, but there are still deeper levels of ambiguity. Failure to recognize different frames of reference in which the term is used often sets people to arguing at cross purposes. What are we talking about when we say "Christian ethics"? The term has five possible meanings, each legitimate in its proper context if that context is defined, but by no means identical.

Do we mean by Christian ethics *the ethics of Jesus?* If so, there is difference of opinion both as to the accuracy of the record and how to interpret it, but the record is there in the Gospels for everybody to look at. If this is Christian ethics, we have at least a manageable set of ideas to talk about.

Or do we mean *the ethics of the New Testament?* Not the words and deeds of Jesus only, but the entire New Testament is the record of the beginnings of Christianity. It has been, and still is, immensely influential in shaping our Christian morality. Were it not so, we should not use it as we do in our Sunday services of worship and our Christian education.

Or do we mean *the ethics of the Bible?* Here the base obviously broadens, and the whole range of matters we have discussed in Chapters Five and Six comes into the picture. Is the Old Testament Christianity? It is, and it is not. Again, a definition of the frame of reference is imperative, but often omitted.

Or do we mean *the ethics of the Christian Church?* Here the three preceding categories must be included, for they have greatly molded the ethics of the Church. But much more must be included with them, for nearly twenty centuries of history, sometimes glorious in Christian insight, sometimes very sordid in conformity to and modification by "the world," have shaped the ethics of the Church. Obviously also, within the Church there are *churches,* and the churches have not agreed either within or among themselves.

Or do we mean *the ethics of Christendom?* Christendom means that part of human society which is nominally Christian, and which has been to a significant degree affected by Christian concepts and ideals. In the current situation Christendom means "the West," in contrast with both the predominantly non-Christian Orient and the officially atheistic but still partly Christian territory of the U. S. S. R. If Christian ethics means the ethics of Christendom, we have a very slippery term to deal with, but a recognition of its many-sidedness may facilitate understanding. The main reason why this book has been written is to point out the variety and richness of the sources of Western morality. However, in view of the inroads of secularism upon current society, it is doubtful whether the ethics of Christendom can now properly be identified with Christian ethics.

In this concluding chapter, we are going primarily to discuss Christian ethics in the first sense—the ethics of Jesus. We shall say something also about the ethics of Paul because of his great contribution both to the New Testament and to the Church. There are ethical insights elsewhere in the New Testament, such as the great ode to faith in Hebrews, the call to add works to faith in James, the portrayal of the new heaven and the new earth in Revelation. But these are elaborations on foundations already laid, and do not call for special analysis.[1] A look at the ethics of Jesus and Paul with what has been said about Hebrew morality will round out a survey of the origins of Christian ethics in the first three senses. The entire book aims at the fifth. The fourth meaning—the ethics of the Christian Church—is a whole story in itself. There are excellent books in this field to which the reader is referred.[2]

2. Jesus and the Ideals of Greece and Rome

In our study of Greek and Roman ethics we have been mov-

[1]My *Toward Understanding the Bible* states briefly the theme of each book.
[2]See note on page 7.

ing among carefully reasoned systems. Their progenitors thought them out as the most satisfactory guides to the moral life, and presented them as statements of belief. They were in a sense gospels, designed to bring others to a new outlook upon life, and we have noted, particularly in Socrates, Plato and the Stoics, religious overtones. Yet all of these Greek and Roman systems were essentially forms of ethical philosophy.

In Jesus we find much that converges with the best in classical pagan thought. But there is much more that is different, and the foundations are worlds apart. The primary difference lies in the fact that Jesus proclaimed, not an ethical *philosophy,* but an ethical *religion*—a personal way of life grounded in faith in God and love for God and one's neighbor. He had no interest in establishing on intellectual grounds a moral system. Yet he influenced moral living more than any other person who ever lived.

There is no evidence that Jesus had any contact with Greek thought, or that he knew Rome except in terms of the ruling political regime. It is futile, therefore, to try to trace influences in him to these sources, as we must to his Hebrew background. But his followers were destined to be greatly influenced by these classic pagan modes of thought, so much so that Christianity to this day is a blend of Hebrew and Greek elements which for centuries were transmitted within the matrix of Roman law. It will be profitable, therefore, to make some comparison of agreements and differences.

Looking back over the past two chapters, we have surveyed six important movements in the Graeco-Roman world which left a permanent stamp on the thought life of the West: the Sophists' relativism with its belief that "man is the measure of all things," the Socrates concept that "knowledge is virtue," the Platonic ideal of harmonious self-realization in conformity with eternal and objective values, the Aristotelian sense of proportion and the right performance of natural functions, the

Epicurean ideal of refined pleasure and enlightened self-interest, the Stoic ideal of self-controlled living actuated by an immanent Logos pervading all nature and all men. To what extent are these philosophies of life—so ancient yet so contemporary—compatible with the outlook of Jesus?

It is apparent that not one of them says what Jesus said, or what he lived and died for. Yet in varying degrees they can be amalgamated with or grafted on to the moral outlook of Jesus.

It has long been customary to compare favorably, if not to equate, the work of Socrates and Jesus. Indeed, until Gandhi came along as a high embodiment of moral purity outside of Christianity, Socrates was the stock example of those who wished to claim that the Christian faith had produced nothing distinctive in the way of moral excellence. This claim has some credibility not only in the fact that both men died as martyrs to their convictions, but in the great moral earnestness and religious devotion of their lives. Socrates' *daimon* which would not let him rest until he convicted men of their error may properly enough be thought of not only as the voice of conscience, but as the voice of God. Nevertheless, at a crucial point there is a radical difference. It was moral error, not sin against God, about which Socrates was concerned, and self-knowledge was essential to release from error. Jesus never taught that right knowing would induce right doing. The oft-quoted, "Ye shall know the truth, and the truth shall make you free" (John 8:32), is usually misquoted, for its context makes it clear that the conditions of such knowledge are faith and Christian discipleship.

The Aristotelian philosophy, with its golden mean and down-to-earth centering in the needs and possibilities of the human situation, has enough to commend it so that St. Thomas Aquinas drew heavily from it and it has still an important place in Roman Catholic thought. It commends itself also to the essentially pragmatic American Protestant temper, and

without being labeled, appears frequently in the ethical outlook of those who decry a "perfectionism" based on Jesus'
absolute demands. But again it falls short of being the ethics
of Jesus. The very fact that Jesus gave an absolute demand to
love without restraint, to trust God unreservedly, to obey without limit sets his moral imperatives sharply at variance with
this view.

The two classical systems that come closest to the outlook
of Jesus are those of Plato and the Stoics. It is not by accident
that neo-Platonism and Stoicism considerably influenced early
Christianity. St. Augustine in a famous passage in his *Con-
fessions* says that he found in Plato everything but the incarnation.[3] There is enough similarity between the moral injunctions of Jesus and the greater Roman Stoics so that it has
been argued that Epictetus and Marcus Aurelius must have
been touched by Christian influence, though there is little
likelihood that they were.

Yet the differences are very great. Centering in a different
view of both God and man, these great classical systems had
a different motivation and looked toward a different goal. Self-
realization through self-development and self-expression, even
in so high a form as health and harmony of the soul through
conformity to universal and objective values, falls short of
humble, outgoing, self-giving service. The urge toward the
supreme idea of the Good, which we more often now term
"the quest for enduring values," has certainly a rightful place
in a humane and civilized culture. But it is not the same as
Christian self-subordination through love of God and one's
neighbor. In short, *agape* is not *eros*, as Bishop Anders Nygren
has shown in an important book devoted to this theme.[4]

Likewise, Stoic self-control has much about it that is ad-

[3]Confessions, Book VII, Sections 13, 14.
[4]See his *Agape and Eros* for an extensive elaboration of this difference.
Also, Reinhold Niebuhr in *The Nature and Destiny of Man,* Vol. I, Ch. 1,
gives a searching analysis of the difference between the classical and the
Christian outlook.

mirable. But as we remarked earlier. Stoicism is altogether too likely to pass over into cynicism when life becomes unmanageable. It is a long step removed from the faith and humility of the Christian who can say, "I know how to be abased, and I know how to abound; . . . I can do all things in him who strengthens me" (Phil. 4:12, 13). An immanent World-Reason or World-Soul is not "the God and Father of our Lord Jesus Christ." And because it is not, Stoic cosmopolitanism is not world brotherhood under one Father, or the natural dignity of man the same thing as the infinite worth of every man in the sight of God, a brother for whom Christ died.

Some other differences, attaching not to any particular system but to the classical spirit as a whole, may be briefly noted. The Greek view of life, we saw, had a place for moral evil but very little for sin. As a consequence, the pagan ideal was one of "life according to nature." Jesus, we are told, "knew what was in man" (John 2:25). Though the context of this passage indicates that he knew the evil that was in man, his total ministry indicates that he knew both the power of evil and the possibilities of goodness in man. His major message was a call to repent of sin and to accept in faith, humility and love the power of God to conquer sin and bring men to newness of life in the kingdom of God.

A marked difference appears also in regard to the focusing of interest in time or eternity. The classical spirit was one of preoccupation with the present life, though with a largely irrelevant belief in the existence of the soul after death. Jesus, though it may be doubted that he was as other-worldly as his followers have often made him, had certainly in his own faith and message the vista of eternity. Regardless of the disputed eschatological passages foreshadowing a great divine intervention and sudden end of the present world, his few but great words on eternal life have given reassurance and hope through the centuries. They are the chief source of the present

Christian faith in personal immortality. Without them, it is doubtful that the intimations of immortality in Greek or Hebrew thought would have survived to have much significance today.

Another contrast lies in the pagan versus the Christian attitude toward the State. Though Jesus said "Render unto Caesar the things that are Caesar's" (Mk. 12:17), these words were incidental to a dominant ethic which put the individual, rather than the State, in the focus of attention. In this the early Christians followed his lead. When the State clashed with a higher loyalty, there stood the word, "We must obey God rather than men" (Acts 5:29). They took this seriously, and for their refusal to worship the emperor they were thrown to the lions.

These differences in general outlook naturally colored the emphasis placed on the virtues. There is no Greek virtue that is not found somewhere in the Christian scheme, yet the *dominant* virtues are quite different. For the great Greek four, we find the Christian ideal summed up in love. Wisdom—the exaltation of reason and intellect—finds its counterpart in faith and the pure heart. Justice is seasoned with mercy. Courage becomes moral steadfastness toward evil.[5] Temperance passes over into the cutting off and the plucking out of whatever may offend the inner life.[6]

We found that the Greek ideal, even at its best, was an aristocratic one, and that the Roman ethic, in spite of its theoretical cosmopolitanism had no great leveling or welding influence in its own day. The Christian ideal, on the other hand, was from its start a socializing agency. Democracy is rooted

[5]"Do not resist one who is evil. But if any one smites you on the right cheek, turn to him the other also" (Mt. 5:39). R. S. V.

[6]"If your hand or your foot causes you to sin, cut it off and throw it from you. . . . If your eye causes you to sin, pluck it out and throw it from you; it is better for you to enter life with one eye than with two eyes to be thrown into the hell of fire" (Mt. 18:8, 9). R. S. V.

in it. It was the common people who heard Jesus gladly, and Christian fellowship and witness within the Church was a great leveling agency. For the Platonic-Aristotelian aristocratic ideal Jesus substituted the supreme worth of every person before God and hence the obligation to regard all men as brothers and neighbors. The whole of ethical development, from a social standpoint, is summed up in an ever-widening concept of the answer to the question which a certain lawyer put to Jesus, "And who is my neighbor?"[7]

3. Jesus and His Hebrew Background

To see Jesus in his proper setting we must view him, not only against a Greek, but still more against a Hebrew background. Jesus himself was a Jew, and except as he passed through Samaria, he never went outside of a Jewish environment. We must now go back in our story to the end of Chapter Six.

Jesus lived and did his work in an atmosphere permeated with three important aspects of post-exilic Judaism which had been gaining in intensity during the inter-Testament period. These were a nationalistic expectation of a political Messiah; the legalistic, ritualistic religion of the Pharisees and Sadducees; and the apocalyptic expectation of a speedy end of this present world.

Jesus clearly repudiated the first two of these concepts, and because he did so was misunderstood. He was not only a religious leader but a loyal Jew, and so devoted was he to his people that he tried to save them from the engulfing nationalism of their own political aspirations which he saw was futilely trying to resist the Roman rule. In Jesus' childhood a rebellion at Sepphoris, only a few miles from Nazareth, was put down with the burning of the city and the crucifixion of two thousand persons. A few years later the tetrarch Archelaus

[7]Luke 10:29.

slaughtered three thousand Jews at a Passover feast, and the furor that ensued led to the deposing of Archelaus, the crushing of revolt by Roman arms, and the formation of a revolutionary party of Jewish Zealots who wanted to overthrow Rome by military force. Such events must have helped to convince Jesus of the futility of political rebellion and the need of a higher force to bring his people out of bondage. It is probable that in the wilderness struggle he faced the question of whether to lead a revolution which might seat him on a Jewish throne. In any case we know that he refused to join the party of the Zealots. Instead of the sword, he chose the way of the cross, and turning his back on political aspiration he met his death under a trumped-up charge that he was claiming to be "king of the Jews."[8]

The legalism, like the nationalism, of his day Jesus tried to correct by the injection of a new spirit. He did not break with the Jewish law, but with its pettiness and anti-moral elements. The Sermon on the Mount rings with "You have heard that it was said to the men of old, . . . but I say to you . . ." For those who would tithe mint and anise and cummin and neglect the weightier demands of human brotherhood, or make clean the outside of the cup while within was all uncleanness, he had a sharp and stinging word.[9]

The current apocalypticism, with its idea of a divine intervention in the established terrestrial order and a great Last Judgment, Jesus seems at least in part to have taken over. There is difference of opinion among Biblical scholars as to whether such passages as Matthew 24, Matthew 25:31–46 and Mark 13 represent Jesus' own outlook or those of a later interpreter; also, whether they are intended as prophecies of the destruction of Jerusalem, which occurred in 70 A.D., or a general destruction which has not yet come. The consensus

[8]Mt. 27:11, 29, 37.
[9]Mt. 23:23 f.

of opinion is that, with all the problems entailed, we must accept the fact that with others of his time Jesus looked forward to a cataclysmic termination of this earthly regime.

But this is not to say, as has been maintained by some, that his ethical injunctions are therefore to be regarded as an "interim ethic."[10] It may explain in part his reticence on such permanent social issues as war and slavery. But it does not make his ethics either less relevant or less difficult. Whether or not Jesus was an apocalyptist, he enunciated principles permanently adaptable and permanently beyond the possibility of full attainment in this life.

Jesus' apocalypticism was in some respects like that of his time. It is not to deny his divinity to say that he was also human, and in some matters the child of his age. Yet the points in which he differs from the prevailing apocalypticism are more significant than his points of agreement. This was largely non-moral; his view is suffused with moral passion. The great Last Judgment scene of Matthew 25 is of profound Christian significance because it is treatment of one's fellow-man that is made the criterion of a place in God's kingdom. The heart of its message lies in the searching requirement, "Inasmuch as ye have done it unto one of the least of these my brethren, ye have done it unto me" (Mt. 25:40). Current apocalypticism was largely pessimistic and fatalistic; that of Jesus is centered in a serious, but joyous and confident, reliance on God. It is these positive elements which have made it possible, in spite of differences of interpretation as to the eschatological framework, to draw from Jesus' words continuing Christian incentive to faith and moral living.

It is a very important fact that Jesus enunciated principles adaptable to all time. He gave little in the way of precise rules for conduct. He was apparently not much concerned with

[10]Notably by Albert Schweitzer in his *The Quest of the Historical Jesus.*

political schemes or plans for immediate social amelioration. What he was supremely concerned about was the forgiving mercy of God, the remaking of the inner life through repentance, obedience and faith, the spread of love and worship among men. This message has been a dynamic ferment working in all ages since. It is as relevant as ever to our time.

In spite of its being so familiar that we often miss its cutting edge, it may be well now to summarize the principal elements in Jesus' ethical message.

4. *Distinctive Elements in the Ethics of Jesus*

There is little in the moral teaching of Jesus—or, for that matter, in his entire religious outlook—that is not to be found somewhere in the Old Testament. Though he was more than a Jewish prophet he was not less, and his mind and spirit were steeped in the wisdom of his fathers. We shall best understand his uniqueness if we see him in direct continuity with his Jewish past. His uniqueness lies, not in this or that element of teaching, but in the immediacy and responsiveness of his relation to God, his complete embodiment of his message in his living, his unerring insight as to what was true and important in his heritage.

(1) The ethics of Jesus are grounded in his religion. Their keynote is that the moral life centers in the worship of God and in glad obedience to his will. Jesus states this ideal in what he calls the Kingdom of God. Its establishment is the first petition of the Lord's prayer, naturally following from the invocation to worship. The concept is summed up in the two great commandments, both found in the Old Testament but given a new meaning in the setting in which Jesus places them:

> Thou shalt love the Lord thy God with all thy heart, and with all thy soul, and with all thy mind. This is the first and great commandment.

And the second is like unto it, Thou shalt love thy
neighbor as thyself. On these two commandments hang
all the law and the prophets.[11]

(2) Interwoven with this double duty to God and man is
Jesus' use of the term *Father* to designate the nature of God.
There are suggestions of the fatherhood of God in Hosea,
Isaiah and the Psalms, and we found Cleanthes and the Stoics
using this term. But with a difference. In spite of the redeeming mercy of God in the Old Testament and notes of human
brotherhood in Stoicism, one never quite gets away from a
feeling of aloofness in Yahweh and impersonality in the Stoic
Logos. The personal Father God of Jesus is the creator, sus-
tainer, redeemer and loving support of His children. The word
Father is of course a symbol—the symbol of the relationship
of a supreme loving Personality to human persons who ought
to look to Him in humility and trust for forgiveness, moral
guidance and saving help.

Is God the Father of all men? Jesus in teaching us to pray
"Our Father" makes no distinctions, and from this follows the
important correlate that all men are brothers. Paul apparently
believed that sonship to God was acquired by accepting Christ
(Romans 8:15-17, 23) and this is reflected in such statements
as "to all who received him, who believed in his name, he
gave power to become children of God" (John 1:12). The-
ologians, therefore, differ in their views on this question, but
the records we have of Jesus' words seem to indicate that he
simply assumed the universal fatherhood of God and hence
the universal brotherhood of men. This distinction has much
moral significance, for if God is the Father of all, our obligation as Christians is thereby intensified—we are obligated to
regard all men, whatever their faith or status, as likewise sons
of God and persons of supreme worth.

(3) Whatever the answer to this question, we certainly find

[11]Mt. 22:37-40. In the Old Testament, Deut. 6:5 and Lev. 19:18.

in Jesus a new estimate of the worth of every individual in the sight of God. Not because a person is by nature or achievement either good or great, but because he is precious to God, he should be to his fellow-men. One comes upon this on almost every page of the Gospels—in the parables of the lost sheep, the lost coin and the lost boy (Luke 15); in Jesus' plea that "not one of these little ones" should perish or be caused to stumble (Mt. 18:6, 14); in making destiny in the Last Judgment depend on how one has treated "one of the least of these my brethren" (Mt. 25:40); in the assurance that the God who cares for the sparrows and the lilies will care for men (Mt. 6:25–30). Much as he hated sin he could see the hidden worth in the sinner, hence his kindness and reassuring word of power to the harlot and adulterer (Luke 7:36–50; John 4:5–26). This principle lies at the root of the Christian impulse to secure a social order in which all men may express their best and be judged by their intrinsic worth.

(4) With love as the central virtue, the accompanying virtues are those, not of conspicuous strength, but of self-effacing tenderness. The blessed are the humble, the compassionate, the pure in heart, the peace-loving (Mt. 5:3–12). The supreme goal is a determined quest for the way of righteousness in the face of opposition, not with any Stoic self-confidence, but with humble and unfaltering reliance on the power of God's living presence (Mt. 6:5–8).

(5) Jesus had a great sense of the integral unity of right *motive* as the source of right behavior and of right *fruits* as the measure of the moral quality of an attitude or act. Both aspects of this insight are illustrated, not systematically but vitally, in the Sermon on the Mount. Those of his followers— and they are not a few—who have emphasized one side or the other of this two-sided moral imperative have failed to follow his leading at this point.

Repeatedly Jesus affirmed that it is not enough to refrain

from the outward forms of evil, or do good for the sake of the plaudits of men. This stress on "ethical inwardness" and right motive is set in sharp contrast in the Sermon on the Mount with a legalistic morality which would find man's whole duty in the keeping of the Commandments.

> You have heard that it was said to men of old, "You shall not kill; and whoever kills shall be liable to judgment." But I say to you that every one who is angry with his brother shall be liable to judgment. . . .

> You have heard that it was said, "You shall not commit adultery." But I say to you that every one who looks at a woman lustfully has already committed adultery with her in his heart. . . .

> You have heard that it was said, "You shall love your neighbor and hate your enemy." But I say to you, Love your enemies and pray for those who persecute you, so that you may be sons of your Father who is in heaven; for he makes his sun rise on the evil and the good, and sends rain on the just and the unjust.[12]

Yet is the motive all that matters? Jesus was not a pragmatist or a utilitarian in the sense in which these terms are generally used. Nevertheless, he had a profound sense of the importance of results—with the results to be measured not by human standards but by God's, and not in earthly success but in spiritual treasure. This appears clearly in the second clause of each of the Beatitudes, and in many such passages as these:

> Beware of practicing your piety before men in order to be seen by them; for then you will have no reward from your Father who is in heaven. . . .

> Let your light so shine before men, that they may see your good works and give glory to your Father who is in heaven. . . .

> Every tree that does not bear good fruit is cut down and

12Mt. 5:21, 27, 43–46. R. S. V.

thrown into the fire. Thus you will know them by their fruits.[13]

(6) Jesus made unqualified demands. He never watered down God's righteousness to easy human performance. To love one's enemies, for example, is no simple or natural achievement. How, then, gain the power? Jesus was apparently not concerned with the moral dilemma posed by what is now called perfectionism.[14] His concern was with living in right relations to God. His answer to the hard demands of life in the kingdom was not an assurance of human sinlessness, but of the new birth by the gift of God. "Truly, truly, I say to you, unless one is born anew he cannot see the kingdom of God" (John 3:3). When Nicodemus cried out in bewilderment Jesus assured him of the reality of this sublime mystery of spiritual birth and baptism into new power—a mystery not to be grasped by thought but accepted as God's loving gift to men (John 3:1–16). The Church has sometimes distorted this doctrine of regeneration and made it the basis of divisive theological strife, but as Jesus stated it, it is a simple and beautiful assurance that God stands ready to give moral cleansing and newness of vision to him who will receive it in penitence and trust.

(7) Again and again Jesus says that the way to true greatness is through service. In other words, the true self-realization—the living of a full, rich, abundant life—is through self-renunciation and self-giving love. "If any man would come after me, let him deny himself and take up his cross and follow me. For whoever would save his life will lose it, and whoever loses his life for my sake will find it" (Mt. 16:24, 25). "Whoever would be great among you must be your servant. For the Son of man also came not to be served but to serve, and to

---

[13]Mt. 6:1; 5:16; 7:19, 20. R. S. V.
[14]See section 8 of this chapter for some further observations on the absoluteness of Jesus' ethics.

give his life as a ransom for many" (Mk. 10:43, 45). In this paradoxical doctrine, so foreign to the classical pagan spirit, lies the perennial power of the Christian gospel to call men away from the allurements of ease, comfort and material reward to live in joyous sacrifice for great ideals.

(8) Finally, the most distinctive element in the Christian ethic is Jesus himself. Other men have taught sublimely, but no other man ever lived with so perfect a harmony of precept and deed. No other man has so challenged the world's allegiance, not alone by what he said, but by what he *was*. Jesus believed himself to have a divine mission to reveal the way of God to men, and he embodied in a life which led him to the cross the self-giving, suffering love of God for men. This is the moral meaning of the incarnation, and if we do not let its creedal wrappings obscure its inner meaning, we shall find in it the high-water mark of ethical idealism.

5. Jesus' Economic Ethics

Such are the general trends of Jesus' ethical teaching. We must ask now what this means in terms of our major human problems.

There is a tendency on the part of some in our time to equate capitalism—the system of free enterprise, private profit and private ownership—with a Christian society if not with the kingdom of God; on the part of others, to decry it as contrary to the teachings of Jesus. The truth lies in between. Jesus, of course, said nothing about capitalism, for except in the general form of the acquisitive impulse of men, it was unheard of in his day. But he denounced selfish money-getting with stinging words. There is nothing clearer in his teaching than his awareness of the perils of wealth to the soul. "You cannot serve God and Mammon" (Mt. 6:24). "It is easier for a camel to go through the eye of a needle, than for a rich man to enter the

kingdom of God" (Mk. 10:25). Those who try to tone down
this statement by making it apply to a mythical hole in the
Jerusalem wall miss the splendid hyperbole by which Jesus
stated the spiritual dangers inherent in wealth-getting. He
knew that no man could serve two masters, and that the selfish
quest of wealth dwarfs and destroys personality and dulls the
sense of brotherhood which is the very essence of the kingdom of heaven. "With God all things are possible" gives no
easy way of escape. Rather, so deep-rooted in man is the love
of possessions that only divine power can break its hold. The
injunction to the rich young man, "Go, sell what you have,
and give to the poor, and you will have treasure in heaven"
(Mk. 10:21), is not a universal summons to voluntary poverty
and alms-giving; it is an affirmation of Jesus' conviction that
only through the rooting out of cupidity can the heart be
opened to receive God's treasure.

Repeatedly, Jesus affirms the supremacy of spiritual over
material wealth. "A man's life does not consist in the abundance of his possessions" (Luke 12:15). "Seek first his [God's]
kingdom and his righteousness" (Mt. 6:33). "Do not lay up
for yourselves treasures on earth, where moth and rust con-
sume and where thieves break in and steal, but lay up for
yourselves treasures in heaven" (Mt. 6:19). Earthly treasures
are perilous and evanescent, spiritual treasures are eternal. The
rich fool wanted to build bigger barns, thinking he had goods
laid up for many years, when God said to him, "Fool! This
night your soul is required of you" (Luke 12:16-21). Thus
unwise, says Jesus, is he that lays up treasure for himself and
is not rich toward God.

Though Jesus clearly puts the wealth of the inner life in the
foreground, it is to distort his words to assume that he had
no concern for the material foundations of life. When he taught
his disciples to say "Give us this day our daily bread," he
probably meant material bread—the physical basis of suste-

nance. He enjoined men not to be overanxious about what to eat or drink or wear, but with no suggestion that these matters are unimportant. "Your heavenly Father knows that you need them all. But seek first his kingdom and his righteousness, and all these things shall be yours as well" (Mt. 6:32, 33). He says comparatively little about almsgiving, save to protest against ostentation in giving (Mt. 6:2–4), but it is clear that he wanted none to suffer from lack of the material necessities of life.

Certain of the parables have an economic reference, though it is difficult to know just how far to push them with fidelity to the simplicity of Jesus' own economic outlook. There is the parable of the talents, with the faithful servants' added reward for diligent use, and the paradoxical, "To every one who has will more be given, and he will have abundance; but from him who has not even what he has will be taken away" (Mt. 25: 14–29). To quote this, as is sometimes done even today, to justify riches as a divine reward for diligence with the inference that the poor are poor only because they are lazy, is to pervert Jesus' teaching.[15] The simpler meaning is the truer one—that every person is expected not to squander or bury his talents, whether material or personal, but to use them as gifts of God in the spirit of stewardship.

There is the parable, still more puzzling from ordinary human standards, of the laborers in the vineyard who stood idle and unemployed until the eleventh hour and then received as much as those who had worked all day (Mt. 20:1–16). Is Jesus here sanctioning the giving of equal pay to those who work and to those who do not? It is in keeping with his spirit that those who are unemployed through no fault of theirs should not be allowed to suffer, but this is probably not the meaning of the parable. Rather, in the free, uncalculating mercy of God

[15]See Max Weber's *The Protestant Ethic and the Spirit of Capitalism* or the author's *John Calvin: the Man and His Ethics* for a discussion of how this idea during the formative period of capitalism gave religious sanction to the acquisitive impulse.

He gives rich reward to those who come late into His kingdom as well as to those who have borne the burden and heat of the day.

6. Jesus and the State

Jesus says much less about the State than about the use of wealth. The reason is easy to discover. He was profoundly concerned with announcing not social or political plans but principles of personal living. The greed for gold ran directly counter to higher loyalties, and must be quenched to enter into the kingdom of God. Political loyalty, on the other hand, could ordinarily exist side by side with loyalty to God. Concerned as he was to set up a new spiritual kingdom, he probably never envisaged clearly the clash of loyalties in which his later followers would find themselves. He foresaw, of course, that like himself they would inevitably be persecuted for their faith; and he saw how political aspiration was quenching the spiritual power of the Judaism of his day. But that nationalism should actually become "man's other religion" was a development which lay in the unborn future. For his own day, it was enough to avoid the compromising of his message by the political entanglements in which the Pharisees tried by trickery to involve him, and with the simple "Render to Caesar the things that are Caesar's and to God the things that are God's" he could pass on to the announcing of the two great commandments of love.

But this does not mean that Jesus had no political wisdom. Without using the word he proclaimed and lived by the democracy that is inherent in the infinite worth of every individual to God. It was Paul who said, "There is neither Jew nor Greek, there is neither slave nor free, there is neither male nor female; for you are all one in Christ Jesus" (Gal. 3:28), but Paul would not have said this had not Jesus set the priceless worth of every soul in the sight of God in the forefront of his teaching. Without a single direct word on the subject of slavery or of sex equality, Jesus set currents moving which were to lead to the abolition of overt slavery throughout the Christian world and go far towards the opening up of equal opportunities to women. Similarly, without a word on democracy as a political system, Jesus gave the major incentive to a trend which, blending with the Stoic concept of world brotherhood, made for the recognition that the spiritual equality of all men has its political correlate.

Jesus announced another spiritual principle of great political significance when he declared that true greatness lies in service and that opportunity entails responsibility. "Every one to whom much is given, of him will much be required" (Luke 12:48). The reply which he gave to the ambitious mother of Zebedee's sons if taken seriously would transform political life (Mt. 20:20–28). Its import is reflected in the aphorism of Grover Cleveland, formerly much quoted and still true, "A public office is a public trust."

This carries us to another of Jesus' magnificent paradoxes, the union of non-resistance to the doer of a personal injury with vigorous action against evil. The doctrine of turning the other cheek and walking the second mile is sublimely Christian (Mt. 5:38–41), but so is the driving of the money-changers from the temple (Mt. 21:12, 13). Jesus would tolerate no wrong, and he did not hesitate to use words, and if necessary whips, to correct the evils he saw in need of remedy. People who say that Christian leaders should not "meddle" in political or economic matters but should give themselves solely to the spread of the spirit of Jesus have missed the fact that one vital aspect of the "spirit of Jesus" is a challenge to evil wherever found. Jesus was perhaps a pacifist, but certainly no "passivist."

The accuracy of calling Jesus a pacifist depends on one's definition of this term. It is impossible to find in his recorded words any clear and unequivocal statement either against or in favor of personal participation in war. This fact has, of course, led equally sincere Christians to hold opposite views on this crucial problem, and has caused anguish of soul to young men who deeply desire to do what is Christian. Texts can be quoted on either side, but an honest reading of the context obliges one to recognize that no single passage is conclusive. "I have not come to bring peace, but a sword" (Mt. 10:34), when seen in its context, can scarcely mean other than a foreshadowing of the persecutions and conflicting family loyalties which the Christian way of life would summon his disciples to face. It is a warning that suffering will come by the sword, not a call to use the sword. But on the other hand, no complete answer to the problem can be drawn from the word spoken in the garden of Gethsemane when one of his disciples impetuously struck off the ear of the servant of the high priest, "Put your sword back into its place; for all who take the sword will perish by the sword" (Mt. 26:52).

Some things we can know with certainty about Jesus' attitude. There is the sublime statement in the Beatitudes, "Blessed are the peacemakers, for they shall be called sons of God" (Mt. 5:9). He enjoined men to love their enemies and to pray for their persecutors (Mt. 5:44). The injunction to minister to the need of the hungry, the thirsty, the stranger, the naked, the sick, the imprisoned (Mt. 25:31–46) is expressed in universal and not in nationalistic terms. The conditions of modern war are in many if not all respects antithetical to these directives—and there is no disputing the fact that these directives accord with the total spirit and message of Jesus. Yet the question remains one on which Christians sincerely differ. One's personal decision must be made on the basis of the fullest possible application of the commandment of love in the situation within which we live.

7. *Jesus and the Family*

Jesus regarded the family as the basic social institution. In this he showed himself a typical Jew, for although the early Old Testament does not give woman a high place, family ties were always highly regarded and the foundations laid for the close-knit family life which has characterized Judaism through the centuries. Hosea's love for his erring wife and the tribute to the virtuous woman in Proverbs 31 portray the family ideal at its best. It is not strange, therefore, that Jesus took the family as his symbol of the relation of all men as brothers, children of the one Father, and this conviction of the basic importance of family love must have been deepened by his own early years in the Nazareth home.

Jesus' teaching regarding the family is full of sublime paradoxes through which runs a consistent demand for purity of the inner life and reverence for personality. There is the assumption that marriage is not only a legitimate and natural but a divinely ordained institution, the closest human tie (Mt. 19:4, 5). Yet he says also that some may need to renounce marriage for the sake of the kingdom (Mt. 19:12), and that the willingness to sever family connections to become his follower is the supreme test of loyalty (Mt. 19:29, 30; Luke 9:57–62). This the medieval church unfortunately interpreted as an injunction to celibacy as the superior moral state. But Jesus was no ascetic, and he probably meant by it only that some of his followers, like himself, must find their widest service in a work that denied to them the joys of family life.

Jesus' teaching regarding adultery shocked many of his contemporaries who believed with the Deuteronomic law that the person guilty of adultery must be stoned. "Neither do I condemn you; go, and do not sin again" (John 8:11) stands in a passage of which the authenticity is disputed on textual grounds, but it is true to the spirit of Jesus. Taken with his words on inner purity in the Sermon on the Mount (Mt. 5:27–32), it is a call to the casting out of sin without treating the sinner as a social outcast. Hester Prynne's accusers in *The Scarlet Letter* are still too numerous among so-called Christians to make this distinction an outmoded concept.

If Jesus' attitude toward adultery seemed to some too lax, his teaching regarding divorce must have seemed intolerant and fanatical. The rabbis of his day were inclined to give a very broad interpretation to the Mosaic[16] provision for a bill of divorcement (Deut. 24:1). Jesus' declaration that adultery is the only lawful ground for the severing of the marriage tie must have caused something of a shock even to his disciples, for they said if this were the case, one had better not marry at all (Mt. 19:7–10)! In the account in Mark, he is even more unequivocal, making no exception, "Whoever divorces his wife and marries another, commits adultery against her" (Mk. 10:11). What we shall make of this as a specific regulation in the present day is a matter of diverse opinion, but the principle is clear—Jesus would tolerate no unions hastily entered into and as easily dissolved, nor would he permit divorces to be bought by a few months' residence for the sake of marrying another. If Jesus' ideal of marriage as a permanent and sacred relation were now dominant instead of hedonistic sensualism, the divorce problem would largely take care of itself.

Jesus exalted the position of woman not so much by what he said as by the whole tenor of his life. Among his closest friends were Mary and Martha whom he seems often to have visited at their home in Bethany, and he was not afraid to accept Mary Magdalene's tribute of understanding friendship (Luke 7:36–50). He healed women as freely as men (Mt. 8:14, 15; 9:18–25; 15:21–28), and some of his greatest words were

---

[16]Modern scholarship does not hold to its Mosaic origin, but it was currently so regarded.

spoken to a woman of a despised race (John 4:5–26). Though he clearly put duty to God above family ties (Mt. 12:46–50), among his last words at the crucifixion was the injunction to the beloved disciple to care for his mother (John 19:26, 27). If these contacts now seem natural and lacking in anything extraordinary, it is because centuries of Christian teaching has lifted the status of women to a position far above that reached in any other culture.

Jesus' exaltation of child life (Mt. 19:13–15) is one of the most original of his teachings, and out of it has come in our own day either directly or indirectly most of our present concern to foster the free development and prevent the exploitation of childhood. In this, as in the position accorded to women, the influence of Christian ideals is very apparent when set in contrast with conditions in the Orient and other non-Christian areas. While Jesus gave parents a new impulse to prize their children as beings of intrinsic worth, "for of such is the kingdom of heaven," he also laid upon children the duty to reverence and care for their parents, and declared that none should evade the fifth commandment by declaring as *Corban* (given to God) what ought to go to one's father or mother (Mk. 7:10–13). In this concern for filial duty he was thoroughly Jewish, yet here as in all his teachings he added a new meaning and incentive to an old idea.

8. Are Jesus' Teachings Practical?

It is not impossible to raise charges against the ethics of Jesus. Not only has his moral outlook been called repeatedly impractical; it has been charged with intolerance, vacillation, asceticism, other-worldliness, effeminacy, disregard of intellectual and civic interests. While these charges are truer of his later followers than himself, and never true of the trend of Christian thought as a whole, both the single-mindedness and the many-sidedness of Jesus' thought made distortion easy. There is in Jesus that which makes his ethic adaptable to every age, and human fallibility in the attempt to apply eternal principles has made rules and followed procedures falling far short of the sublime insights of the man of Nazareth.

Yet to say that the ethical teachings of Jesus either do not or cannot "work" is to fall into a too easy oversimplification. Work for what? For the improvement, enrichment and lifting of human welfare and happiness, or for the complete elimination of human sin and misery to usher in a utopian society? Those who charge impracticality against the perfectionism of Jesus tacitly assume the second of these alternatives as their standard of reference, and then point out the disparity between the best human achievement and this goal. "You, therefore, must be perfect, as your heavenly Father is perfect" (Matt. 5:48), says Jesus, and it is obvious that no Christian is perfect and no society perfectly Christian. Does this, then, rob his words of relevance to our sinful, tragic human plight?

By no means. The absolute demands of Jesus, centering in the requirement of perfect love to God and one's neighbor, have been through the ages and are today the most effective force in the world for the improvement of individual and social living. This is not to say that on earth the requirement will ever be fully met. The verb is "must," not "shall be."[17] This eternal *must* is a perennial challenge to the widening and deepening of Christian love, to an awareness of individual and social sin, to a determined attack on every form of evil through the power and grace of God. The absolute imperatives of Jesus carry with them not prediction of complete fulfillment, but as imperatives and goals and sources of judgment the profoundest ethical realism.

To say that the Christian ethic does not or cannot work in

[17]Note that at this point, both the King James and the Revised Standard Versions are more accurate than the futuristic rendering of the American Standard Version.

practice is to blind ourselves to the evidences; for tested by
Jesus' own pragmatic standard, "By their fruits ye shall know
them," it *has* worked. Early in Christian history it led to the
abolition of infanticide and the cruelty of gladiatorial orgies,
and through the centuries it has been fostering an humanitarian concern for healing of mind and body, care of the weak,
the poor and the unfortunate, and the enlargement of life for
all. Christian ideals have permeated and created some of the
world's greatest art, music and literature. In the Dark Ages,
the Church kept learning alive; and to our own day it has
spread learning in the founding and maintenance of schools
and colleges, in movements for universal education, in the extension of education through missionary effort around the
world. Christian idealists actuated by the message of Jesus are
among the most active leaders in movements for racial and
international peace, economic justice, domestic purity, preven-
tion of crime and social maladjustment; and many who have
severed connection with the Christian Church owe their social
ideals to a family or community environment permeated with
its influence. Jesus' ideal of the infinite worth of persons has
lifted child life and womanhood wherever it has gone; it has
abolished many forms of slavery; it lies at the root of democracy. There are long steps yet to take, but we have gone far
enough to prove the basic practicality of Jesus' way of life.

9. *The Ethics of Paul*

Were we to use the term "Christian ethics" in the first sense
indicated at the beginning of this chapter, that is, as the ethics
of Jesus, it would be possible now to close the book and call
the task, if not completed, at least concluded. But while Christian ethics ought always to center in the life and teachings
of Jesus as its primary source, there are two reasons why we
cannot thus limit the term. The first is that, historically, the

record of the life and words of Jesus stems from the experience of the primitive church. Jesus lived and taught before there was any church, but what we know of him comes from the memories and fragmentary records preserved by the Church. Consequently, Paul's letters considerably antedate the Gospels.

The second reason is that in the structure of Christian worship and teaching through the centuries, Paul's letters have ranked with the Gospels as scripture "inspired by God and profitable for teaching, for reproof, for correction, and for training in righteousness" (II Tim. 3:16). The basing of Christian morality equally on all parts of the New Testament, and on Pauline theology equally with the less theological but more vital insights of Jesus, has had far-reaching consequences. Some of these consequences have been very helpful, for Paul has much to teach us; some have led to a distortion of the sources, and hence of the true nature, of Christian morality.

We shall not attempt to deal with the ethics of Paul at such length as has been accorded to this, at best cursory, analysis of the ethics of Jesus. This is because the moral insights of Jesus are primary for Christian thought, Paul's are secondary and derivative. But let us see what he has given us. And, first, let us see what there is about the man and his experience that has to be borne in mind as we look at his moral admonitions.

a. *The setting of Paul's teaching.* We must note, to begin with, that he was a Jew, "a Pharisee, a son of Pharisees" (Acts 23:6) who by a dramatic conversion had become a Christian. His words to the Corinthian church, "Therefore, if any one is in Christ, he is a new creation" (II Cor. 5:17), apply to no one more aptly than to Paul himself. As a consequence, he broke with Judaism far more radically than Jesus did. Jesus could say, "Think not that I have come to abolish the law and the prophets; I have come not to abolish them but to fulfil them" (Matt. 5:17). Paul, though he regards the law as our school-

master, or custodian, to bring us to Christ (Gal. 3:24), speaks
many words about its inadequacy to one who has been justified by faith in Christ. In fact, so sharply does he contrast the
law with the gospel in depreciation of the former that he has
been charged with antinomianism, though the frequency and
intensity of his moral admonitions give evidence that it is
the Jewish *ceremonial* and not the *moral* law that he is abro-
gating.

In the second place, Paul's was a volatile and many-sided
personality, and not every side of his nature was exemplary.
The sinlessness of Jesus, though sometimes disputed, has on
the whole been regarded as a fact—indeed, as a necessary fact
if we are to see in him the perfect incarnation of God. Paul's
words, as we noted above, have often been taken as "gospel
truth." But Paul himself has rarely, if ever, been regarded as
a perfect person. It is not to impugn but to high-light his greatness to say that there are paradoxes in his nature, and that
his human frailties were not all purged away by his conversion. He had a "sharp contention"—we might call it a first-rate
quarrel—with Barnabas, so that they parted company (Acts
15:39). He could be tender and understanding towards the
sinful (Gal. 6:1); he could also upon occasion use harsh and
stinging words (Rom. 1:28–32; Gal. 2:11; 3:1; 5:19–21). He
could be humble, calling himself the least of all the saints
(Eph. 3:8) and glorying only in the gift of God's strength in
his weakness (II Cor. 12:9). But he could recount, apparently
with considerable satisfaction, all that he had endured for
Christ (II Cor. 11:16–32)! He could in immortal words call
men to the pursuit of the best things, then cap the injunction
with the appeal to follow the example they had seen in him
(Phil. 4:8, 9). Paul was a stalwart, a courageous, a truly great
man; he was not always humble, forgiving, or free from prejudice.

A third thing to remember in interpreting Paul's words—and

failure to remember it has caused much distortion and narrowness—is that almost everything he wrote was "situation-condi-
tioned." That is, he wrote to give needed counsel when situations had arisen in the churches which in his judgment required
such Christian counsel. He never had any idea that he was
writing Scripture, or that nineteen centuries later his words
would be read as "gospel truth." He simply wrote what he
felt the Lord had moved him to write in his capacity as missionary and pastor-at-large. In fact, he was not always sure
that the Lord had thus given him the right word, and with
more honesty than some of his successors he says so in I Cor.
7:25, "Now concerning the unmarried, I have no command of
the Lord, but I give my opinion as one who by the Lord's
mercy is trustworthy." He goes on to say that in view of the
impending distress the married should stay married but the
unmarried should not marry—a bit of advice hardly now applicable to all cases. He advised the Corinthian women to keep
silent in church (I Cor. 14:34) and not to attend worship with
their heads uncovered (I Cor. 11:13)—counsel that had a
reason in a day when only women of loose morals made themselves publicly conspicuous, but not to be taken as injunctions
for all time. One of his greatest utterances is, "Where the
Spirit of the Lord is, there is freedom" (II Cor. 3:17), and one
of the things he would have least desired would be the citing
of his words to place fetters on Christian speech and action
in years to come.

b. *The law and the gospel.* The element in Paul's teaching
which most directly sets a framework for his ethics is what
he says about the relations of the gospel to the law. In the
numerous passages where he speaks of the law he does not
distinguish whether he means by it the Shema, or the Decalogue, or the many provisions of the various Judaic codes,
often more ritualistic than moral, or the Pentateuch, or the

entire Old Testament way of viewing God's commands under the covenant with Israel. Though it would have been helpful to us if he had drawn sharper distinctions at this point, he did not ask our questions. He did not do so because the overwhelming experience of his conversion to the Christian faith, which had made him a "new creation," led him to put most of his emphasis on the difference Christ makes.

For Paul, to be "in Christ" apparently meant not only to be in a new relation to God the Father, but to be in the Spirit, and in the Christian community, and by anticipation, in the Kingdom of God. All are aspects of one experience—that of being a changed man by the grace of God in Christ. He does not elaborate a doctrine of the Trinity—indeed, as a *doctrine* the Trinity had not emerged in Paul's time though there are foregleams of it in II Cor. 13:14. What he is very sure of is that God through His redemptive act in Christ has made it possible for men to be "more than conquerors through him who loved us" (Rom. 8:37). And through this divine act, the difficulties and problems men encounter in the attempt to keep the law (Rom. 7) melt away before a great new power that gives victory and hope. From the human end, what is required of us is not moral perfection or legal exactitude, to which in our best efforts we cannot attain, but simply *faith* and *love*.

Paul's doctrine of justification by faith, the keynote of his letters to the Romans and Galatians, and his ode to love as the highest of spiritual gifts in I Cor. 13, are imperishable contributions of his mind and heart. It is not by accident that the first became the basis of the Protestant Reformation and the second is among the greatest and most familiar passages of all literature. What is sometimes overlooked is that Paul stressed both notes equally, and both faith and love are required for meeting the high demands of the gospel. Where they exist the law is inconsequential; where they are not found the law has no redemptive power.

As we noted earlier, it is to misread Paul to suppose that his attitude toward the law meant anything like moral anarchy. There is scarcely a chapter in his writings in which he does not plead for a high morality on the basis of faithful obedience to God as He has come to us in Christ, and more loving concern for one another in Christian fellowship. This is not to say Paul was right on every concrete issue. At some important points his vision was limited. But in his basic moral outlook, he was at one with Jesus in his insistence on faith and love as the foundations of right living, with hope as the fruit of both.

c. *Paul's social ethics.* It is when we look at what Paul says on matters like family relations, economic conditions and the Christian's relation to the State, that we see most clearly both his moral wisdom and its limitations. There is a great charter of democracy in Gal. 3:28, "There is neither Jew nor Greek, there is neither slave nor free, there is neither male nor female; for you are all one in Christ Jesus." Yet he had very little idea of the Christian family as an equal partnership of the sexes. He seems to have thought celibacy the preferable state, with marriage as a sort of prophylaxis against incontinence (I Cor. 7:9), and wifely subjection to one's husband is enjoined. If Paul wrote the letter to the Ephesians, he made a rather drastic affirmation of male superiority when he said, "Wives, be subject to your husbands, as to the Lord. For the husband is the head of the wife as Christ is the head of the church" (Eph. 5:22, 23). In similar vein is the statement, "Neither was man created for woman, but woman for man" (I Cor. 11:9).

Social distinctions were not abrogated, but transcended in Christian love, when Paul sent Onesimus back to his master Philemon with the word, "No longer as a slave but more than a slave, as a beloved brother" (Philemon v. 16). The early Christian fellowship apparently embraced not only both men and women, but people of many occupations whom Paul freely welcomed as being with him in Christ. Yet his "Servants, obey in all things your masters" (Col. 3:22; Eph. 6:5), and "Everyone should remain in the state in which he was called" (I Cor. 7:20) indicate little awareness of economic democracy, and have many times been quoted as a bulwark of social conservatism.

Paul was undoubtedly wise in counseling the little Christian group, living as citizens of the kingdom of God in occupied Roman territory, not to launch a political revolution. In this setting, "Let every soul be subject unto the higher powers" (Rom. 13:1) is prudential realism. But this with the sentence that follows it, "The powers that be are ordained of God," has repeatedly been used to reinforce the *status quo*, to defend a theory of the divine right of kings, to sanction acquiescence even in Nazi tyranny up to the point when the ruler as anti-Christ defied the lordship of Christ.

Of such passages two comments must be made: first, that Paul was a man of his age, of far-reaching vision but without a full awareness of where the ethics of Jesus might lead when applied to the problems of human society, and second, that he had a greatness of insight lacking in the view of many who have quoted his words to reinforce their prejudices. It is significant that just a few lines beyond Romans 13:1 we come upon the timeless words, "Love does no wrong to a neighbor; therefore love is the fulfilling of the law" (Rom. 13:10).

Here our study must end. It is not finished, for nineteen centuries have been painting an increasingly intricate design upon the canvas where the outlines were sketched so long ago. But lest we lose the outlines in preoccupation with the often glorious, often sordid, many times baffling details of the picture, it is well to call to mind the great, basic, bold strokes that set the pattern of our civilization and our morals. These strokes we have tried as faithfully as possible in these pages to portray.

SELECTED BIBLIOGRAPHY

A. GENERAL SURVEYS

Dewey, John and Tufts, J. H., *Ethics,* Part I. (New York: Holt, 1908, 1925)

Hobhouse, L. T., *Morals in Evolution.* (New York: Holt, 1921)

Kropotkin, Petr A., *Ethics, Origin and Development.* Translated from the Russian by L. S. Friedland and J. R. Proshnikoff. (New York: Dial Press, 1936)

Myers, P. V. N., *History as Past Ethics.* (Boston: Ginn, 1913)

Riley, Woodbridge, *Men and Morals.* (New York: Doubleday, 1929)

Saunders, Kenneth, *The Ideals of East and West.* (New York: Macmillan; Cambridge: Cambridge University Press, 1934)

Sneath, E. H., ed., *The Evolution of Ethics.* (New Haven: Yale University Press; London: Oxford University Press, 1927)

Toynbee, Arnold J., *A Study of History.* Abridgement by D. C. Somervell. (New York and London: Oxford University Press, 1946)

Wells, H. G., *The Outline of History.* Vol. I. (New York: Macmillan, 1920)

Westermarck, E. A., *The Origin and Development of the Moral Ideas.* Vols. I and II. (London and New York: Macmillan, 1906–08)

Wright, William K., *General Introduction to Ethics.* Part I. (New York: Macmillan, 1929)

B. PRIMITIVE MORALITY

Breasted, J. H., *The Conquest of Civilization.* Part I. (New York and London: Harpers, 1926)

Fraser, James G., *The Golden Bough.* Abridged edition. (New York: Macmillan, 1922, 1940)

Malinowski, B., *The Foundations of Faith and Morals.* (London: Oxford University Press, 1936)

Mead, Margaret, *Cooperation and Competition Among Primitive Peoples.* (New York: McGraw Hill, 1937)

Sumner, W. G., *Folkways.* (Boston: Ginn, 1907, 1913)

245

C. EARLY CIVILIZATIONS

Breasted, J. H., *The Conquest of Civilization*. Part II. (New York and London: Harpers, 1926)

Breasted, J. H., *The Dawn of Conscience*. (New York and London: Scribners, 1933)

Brodeur, A. G., *The Pageant of Civilization*. Chs. I–IV. (New York: McBride, 1931)

Childe, V. G., *New Light on the Most Ancient East*. (New York: Praeger, 1953)

Durant, Will, *The Story of Civilization*. Vol. I. (New York: Simon and Schuster, 1935)

Finegan, Jack, *Light From the Ancient Past*. (Princeton: Princeton University Press, 1946)

Frankfort, Henri, *The Intellectual Adventure of Ancient Man*. (Chicago: University of Chicago Press, 1946)

Wilson, John A., *The Burden of Egypt*. (Chicago: University of Chicago Press, 1951)

D. GREEK AND ROMAN ETHICS

Brodeur, A. G., *The Pageant of Civilization*. Chs. V, VI. (New York: McBride, 1931)

Dickinson, G. Lowes, *The Greek View of Life*. (New York: Doubleday, 1925; Boston: Beacon Press, 1951)

Durant, Will, *The Story of Civilization*. Vols. II and III. (New York: Simon and Schuster, 1939, 1944)

Durant, Will, *The Story of Philosophy*. Chs. I, II. (New York: Simon and Schuster, 1926)

Hyde, William D., *Five Great Philosophies of Life*. (New York: Macmillan, 1911)

Tsanoff, R. A., *The Moral Ideals of Our Civilization*. Ch. I. (New York: Dutton, 1942)

Warbeke, John M., *The Searching Mind of Greece*. (New York: Crofts, 1930)

See also any standard history of philosophy. Basic primary sources are Plato, *The Republic, Apology, Crito, Phaedo;* Aristotle, *Nichomachean Ethics;* Marcus Aurelius, *Meditations;* Epictetus, *Discourses;* Cicero, *De Finibus, De Amicitia.*

E. HEBREW MORALITY

Baab, Otto J., *The Theology of the Old Testament*. Chs. V, VI. (New York: Abingdon, 1949)

Kent, Charles F., *Israel's Laws and Legal Documents*. (New York: Scribners, 1907)

McCown, C. C., *The Genesis of the Social Gospel*. Chs. V–IX. (New York and London: Knopf, 1929)

Mitchell, H. G., *The Ethics of the Old Testament*. (Chicago: University of Chicago Press, 1912)

Scott, R. B. Y., *The Relevance of the Prophets*. (New York: Macmillan, 1944)

Smith, J. M. P., *The Moral Life of the Hebrews*. (Chicago: University of Chicago Press, 1923)

Smith, J. M. P., *The Origin and History of Hebrew Law*. (Chicago: University of Chicago Press, 1931)

Snaith, Norman H., *The Distinctive Ideas of the Old Testament*. Chs. III–VI. (London: Epworth Press, 1944)

F. THE ETHICS OF THE NEW TESTAMENT

1. *Inclusive Treatments*

Cave, Sydney, *The Christian Way*. (London: Nisbet, 1949)

Grant, F. C., *An Introduction to New Testament Thought*. Ch. XII. (New York: Abingdon, 1950)

Ramsey, Paul, *Basic Christian Ethics*. (New York: Scribners, 1950)

Scott, C. A. A., *New Testament Ethics*. (New York: Macmillan, 1930)

Spencer, F. A. M., *The Ethics of the Gospel*. (London: Allen and Unwin, 1925)

2. *The Ethical Teachings of Jesus*

Branscomb, Harvie, *The Teachings of Jesus*. (Nashville: Cokesbury, 1931)

Bultmann, Rudolf, *Jesus and the Word*. (New York: Scribners, 1934)

Dibelius, Martin, *Jesus*. Chs. V–VIII. (Philadelphia: Westminster, 1949)

Dibelius, Martin, *The Sermon on the Mount*. (New York: Scribners, 1940)

King, H. C., *The Ethics of Jesus*. (New York: Macmillan, 1910)

Knox, John, *The Man Christ Jesus*. (Chicago: Willett Clark, 1942)

Manson, T. W., *The Teachings of Jesus*. (Cambridge: Cambridge University Press, 1943)

Scott, E. F., *The Ethical Teaching of Jesus*. (New York: Macmillan, 1924)

Wilder, A. N., *Eschatology and Ethics in the Teachings of Jesus*. (New York: Harpers, 1939)

3. *The Ethical Teachings of Paul*

Andrews, Mary E., *The Ethical Teachings of Paul*. (Chapel Hill: University of North Carolina Press, 1934)

Enslin, M. S., *The Ethics of Paul*. (New York and London: Harpers, 1930)

Rall, H. F., *According to Paul*. (New York: Scribners, 1945)

INDEX

Abraham, 91 n., 92, 93, 105, 126
Absalom, 96, 104, 114
Absolute demands of Jesus, 217, 227, 237
Academy, 180, 190, 192
Achan, 18, 19
"Admonitions of Ipuwer," 52 f.
Adoni-bezek, 102 f.
Adultery, 23, 80, 81, 106, 134, 196, 234 f.
Aeschylus, 151, 158, 159 n., 166, 167
Agape, 189, 217. See Love.
Agricultural society, primitive, 15, 17, 18, 21; Egyptian, 40; Babylonian, 82; Hebrew, 88, 94, 99, 109, 117, 134; Greek, 153, 155
Ahab, 111, 120
Ahriman, 74, 83
Ahura Mazda, 74, 83
Akkad, Akkadians, 61, 63 f., 66
Alabaster, carving in, 67, 69
Albertson, C. C., 58 n., 183 n., 185 n.
Alexander the Great, 46, 98, 142, 177, 191
Alexandria, 46 f., 98, 146
Aliens, treatment of, 23 f., 101–05, 108, 141, 161, 198
Alphabet, origins of, 41, 67, 156
Amenhotep IV. See Ikhnaton.
Amorites, 64, 72, 104
Amos, 97, 111, 119, 120–23, 130, 143, 156
Anaximander, 168
Anaximenes, 168
Animism, 30, 38, 48
Anthropology, 9, 37
Anthropomorphism, 31, 92, 149, 151, 165
Antinomianism, 240

Antiochus Epiphanes, 98
Antisthenes, 176 f.
Apatheia, 203
Apocalypse, apocalyptic, 143 f., 220 f.
Apocrypha, 143 n., 146
Aphrodite, 65, 165
Aquinas, St. Thomas, 193 n., 198, 216
Arabian Desert, 60, 66, 94
Arameans, Aramaic, 67 f., 69
Aristippus, 175 f., 200
Aristocles, 180
Aristocracy, 161, 173, 197, 198, 219 f.
Aristophanes, 159 n., 166, 168
Aristotle, 157, 158, 161, 165, 167, 181, 190–99, 209, 215
Art, 66, 69, 152, 158, 160, 171, 238
Asceticism, 171, 177, 179, 206, 234
Asia Minor, 60, 66, 72, 155
Assur (city), 61 n., 66, 67, 69
Assur (deity), 67, 74
Assurbanipal, 68, 69
Assyria, Assyrians, 61, 66–70, 73, 83, 84 f., 97, 123, 124, 126
Astarte, 74, 82
Astronomy, 43, 71
Ataraxia, 201, 203
Athens, 154, 159 ff., 172, 173, 180, 191
Aton, 45 n., 50, 53, 54. Hymn to Aton, 53, 57 f.
Augustine, St., 217

Baal, Baalism, 74, 82, 84, 95, 104 f., 120, 131
Babel, Tower of, 63, 71
Babylon, Babylonians, civilization, 25, 37, 61, 62–66, 69, 72–85; in relation to the Hebrews, 89 f., 97, 98, 99, 111, 129, 135 ff.

249

Bar-Cochba rebellion, 99
Bathsheba, 96, 106
Bel, 74, 75, 136
Belshazzar, 72
Bennett, John C., 2 n.
Bethel, 120, 132
Blood revenge, 25–28, 112, 135, 138
Book of the Dead, 46, 55
Breasted, J. H., 38, 40, 52, 54, 58,
   60, 65 n., 76 n.
Bribery, 110, 112, 121, 125, 146
Bride price, 14 f., 80
Brotherhood of man, 205, 208, 218,
   224, 232
Browne, Lewis, 87 n.

Calendar, Egyptian, 41
Calvin, John, 92 n., 110, 133
Canaan, Canaanites, 82, 94 f., 100,
   101, 102, 104, 115
Cannibalism, 12
Capitalism, 18 n., 110, 121, 157, 197,
   228, 230 n.
Celibacy, 234, 243
Chaldeans, 61, 65, 69, 70–72, 128
Chosen people, Hebrews as, 91, 119,
   122, 152. See Covenant.
Christendom, 1, 2, 7, 39, 59, 213 f.
Christian Church, 17, 107, 207, 213 f.,
   220, 227, 238 f.
Christian ethics, meaning of, 212–14
Christianity, 2, 203, 206, 210 f., Ch.
   IX
Chrysippus, 204
Cicero, 208 f.
Circumcision, 103
Cities of refuge, 135
City-states, 84, 154 f., 159, 207
Civilization, emergence of, 36–38
Class distinctions, 20, 33, 55, 111,
   162. See Equality.
Cleanthes, 203, 224
Clisthenes, 157
Code, Covenant, 25, 100 f., 103, 106,
   107, 109 f., 112 f., 115, 132 ff.;
   Deuteronomic, 132–35, 136, 140,
   234; Holiness, 140; of Hammu-
   rabi, 25, 64, 73, 79, 82, 115
Codrus, 180

Collective responsibility, 25–28, 95,
   112, 138, 150
Commercial civilization, 64, 67, 71,
   84, 135
Communism, primitive, 17–22, 111;
   Plato's, 186 ff.; Marxist, 2, 4, 20,
   21 f., 117
Concubinage, 14, 15, 80 f., 105
Council of elders, 23, 112, 156
Courts, 25, 79, 84, 110, 112, 121, 125,
   134
Covenant, Hebrew, 89, 90, 91, 111,
   152, 242; new, 130 f.
Creation stories, 74 f., 93, 101
Crime, punishment for, 23–25; 33.
   See Adultery; Theft; Murder;
   Death penalty.
Cross, 139, 211, 228
Cubberley, E. P., 161 n.
Cynics, 175 ff., 179, 204 f.
Cyrenaics, 175 ff., 179, 180, 195, 200 f.
Cyrus, 72, 98, 140

D document, 100, 136
Damascus, 68, 121
Daniel, Book of, 72, 143
David, 92, 96, 103, 104, 105, 106, 114,
   120, 147
Day of the Lord, 122, 143
Dead, ceremonials for, 31. See Book
   of the Dead.
Death, attempted conquest of, 47,
   49, 51, 54 ff., 75
Death penalty, 23 f., 106 n., 109, 113,
   133, 134 f.
Deborah, 16, 95; Song of, 101, 104
Decalogue, 23, 90, 91, 94, 100, 109,
   113, 149, 226, 241
Democracy, 4, 23, 55, 72, 83 f., 117,
   197; Greek sources of, 72, 154–59,
   211; Christian sources of, 219 f.,
   231 f., 238, 243 f.
Democritus, 166, 168, 200
Determinism, 5, 36
Deutero-Isaiah, 98, 124, 136, 138–40,
   143, 149 f.
Deuteronomy, 100, 113 n., 133, 136.
   See Deuteronomic Code.
Dewey, John, 5, 7, 208 n.
Diaspora, 98, 142

Diogenes, 177
Diogenes Laertius, 179 f.
Divorce, 80, 134, 235
Draco, 153, 157
Drunkenness, 97, 121, 125, 146

E document, 100, 136
Ecclesiastes, 98, 145
Ecclesiasticus, 98, 146
Economic forces, 7, 10, 17, 36; or-
  ganization, 17–22; oppression, 45,
  96 f., 111 f., 121, 125, 134, 146, 162,
  207. *See* Property rights.
Education, 5, 10, 32, 142, 165, 238;
  Socratic, 171 f., 174; Plato's views
  on, 187, 197
Egypt, 1, 25, 67, 84, 117, 155; his-
  tory, 38–47, 99; religion, 47–50,
  74; morals, 50–58; in relation to
  Assyria, 66, 69, 73; in relation to
  the Hebrews, 89, 92, 93, 97, 98,
  103, 107, 123, 126, 130, 135, 141
Eleatics, 168
Elijah, 97, 120, 132
Elisha, 97, 120
Elkanah, 105
"Eloquent Peasant," 52, 117
Empire, Egyptian, 44 ff., 99; Baby-
  lonian, 63–66; Assyrian, 65–70;
  Chaldean, 65, 70–72; Roman, 46,
  98 f., 159, 207
Endogamy, 13
Engineering, 37, 39, 42, 43, 207
Enlil, 73, 75
Ephebic oath, 161
Epictetus, 209 f., 217
Epicurus, Epicureans, 145, 176, 195,
  199–202, 203, 216
Equality of all men, 208, 209, 211,
  232
Eros, 184 f., 190, 217
Esarhaddon, 68, 69
Eschatology, 143 f., 218, 221 f.
Esther, Book of, 144
Eudaemonism, 195
Euphrates, 36, 44, 59 f., 99
Euripides, 158, 159 n.
Exile, Hebrew, 70, 83, 89, 98, 100,
  124, 127, 130, 133, 135–40, 144

Exodus from Egypt, 45, 82, 89;
  Book of, 90, 100
Exogamy, 13
Ezekiel, 98, 136–38, 140, 143, 150
Ezra, 140

Factionalism, 159, 162, 207
Faith, basic to Christian ethics, 215,
  240, 242 f.; justification by, 240,
  242
Family relations, primitive, 10–17;
  Babylonian, 80 f.; Hebrew, 105
  ff., 234; Greek, 163; Plato's view
  of, 187, 189; Jesus' view of, 234–
  36; Paul's view of, 243. *See* Mon-
  ogamy; Polygamy; Position of
  women.
Fatherhood of God, 224
Fertile Crescent, 60, 61, 68, 70, 72
Feudal society, 19, 43, 79, 110, 117
Finegan, Jack, 65 n.
Flood, the, 63, 93
Forgiveness, Divine, 124, 125, 199,
  223
Form and matter, 183, 194
Frankfort, H. and H. A., 73 n.
Frazer, J. G., 13 n.

Galatians, Book of, 242
Gandhi, 216
Garden of Eden, 61
Gautama, 201
Genesis, Book of, 87, 93, 100 f.
Gentiles, 119, 138 f., 141, 148, 150
Gideon, 95
Gilgamesh, Epic of, 75
Gods, moral compulsion of, 17, 23,
  29–32, 38, 48, 151 f., 153, 200 f.
  See names of principal deities.
Golden age of innocence, 21, 52, 61,
  78
Gorgias, 169
Gospels, 173, 213, 225, 239
Government, centralized, 37, 39, 40
  n., 41, 42, 43, 95. *See* Political re-
  lations.
Grace, divine, 54, 57, 119, 190, 242.
  See Forgiveness.
Greece, Greeks, 1, 23, 36, 41 n., 46,
  117, 142; the Hebrew versus the

Greek spirit, 151–54; birth of democracy, 72, 154–59; moral consciousness, 159–63; early Greek morality, 163–66; philosophical schools, 145, 166–206; Jesus and the ideals of Greece, 214–20

Grotius, 211

Habakkuk, 128, 149
Habiri, 99
Haggai, 140
Hall, T. C., 7 n.
Hammurabi, 25, 64, 67, 71, 72, 75, 78, 79, 81, 84. *See* Code of Hammurabi.
Hannah, 16, 105
Harmony theory of value, 160, 178, 182, 184, 189
Hatshepsut, 45
Hebrews, 1, 22, 23, 58, 59, 84, 85, 179; contributions, 86–89, 149 f.; relation to Yahweh, 38, 50, 89–93; history, 45, 46, 67, 82, 93–99; pre-prophetic morality, 99–115; prophets, 116–140; pre-exilic prophecy, 119–131; Deuteronomic reform, 131–35; exile, 135–40; rise of Judaism, 140–42; post-exilic literature, 143–49; Hebrew versus Greek, 151–54; Jesus and his Hebrew background, 220–23
Hedonism, 174, 175 f., 195, 199–202; hedonistic paradox, 176
Hegesias, 176
Heliopolis, 41, 48, 50
Hell, 56, 144
Henotheism, 50, 74, 94
Heraclitus, 168, 204
Herodotus, 43, 69, 158, 166
Hesiod, 117, 156, 165
Hippocrates, 158, 159 n.
Hittites, 46, 65, 67, 104
Hobbes, Thomas, 10
Hobhouse, L. T., 9
Homeric poems, 14, 156, 157, 163 ff., 165
Horus, 48 f.
Hosea, 97, 123 f., 130, 224, 234
Hospitality, 18, 20, 28, 93, 103 f., 164

Humanism, 5, 175
Hunting stage, 17, 18
Hyde, W. D., 179
Hyksos invasion, 40 n., 44

Ideas, Plato's theory of, 182–84, 189
Idolatry, 113, 132 f.
Ikhnaton, 45, 53 f., 57 f.
Iliad, 156, 157, 163
Immortality, Egyptian view of, 31, 39, 47, 49, 51, 54–58; Babylonian, 75; Hebrew, 143 f.; Socratic, 172; Christian, 218 f.
Incarnation, 48, 217, 228, 240
Incest, 13, 23
Individualization, 11, 20, 33, 73, 88, 137, 150
Infanticide, 24, 106, 163, 238
In-group and out-group, 19, 32, 36, 101, 115. *See* Aliens.
Inheritance, 15, 19, 79
Interim ethic, 222
Intermarriage, 13, 95, 104 f., 144
Internationalism, 127, 150, 210
Intichiuma, 13
Iroquois, 13, 23
Isaac, 15, 93
Isaiah, 98, 124–27, 130, 150. *See* Deutero-Isaiah.
Ishtar, 65, 71, 74, 82, 84
Isis, 49
Israel, 96 f., 99, Chs. V, VI. *See* Hebrews.

J Document, 100
Jacob, 15, 93, 95, 105, 107
Jacobsen, T., 73 n., 84 n.
Jael, 101, 104, 165
Jephthah, 95, 114
Jeremiah, 98, 128–31, 132, 138, 149, 150, 173
Jericho, 94
Jeroboam, 96
Jerusalem, 96, 125, 127, 132, 136, 137, 147; besieged, 68, 97; conquered, 70, 98, 99, 135, 221; rebuilt, 140
Jesus, 1, 49, 68, 142, 148, 175; Hebrew background, 220–23; death, 139, 211, 238; ethical teachings,

87 f., 127, 212–38; compared with ideals of Greece and Rome, 214–20; compared with Socrates, 170, 174, 216

Jesus, ben-Sirach, 146

Jezebel, 120

Job, 98, 144 f., 147 f., 150, 166

Jonah, 144, 150

Jonathan, 114

Jordan, 94

Joseph, 93

Joshua, 94

Josiah, 100, 131 f.

Judah, 68, 69, 96 ff., 100, 138

Judaism, 13, 140–42, 239

Judas Maccabeus, 98

Judges, 22, 84, 95, 105, 112; Book of, 101 f.

Judgment, divine, 39, 49 n., 55, 58, 75, 83, 116, 119, 137, 143 f. *See* Last Judgment.

Justice, corrective and distributive, 197; origins, 24, 33, 51; social, 52, 58, 87, 92, 109 ff., 115, 116–42, 161. *See* names of prophets.

Justification by faith, 240, 242

Kant, Immanuel, 202

Karnak, 44 f.

Kassites, 65

Kidinnu, 71

Kingdom of God, 218, 222, 223, 227, 228 f., 231, 234, 242, 244

Kinship stage of development, 10–17, 22, 32, 40, 95

Knowledge as virtue, 174, 196, 205, 215

Koheleth, 145, 147

La Farge, Oliver, 13 n.

Laban, 107

Lamentations, Book of, 135

Lansbury, George, 61

Last Judgment, 144, 221 f., 225

Law, codification of. *See* Code.

Law, Roman, 203, 207, 215

Law, the (Hebrew), 88, 89, 91, 94, 142, 147, 150; law and gospel, 241–243; legalism, 220 f., 226

Lecky, W. E. H., 7 n.

Levirate marriage, 134

Leviticus, 140

Lex talionis, 25, 80, 112, 135

Lippmann, Walter, 3

Locke, John, 19

Logos, 51, 203, 204 f., 216, 224

Lots, sacred, 112 f.

Love, basic to Christian ethics, 189, 212, 215, 217, 219, 225, 233, 242 f., 244

Lowry, Charles, 2 n.

Lucretius, 200

Lyceum, 191

Maat, 52, 55

Maccabean period, 98, 147

Macedonia, 159, 190, 191, 199

Magic, 30, 46, 55 f., 57, 74, 77 f.

Malachi, 147

Man, doctrine of, 174, 185 f., 194, 218, 224 f. *See* Brotherhood; Worth of persons.

Mana, 31, 113 n.

Manumission of slaves, 108

Marcus Aurelius, 53, 210 f., 217

Marduk, 65, 71, 74, 81

Materialism, 166, 199 f.

Maternal family (matriarchate), 11, 12–14

Mean, doctrine of the, 195, 216

Medes, 69, 70

"Memphite Theology," 50 f.

Mesopotamia, 1, 35, 38, Ch. IV, 155

Messianic hope, 52, 119, 136 f., 143, 220 f.

Metals, use of, 37, 41, 62, 64, 67

Micah 98, 127 f., 150

Militarism, 3, 44, 67, 70, 84, 175

Miller, Alexander, 2 n.

Mitanni, 67

Moab, 94, 104, 121

Moderation, principle of, 153, 160, 176, 179, 199. *See* Mean.

Mohammed, 86

Moira, 165, 166

Monogamy, 12, 14 n., 16, 80, 163

Monolatry, 92, 94, 98, 149

Monotheism, 48, 74, 94; emergence of, 31, 45, 53, 58, 98, 130 f., 136,

138; ethical, 83, 149, 165; philosophical, 152, 184, 194, 203, 209 f.
Moore, G. F., 77 n.
Moses, 90, 91, 93 n., 94, 102, 112 n., 120, 132
Murder, 24, 135, 196
Myers, P. V. N., 74 n.
Mystery cults, 48 f.
Mythology, 29, 31, 74, 84, 181

Naaman, 120
Naboth, 111, 120
Nabu-rimannu, 71
Nahum, 128
Nathan, 120
Nationalism, 3, 4, 104, 128, 140 f., 143, 148, 220 f.
Natural law of morality, 209, 211; natural rights, 211
Nebuchadnezzar, 70 f., 72, 97, 135
Negative Confession, 46, 55, 77
Nehemiah, 140
Nemesis, 151, 166
Neo-Babylonian empire. See Chaldeans.
Nero, 209
New Testament, 1, 8, 83, 99, 144, Ch. IX
Nichomachean Ethics, 194 ff., 199
Niebuhr, R., 217 n.
Nile, 36, 38, 40, 43, 48
Nineveh, 35, 61, 66, 68, 69, 70, 128, 144
Noah, 126
Nomadic society, primitive, 15, 17, 18; Akkadian, 64; Hebrew, 82, 88, 93, 94, 99, 109, 115, 117, 120; early Greek, 153, 155
Non-resistance, 232. See Pacifism; War.
Northern Kingdom, 68, 96 f., 100, 120, 124
Nygren, A., 217

Oath before God, 81. See Vow.
Objectivity of values, 189, 215, 217
Odyssey, 156, 157, 163
Old Testament, 46, Chs. V, VI, 197, 213, 223, 234, 242; examples of primitive society in, 15, 16, 18,

26 ff., 31; compared with early Greek period, 14, 31, 163
Olympic games, 156
Olympic pantheon, 152, 155
Osiris, 38, 48 ff., 54–57, 74
Ostracism, 157

P document, 100, 136
Pacifism, 78, 175, 232 f.
Palestine, 36, 46, 67, 68, 82, 94, 97, 98, 99, 135; topography of, 60, 66, 153
Pantheism, 205 f.
Parthenon, 158, 167
Passover, 103, 132 f., 147, 221
Pater, Walter, 202
Patriarchal society, 11, 14–16, 22, 87, 88
Paul, 81 n., 175, 203, 214, 231; ethics of, 238–44
Pentateuch, 142 n., 241. See J, E, D, P documents.
Perfectionism, 217, 227, 237
Pericles, 158, 166
Peripatetic school, 191
Persia, Persian, 72, 83, 98, 140, 144, 157, 166
Persian Gulf, 60, 69
Personality. See Worth of persons.
Pharisees, 142, 220, 231, 239
Phidias, 158, 159 n., 166
Philip of Macedon, 159, 191
Philistines, 46, 94, 96, 103, 122
Philosophy, 6, 47, 98, 142, 143, 153; Jewish, 144–47; Greek, 160, 166–206, 215; Roman, 206–11
Phoenicians, 41 n., 67, 156
Pindar, 153, 165
Pisistratus, 157
Plato, 158, 159 n., 165, 167, 177, 199, 215, 217; life and influence, 180–82; doctrine of ideas, 182–84; of Eros, 184 f., of man, 185 f., of the State, 186–88; relation to Socrates, 170 f., 173; to Aristotle, 190. 192, 198
Political relations, primitive, 22–28; Egyptian, 51–55; Babylonian, 62–66; Assyrian, 66–70; Chaldean, 70–72; Hebrew; 93–99; Greek,

154–59, 161; Roman, 207. *See* Government; Law.
Polygamy, 14, 16, 105
Polytheism, 22, 48, 73, 82, 149, 151, 165, 200
Pompey, 98
Post-exilic literature, 143–49
Pragmatism, 168, 169, 226
Priests, power of, in primitive society, 22, 30; in Egypt, 46, 48 f., 57; in Babylonia, 63, 73; in Judaism, 128, 136, 142, 149
Primitive society, 1, 88, 90; family relations, 10–17; economic organization, 17–22; civic relations, 22–28; religion, 28–32; achievements, 32–34
Private ownership, 21, 111, 188, 228
Property rights, 17–19, 24, 33, 79, 108, 109–12, 188
Prophets, Hebrew, 58, 83, 87, 97 f., 111, 115, 116–40, 153, 223
Proportion, Aristotelian sense of, 179, 195, 215
Prostitution, 36, 163; temple, 76, 81, 132
Protagoras, 168 f.
Proverbs, Book of, 54, 98, 146, 234
Providence, 206, 209
Psalms, 53, 76, 87, 98, 143, 147–49, 224; imprecatory, 92, 142, 148
Ptah, 51
Ptolemies, 46, 98
Pyramids, 31, 42 f., 47, 51, 53, 55; Pyramid Texts, 47, 51, 54

Rachel, 16, 105, 106
Racial exclusiveness, 36, 177. *See* Aliens; In-group.
Rameses, II and III, 45
Re, 38, 48, 50 f., 54, 74
Reason, as guide to morals, 176, 182, 194, 195 f., 202
Rebekah, 15, 16
Recollection, Plato's doctrine of, 183
Redemption, of a slave, 108, 123. *See* Salvation.
Regeneration, 227
Rehoboam, 96, 111

Relativism, 168, 169, 182, 215
Religion, 4, 10; primitive, 17, 28–32, 33 f.; Egyptian, 47–58; Babylonian, 72–78; Hebrew, 86–93, 113 f., 116–50; Greek, 151 ff., 165; of Jesus, 220–28; of Paul, 239–43
Remnant, doctrine of, 119, 126 f., 128, 130
Republic, 186 ff.
Resurrection, 49 f., 57
Revelation, Book of, 87, 143
Riley, Woodbridge, 164, 204 n.
Ritualism, 98, 114, 122, 124, 132 f., 136, 140
Romans, Book of, 242
Rome, Romans, 1, 23, 41, 49, 111, 122, 206–08, 215; Roman Empire, 2, 39, 46, 53, 98, 159; law, 203, 207, 215; philosophy, 179, 203, 208–11, 217
Rousseau, J. J., 10, 177
Ruth, 106, 144, 150

Sabbath, 103, 108, 110, 113, 136, 141 f.
Sacrifices, 30, 63, 113, 124, 133, 165
Sadducees, 142, 220
Salvation by divine grace, 39, 49 f., 54, 57 f.; 119, 139, 190
Samaria, 68, 96, 124, 220
Samson, 95, 106
Samuel, 95, 105, 120
Sargon I, 63 ff., 67; II, 68
Satan, 83, 144
Saul, 95 f., 103, 104, 114
Schweitzer, A., 30 n., 222 n.
Secularism, 2, 17, 159, 214
Seleucids, 46, 98
Self-realization, 186, 195, 212, 215, 217, 227
Semites, 63 f., 66, 82, 93, 154
Seneca, 209
Sennacherib, 68 f., 97, 124
Sermon on the Mount, 225 f., 235
Set, 49, 74
Sex equality, 16, 106, 187, 189, 232, 243. *See* Women.
Shalmaneser I, 66; V, 68
Shamash, 65, 74, 76, 78, 81
Shema, 86, 241

Sheol, 75, 114, 144
Shillito, Edward, 4
Sin, Greek versus Hebrew concepts of, 153, 194, 199, 216, 218. *See* Judgment.
Sinai, Mt., 90, 94
Sisera, 95, 101, 104, 165
Sky-god, 48, 73
Slavery, 20 f., 198, 209, 222; Egyptian, 38, 42, 51; Babylonian, 81; Hebrew, 101, 107–09, 111, 115; Greek, 162
Smith, Adam, 197
Sneath, E. H., 78 n.
Social contract theory, 10
Social solidarity, 11, 17 ff., 29, 101, 150. *See* Government.
Socrates, 158, 159 n., 161, 165, 167, 168, 169, 194, 199, 215 f.; life and thought, 170–75; relation to Cyrenaics, 175; Cynics, 177; Plato, 180, 181, 182, 184, 185; Stoicism, 204 f.
Solomon, 96, 105, 111, 114, 140, 146
Solon, 153, 157, 160, 180
Somervell, D. C., 39 n.
Sophists, 158, 166–70, 172, 175 f., 182, 201, 215
Sophocles, 158, 159 n., 163, 167
Southern Kingdom, 96 f., 100, 124
Sparta, 154 f.
Speucippus, 191
State, Greek devotion to the, 152, 161, 199; Plato's view of, 182, 186–88; Aristotle's, 197 f.; Jesus', 219, 231–33; Paul's, 243 f. *See* Government; Political relations.
Stoics, Stoicism, 179, 199, 203–06, 208–11, 215 f., 217, 224 f., 232
Subjectivism, 169
Suffering servant, Israel as, 98, 119, 136, 138 f., 150
Suicide, 176, 178, 203, 206
Sumer, Sumerians, 61, 62 f., 66, 72, 82
Sun-god, 41, 48, 50, 51, 52, 74
Synagogue, origins of, 136, 142
Syria, 46, 60, 66, 67, 98, 122

Taboo, 12, 22, 30

Talmud, 142
Tawney, R. H., 197 n.
Taxation, 40, 43, 96, 111
Tekoa, 120
Tell el-Amarna, 46, 53, 99
Temple, at Jerusalem, 96, 98, 99, 100, 131 f., 137, 140, 142, 147
Ten Commandments. *See* Decalogue.
Thales, 168
Thebes, 40 n., 44, 53
Theft, 19, 24, 81, 93, 109, 112, 196
Thucydides, 158 n.
Thutmose III, 44, 45, 99
Tiamat, 75
Tiglath-pileser, 68
Tigris, 36, 59 f., 66, 67
Titus, 99
Tools, use of, 37. *See* Metals.
Torah, 142
Totemism, 12, 13, 22
Toynbee, Arnold, 39 n., 40 n., 82 n., 159 n.
Troeltsch, Ernst, 7 n.
Troy, 46, 155, 163
Tufts, J. H., 208 n.
Tutankhamen, 31, 45, 53
Tyre, 35, 121

United Kingdom, 97, 120
Universals, 172, 182 f., 189, 193 n.
Unmoved Mover, 194
Ur, 60, 61 n., 62, 64, 67
Uriah, 96, 106, 120
Urim and Thummim, 112
Urwir, 17
Usury, 110, 197
Uzziah, 124 f.

Virtues, Greek cardinal, 160, 171, 185, 219
Vow, binding nature of, 27 f., 95, 114

Wage system, 107, 134
War, ethics of, 24, 36, 70, 102, 127, 134, 212, 222, 232 f.
Warbeke, John M., 171 n., 178 n.
Weber, Max, 230 n.
Westermarck, E. A., 9, 13 n.
Wilson, John A., 45 n., 51 n., 53 n.

Wisdom literature, 144–47
"Wisdom of Amenemope," 54
Women, position of, in primitive society, 12, 14, 16, 26 ff.; Babylonian, 80; Hebrew, 105–07, 115, 134 f., 146; Greek, 163; in Plato's thought, 187; Aristotle's, 198; Jesus', 232, 235, 238; Paul's, 243
Worth of persons, 54, 198, 220, 224 f., 231, 236, 238
Wright, W. K., 13 n., 150 n.
Writing, invention of, 37, 39, 41; hieroglyphic, 41; cuneiform, 62, 64, 65, 66, 67

Xanthippe, 171

Xenophon, 69, 170
Xerxes, 72

Yahweh, 27, 38, 50, 82 f., Chs. V, VI, 152, 224. See Covenant; Chosen people; Judgment; the Law.

Zealots, 221
Zechariah, 140, 151
Zeno, 199, 203
Zephaniah, 128, 131
Zeus, 151, 165, 166, 200. Hymn to Zeus, 203 f.
Zoroastrianism, 74, 83, 144

KANSAS BIBLE CHAIR
MYERS HALL,   Lawrence, Kansas
PRIVATE LIBRARY

PRIVATE
LIBRARY

H. HILL